A BOOZY HISTORY

· of ·

ATLANTA

A BOOZY HISTORY

· of ·

ATLANTA

People, Places & Drinks that Made a City

CAROLINE EUBANKS

AMERICAN PALATE

Published by American Palate
A division of The History Press
An imprint of Arcadia Publishing
Charleston, SC
www.historypress.com

First published 2025

Manufactured in the United States

ISBN 9781467159456

Library of Congress Control Number: 2025931106

I'd like to dedicate this book to the memory of three men: my grandfather Robert Eubanks, my uncle Dan Murray and, in particular, my uncle Brian Poore, who loved a good beer, especially while sitting around the fire on a camping trip in North Georgia.

CONTENTS

PREFACE

I've lived in Atlanta for my entire life, watching much of the development from the northern suburb of Marietta. When I was old enough, I escaped in favor of the neon-lit bars of Buckhead, not yet mindful of the city's drinking legacy and opting for an excess of cheap beer and vodka sodas. There were the nights I spent eating Goldfish-covered burgers from a trailer parked in front of Moondogs, a labyrinthine series of inner bars popular with the post-college crowd. Other nights, my friends and I would hit the drive-through ATM before a wild night at the Clermont Lounge, first interacting with a woman called Blondie with single bills tucked into her bra. We rehashed the prior evenings' events on the smoky patio at 97 Estoria or the rooftop at Republic Social House, with Oakland Cemetery below.

I surprised friends after their engagement at Manuel's Tavern, or "Manny's," as we affectionately called it, and rang in the New Year at the bars of Virginia Highland. I celebrated birthdays at a series of since-closed cocktail bars and excitedly debuted my first book with friends over drinks and oysters at Beetlecat and, later, dancing in the basement-level Den. These spaces feel like part of my history, running alongside my big life events.

Before that, my parents were doing much the same, as my mother had her first drink at the age of eighteen, before the law was changed, and danced at Flanigan's, a bar off Powers Ferry Road. One of my parents' first dates was at Alex Cooley's Champagne Jam in 1978, and my aunt and uncle had their first date at Moe's and Joe's. Even my teetotaling grandparents also shared tales of finding a still on their rural farm and being offered money to drive moonshine into the city.

In eighth grade, I took the required Georgia history class. We learned a series of facts about the highest peak (Brasstown Bald) and the state bird (brown thrasher). But there was plenty left out. Like Atlanta's first mayor, who was a candidate from the "Rowdy" Party. Or John Pemberton, who created a cocaine-laced wine before "inventing" Coca-Cola. And the controversial theater performance that led to Atlanta's reputation as the capital of strip clubs. Atlanta may not have the reputation of other debaucherous cities, like New Orleans or Las Vegas, but it certainly has stories to share.

In the many (don't ask how many) years since the bright red "under 21" bar was removed from my driver's license, I've become a frequent fan of the city's craft beer scene and upscale cocktail lounges that would have been lost on me as a twenty-something. It's become part of my career, as I've written about spirits and booze history for national publications. I love the stories behind them, especially the people. I even took a spin behind the bar for a few years, although I mostly poured beers and looked up recipes for the most basic of cocktails.

I, of course, wasn't able to cover every important drinkery in Atlanta's past and present. But it's these wild tales that I hope will serve as a connection point for the city's history and to honor the places where we celebrate and commiserate. If I've learned anything during the research, it's that everything is connected. You'll notice lots of overlap and threads between the places, past and present, forming an almost spiderweb of influences.

This book serves as a guide to the past and present, in which you can see where important events in Atlanta's history took place and also belly up to functioning bars. I've also created a Google Map that can be used as reference to see where each of these places is located and where others used to be, all with notes. You can find it at https://maps.app.goo.gl/Janvp8qpknQCCBWBA.

And if you visit any of these places or share memories of Atlanta watering holes past on social media, use the hashtag #atldownthehatch.

INTRODUCTION

The story of Atlanta, Georgia, is a long and complicated one that's difficult to cover in one book. Thankfully, plenty of ink has been spilled on the city already, from the music history to specific historic events, many of which are outlined in the extensive bibliography of this book. It's a railroad town turned state capital, a city of ruins, a phoenix among the flames. A city of neighborhoods. A place that's said to be "too busy to hate" since the time of Mayor Ivan Allen.[1] And it impacts the world, according to a local creative agency.[2] "Atlanta influences everything" has become the city's unofficial catchphrase, with the words on shirts donned by everyone from Billie Eilish and Lil John to Mayor Keisha Lance Bottoms.

But one of the threads that has connected the city's history over the past century-plus is its nightlife. People have always traveled here to party, even when they traveled by horse and wagon, the watering holes were covered with sawdust and the drinks offered were of questionable origin. Every generation has its own story, whether it's the college students who flocked here for Freaknik, the boomers who remember the original bars of Underground or the locals today who can now (finally!) enjoy a brunch cocktail before noon.

Atlanta isn't associated with classic cocktails like the Sazerac, Old Fashioned or the Negroni. The history isn't even always about the drink itself. Sometimes it's about little more than a canned beer in a crowded room, watching a band perform before they hit it big. The watering holes also aren't household names across the nation.

But the cast of characters from Atlanta's drinking history are too wild to be fictional: the early mayor busted for public intoxication and visiting brothels, the ski bum who kept live crocodiles at his bar, the nightclub drag troupe who provided essential care during the AIDS crisis, the cannon-shooting first local political party, the former divinity scholar who oversaw a bar filled with Ping-Pong tables and delightfully blasphemous art and the exotic dancer known for crushing beer cans between her bosom.[3]

One thing is certain: it could happen only in Atlanta.

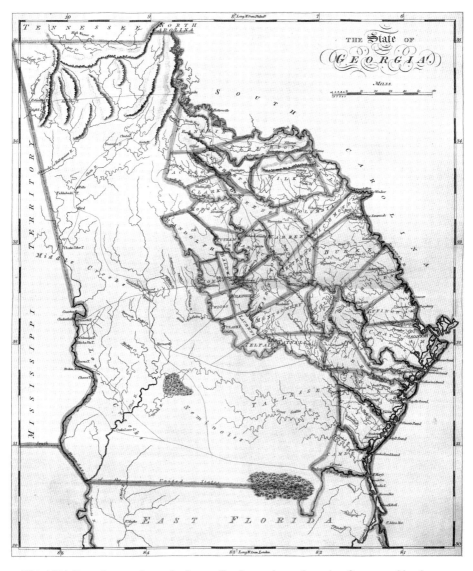

This 1814 Georgia map shows the few outlined counties and swaths of unnamed land. Atlanta is not yet listed, but Savannah is. *New York Public Library Digital Collections.*

.

TIMELINE OF RELEVANT EVENTS

1525   The first known Europeans arrived in the mouth of the Savannah River, led by Pedro de Quejos.[4] Hernando de Soto and his crew followed, arriving at the state's modern southern border in 1540.

1732   The thirteenth and final colony of Georgia was founded along the coast between the Savannah and Altamaha Rivers in the name of King George of England.[5] Of course, there were already Native people living in the colony's boundaries. Most of the tribes in the area that became Atlanta, Creek and Cherokee, were gone within the century due to wars and their forced exile on the Trail of Tears.[6]

1733   George Walton, Archibald Bulloch, John Houstoun and Noble W. Jones met at Tondee's Tavern in Savannah to discuss the "intolerable acts" of the Crown, which led to Georgia's inclusion in the Revolutionary War.[7] All four men went on to become involved in Georgia politics, and three served stints as the state's governor.

1735   The trustees who oversaw the Georgia colony banned the importation of rum, brandy and other types of "strong drink." Slavery, Catholicism and practicing law were also forbidden in the colony—but not for long.[8] Rum was legalized in 1742, and slavery was legalized in 1751.

1776   America declared its independence from England, severing ties between the colonies and the Crown. Walton signed the Declaration of Independence alongside Button Gwinnett and Lyman Hall, two fellow future governors.

1785   The University of Georgia was founded in then-rural Athens, as the founders of American universities believed that students should be kept away from the alcohol and the depravity of cities like Atlanta and instead study in the countryside.[9] Ultimately, the joke was on them, as in 2010, the University of Georgia was named the top party school in the nation by *The Princeton Review*.[10]

1788   Georgia became the fourth state to join the United States of America.[11] The state's boundaries then reached beyond the Mississippi River to what is now Alabama and Mississippi.[12] The land to the west was ceded in 1802.

1791   The United States government attempted to pay its Revolutionary War debts with an excise tax on distilled spirits, including whiskey.[13] This hit the small-scale distillers hardest, many of whom continued illegally, but for others, their costs were passed on to the consumers. This would spark a rebellion in Pennsylvania and beyond.

1837   The planned terminus of the Western and Atlantic Railroad was determined in then-rural Georgia. Several other train lines also arrived nearby, earning the burgeoning community the uninspired name of "Terminus."

1843   Atlanta is renamed Marthasville in honor of the daughter of former Georgia Governor Wilson Lumpkin.[14]

1860   The state's alcohol industry was on the rise. By this year, Georgia was producing more wine than any other state, an estimated twenty-seven thousand gallons annually.[15]

1861   After holding a landmark convention in Milledgeville, Georgia becomes the fifth state to secede from the Union, joining the Confederacy. A few weeks after the convention was dismissed, the first shots of the Civil War were fired at Fort Sumter in South Carolina.

1862   The Civil War government outlawed distillation because the grain was needed for the war effort.[16] It was another step toward Prohibition, which would follow forty-five years later.

1864   The Civil War, which had been fought throughout the South, came to Atlanta, resulting in the infamous burning of the city at the hands of General William T. Sherman.[17] During the war, the South's saloons served as a Confederate spy network.[18]

1868   The newly rebuilt city of Atlanta officially became Georgia's state capitol under its current name after the capital was earlier located in Savannah, Augusta, Louisville and Milledgeville. Atlanta adopted the phoenix as its symbol, rising from the flames.

1881   A series of expositions in the next decade, starting with the International Cotton Exposition, brought national and international attention to the growing city and its business opportunities. The city's chamber of commerce was founded a decade prior to promote Atlanta for businesses.[19]

1885   Local laws in Atlanta allowed for the production of wine within the city, but they also banned imported wines.[20] Fulton County also voted against allowing the production of liquor.[21]

1906   Several Black Atlantans were killed in a four-day race massacre. It wasn't the last time there was violence against the Black community in Atlanta. Segregation followed this period and continued until the civil rights movement.

1907   After the increasing efforts of the temperance movement, Georgia enacted a statewide prohibition of the consumption and sale of alcohol several years before the rest of the United States followed suit.

1917–18   The United States entered World War I, bringing several military camps to Georgia.

1917   A devastating fire swept through Atlanta, mostly affecting the poorest neighborhoods. Nearly two thousand buildings were burned, and intentional fires were set to stop the spread. One thousand residents were left homeless.[22]

1929–41   The Great Depression forced many Americans into poverty, especially due to the boll weevil insect infestation that ravaged southern farmlands and took down "King Cotton," which had been Georgia's cash crop for generations.

1935   Prohibition is finally repealed within Georgia to avoid an economic crisis, but some counties remained "dry" for years. But within days of this repeal, the city of Atlanta issued new licenses to bars, liquor stores and alcohol wholesalers.[23] Winemaking was again legalized, but distilling continued to be illegal in Georgia and remained so for the better part of a century.[24]

1941–45   The United States entered World War II, but the war effort put many Atlantans back to work after years of struggling, as federal funding went into the military infrastructure within the state.[25]

1964   The civil rights movement, which included the tireless work of Atlantans like Hosea Williams and Martin Luther King Jr., culminated in the national passage of the Civil Rights Act, which banned segregation in public spaces like hotels, restaurants and bars. Of course, it took time for the act to be enforced in Atlanta.

1972   Toward the tail end of the Vietnam War, Georgia set the drinking age at eighteen, allowing for more adults to frequent the city's growing nightlife scene.[26]

1978   Then-President Jimmy Carter, a peanut farmer from small-town Plains, Georgia, signed a national bill to allow for the brewing of beer at home, setting the stage for the modern craft beer industry.[27] But this wouldn't be legal within Georgia until 1995.[28]

1980–86   Georgia's drinking age again rose, to nineteen. Five years later, it rose to twenty, and then the next year, it rose to twenty-one, which remains the nationwide drinking age.

1995   State laws expanded drinking opportunities just in time for the Atlanta centennial summer Olympics, including GH Bill 374, which allowed for brewpubs to open.[29]

1996 Atlanta hosted the centennial summer Olympic Games to much fanfare following years of preparation. But most remember the negative events, specifically the bombing at the hands of terrorist Eric Robert Rudolph, which left two people dead and one hundred injured. Rudolph also later struck a local gay bar.

2001 After a fatal stabbing on the night of the Super Bowl in 2000, Atlanta took swift action to change the city's party scene. All-night licenses were not renewed. The eighteen to party, twenty-one to drink clubs were also outlawed.[30]

2004 Legislation allowed for high-gravity beer to be sold, with alcohol by volume increasing from 6 to a maximum of 14 percent, where it remains.[31]

2005 A citywide smoking ban affected formerly all-ages spaces. Bars and restaurants now had to decide whether to allow smoking, welcoming only patrons over eighteen, or to ban smoking and allow all ages.[32]

2009 The state's first distillery since Prohibition, 13th Colony Distilling in the South Georgia town of Americus, opens, paving the way for others in Atlanta and beyond.[33]

2011 A bill was signed to allow counties to decide whether to discontinue "blue laws" or allow for the Sunday sale of alcohol.

2015 A new law allowed for the on-site sale of alcohol at breweries. It no longer had to go directly through distributors, but it was limited to no more than two pints per person for onsite consumption.[34]

2018 The so-called brunch bill was passed in Atlanta, allowing for the sale of alcohol on Sundays starting at 11:00 a.m. at restaurants and bars instead of the previously outlined time of 12:30 p.m.[35] The following years also brought new open-container districts around Atlanta, including in Roswell, Kennesaw, Smyrna and Acworth.

2020 During the global COVID-19 pandemic, all bars and restaurants were forced to shutter for months, but several stayed afloat creatively, with distilleries making hand sanitizer. The city allowed for a period of to-go alcohol sales and expanded delivery options, at least temporarily.

BEFORE GEORGIA AND BEFORE ATLANTA

Before there was Atlanta, there was Georgia, a colony founded in honor of King George in 1732. It was originally planned as a debtor's colony for the nation's criminals, but the trustees sought skilled people. These skilled laborers would create wine and silk to send back to England in exchange for a new life and opportunities abroad, far from the cramped quarters of London.[36]

When the English colonists arrived on the coast aboard the ship *Anne*, it was unsafe to drink the water for risk of illness. Instead, an alternative was offered, as the state's first brewery was established on Jekyll Island, where its ruins can still be seen at the Horton House Historic Site.[37] William Horton, the island's first English resident, brewed beer using hops, rye and barley he grew on site, and he sold the final product to the soldiers stationed on neighboring St. Simon's Island.

There were also attempts at making wine using native grapes, blackberries and scuppernongs, but these attempts largely failed for many years.[38] Instead, Madeira wine was among the most popular imports from Europe.

James Oglethorpe, the colony's founder, set strict guidelines for the alcoholic drinks he allowed in Georgia. In 1735, the trustees decided that there would be a ban on imports of rum, brandy and other "strong drink," making it one of the first acts of alcohol prohibition in America.[39] Oglethorpe believed that the settlers were becoming too wild and even blamed deaths in the colony on rum, rather than the more likely culprit—polluted water.[40] The only vice allowed was English beer, imported straight from the motherland.

Left: The Horton House ruins as seen in 1933 as part of a buildings survey. *Library of Congress.*

Below: This 1895 drawing from artist W.P. Snyder depicts a meeting between Oglethorpe and Tomochichi. *New York Public Library Digital Collections.*

But this prohibition didn't last long, as taverns were legalized by 1786, popping up in the future capital city of Savannah and beyond, with sugarcane grown along the coast to support the colonists' desire for rum. The colonists' taste for the spirit was insatiable and extended to the Yamacraw Native people who lived in the area. The leader of the group, Tomochichi, asked Oglethorpe to end the sale of rum for the good of his people. By 1735, it was all but banned. It would take another century, but this wasn't the last time Georgia banned alcohol.

Trustee rule ended in 1752, as did the strong drink bans, as Georgia sought independence, despite the colonists being a mix of English Loyalists and those against English rule.[41] The thirteenth colony joined the Revolutionary War in 1775 and became the fourth state to join the Union in 1788. From then on, rum was imported continuously to the colony until trade routes were disrupted during World War I.[42]

1837–1906

The Tavern with White Walls

In the mid-1700s, the Muscogee (Creek) village of Standing Peachtree sat where the Chattahoochee River and Peachtree Creek meet. European settlers moved inland from the coast, settling in the area, some for the short term and others for the long haul, thanks to a series of land lotteries starting in 1805.[43] Little by little, the Creek and Cherokee were pushed out through treaties and a forced removal in 1838 on the "Trail of Tears."

The city that would become Atlanta was established in 1837, first given the name "Terminus," which was initially assigned the city because there was no certainty that anyone would want to live there permanently.[44] In the words of the Western and Atlantic Railroad's chief engineer, it was "a good place for one tavern, a blacksmith shop, a grocery store, and nothing else."[45] For travelers taking the stagecoach routes through the South before the official establishment of the city, this was accurate. That first tavern was the Whitehall Tavern, which was then the only place to spend the night between parts of Georgia and Tennessee.[46] Named for its white-painted walls, a novelty in its time, the tavern was opened in 1835 at Newnan and Sandtown Roads and was used as a landmark.[47] A stay at the eight room-accommodation also came with a daily meal.[48]

Whitehall Tavern's owner, Charner Humphries, ran the two-story inn and tavern, which also became the area's post office, gambling hub and,

Photographer George N. Barnard snapped this image of the city not long before the Battle of Atlanta, with a saloon right along the train tracks. *Library of Congress.*

later, a voting precinct.[49] His daughter Elizabeth married Joshua Gilbert, the city's first doctor.[50]

It continued to operate for the next twenty years until Humphries' death in 1855. Charner and his wife were interred near the tavern, and their remains were later relocated to the historic Westview Cemetery. A community popped up around the tavern, with two breweries operating there by the 1860s in a burgeoning liquor trade.[51] While the tavern was later torn down, Whitehall lent its name to a street that became a part of Atlanta's drinking culture for many years to come.

But Whitehall wasn't the only watering hole in the growing town. In later years, the city's train station and hotels had their own saloons. Rough and Ready Tavern was another stagecoach stop located south of the city. It was rumored to have been a gathering place for Confederate spies, and it also operated as a post office before it was ultimately demolished in 1917. There were several other taverns in the larger cities nearby, like Marietta and Decatur.[52]

Other bars gave way for the names we recognize around the city today. Henry Irby's Tavern had a mounted deer head, and this is believed to be the origin of the Buckhead neighborhood's name.[53] Pace's Tavern in modern-day Vinings gave the name to the ferry where travelers had to cross the river, and Kile's Tavern gave way to Kile's Corner near today's Five Points.[54]

At these spots, people who found their way to town could come for a homemade beer brewed from corn and molasses or whiskey, which was being made in Virginia as early as the 1600s.[55] Refrigeration wasn't created stateside until 1865, so drinks weren't exactly refreshing in the humid South.[56] Railroad Ale House was the first Atlanta bar to have refrigeration.[57]

A "free with purchase" lunch included cheese, meat and crackers, almost like modern charcuterie. There were no bar seats, so patrons, almost exclusively male, were expected to stand amid the sawdust, which was used to clean up spills and anything else that found its way to the bar floor.

By 1850, the title of "saloon" or "tavern" took on a negative association, as the temperance set pushed for their abolishment, but during the frontier days of the city, Whitehall was a welcome respite for weary and thirsty travelers.[58]

Are You a Moral or Rowdy?

The early days of the city that became Atlanta were relatively lawless, despite a strong religious presence, namely the enclaves of Methodists, Presbyterians and Baptists.[59] An 1850 survey of the city found that of the 2,500 then-residents, 85 had no form of employment, and most residents were transient, following whatever short-term jobs were available.[60] This was also when the city's first recorded party took place, and it surely set a precedent for the future.[61]

The vices of sex work, gambling and drinking were especially abundant, particularly in neighborhoods like Tight Squeeze, Humbug Square, Murrell's Row, Slab Town and Snake Nation. The section of taverns between Decatur and DeKalb was called Rusty Row, a notorious hangout zone.[62] Each borough had its own unsavory reputation.

Snake Nation took its name from the "snake oil" salesmen and rough characters typically found there ("mean as a snake"), now part of modern-day Castleberry Hill (see "From Snakes to Castles" section). It wasn't uncommon to find the bodies of murder victims on the train tracks of the Macon and Western Railroad that came through the neighborhood.[63] It also served as the city's red-light district, where mostly immigrant sex workers lived and worked until an 1850 ordinance attempted to push them out.[64]

Tight Squeeze was a popular spot for pickpockets and thieves, as the section of old Peachtree Street curved sharply around a ravine.[65] Humbug Square featured "freak shows" and fortune tellers.[66] Slab Town, near today's Old Fourth Ward, was given its name for its shoddily constructed buildings with dirt floors made for the poor using the scraps from future Mayor Jonathan Norcross's lumber mill.[67] His downtown sawmill also supplied wood for the growing railroad business.[68]

Murrell's Row was described in an 1894 *Atlanta Journal* article as being full of a "hard class of people" who would fight, host chicken fights and gamble over cards with little police interference.[69] It's appropriate that it was named for thief and murderer John A. Murrell, whose likeness appeared in *The Adventures of Tom Sawyer*, published in 1876.[70]

The railroad brought in many people, especially immigrants from Scotland, Ireland and Germany, who developed their own communities and social events.[71] With little work to go around and plenty of places to drink, it was easy for these newcomers to get into trouble. In fact, even the train station had a bar, so new Atlantans could start hitting the bottle as soon as they arrived.[72]

The saloons and grocery stores that transformed into bar rooms at night were gathering places for these low-income workers, offering free lunches, pool tables and back rooms in which to mingle with sex workers.[73] The booze was always flowing, specifically five-cent beer, corn whiskey and peach brandy, and violence was common.[74]

With this in mind, a "moral majority" grew within Atlanta to crack down on the city, which, by the middle of the century, had forty saloons, like The Big Bonanza, reportedly owned by a future Atlanta mayor, and The Girl of the Century, where Wild West legend Doc Holliday, who was born in a nearby suburb, is rumored to have drunk.[75]

Since America's founding, politicians have had a stake in the alcohol business, often firsthand. In 1847, the Moral (or Orderly) Party chose the aforementioned Norcross, the son of a preacher man, as their candidate to lead the city.[76] But it didn't take long for an opposing faction to rise. As the name would imply, the Free and Rowdy Party was in favor of the drinking crowd, led by saloon owner Moses W. Formwalt, a self-made man who had earned his wealth through the production of tinware and copper stills for whiskey and who had a warehouse on the border with Murrell's Row.[77] He was elected in 1848 for a one-year term as Atlanta's first mayor, thanks in part to the whiskey passed out by the Rowdies in exchange for votes.[78] The Moral Party, on the other hand, passed out apples and candy.[79]

ERECTED
BY
THE CITY OF ATLANTA
TO THE MEMORY
ATLANTA'S FIRST MAYOR
MOSES W. FORMWALT
1848

Both Moses Formwalt and Jonathan Norcross are buried in Oakland Cemetery. *Photograph by the author.*

The Rowdies would hold power for two additional terms after Formwalt's win, but in 1851, Jonathan Norcross claimed victory against Rowdy candidate Leonard C. Simpson. The Rowdies shot off cannons at Norcross's dry goods store in defiance of his leadership and burned much of Slabtown and Snake Nation to the ground, but Norcross recruited one hundred men to quell the violence.[80]

In 1860, a new, more permanent jail was erected in the city to deal with the melee, and after chaos erupted in Murrell's Row in 1873, the city's first police force was founded.[81] The wild era of these neighborhoods mostly ended with the arrival of the Civil War in 1861.[82] Snake Nation was attacked by a "vigilance committee" of disguised white citizens armed with axes and torches in 1917.[83] They kidnapped women, beat men and set buildings aflame.[84]

After his term was up, Formwalt became the deputy sheriff in DeKalb County, where, in 1852, he was stabbed by a prisoner he was escorting to the courthouse.[85] Norcross made an ill-fated attempt to reach the governor's mansion in 1876 before his death in 1898.[86] Rivals Norcross and Formwalt did meet again, in a way. Both were buried in Oakland Cemetery, along with several other Atlanta mayors.

The Rowdies may have been the first of Atlanta's controversial politicians, but they certainly weren't the last over the city's nearly two-hundred-year-long history. Atlanta's "rowdy" heyday has since been memorialized in—what else—a drink by Murrell's Row Spirits, which was started in 2015.[87]

A Grand Hotel for the "New South"

Atlanta was left in literal ruins after the Civil War ended in the spring of 1865. Sherman had torched the city on his way to the coast, and the people were desperate for essentials like food and shelter as soldiers burned fields and killed livestock. The once-bountiful plantation tables were now empty. The rail depot and countless other buildings were decimated, with the remaining hotels and structures serving as makeshift hospitals for the wounded and morgues for the dead.

Historian Willard Range described it this way:

> The aftermath of the Civil War in Georgia and especially in Atlanta was a time when men had to fight for even clothes, food, and shelter.[88]

This photograph shows the ruins of Atlanta following the Civil War. *Library of Congress.*

It was a slow climb to bring Atlanta back out of the ashes, but little by little, the city rebuilt.

Henry Grady, the young editor of the *Atlanta Constitution*, who wielded his power through the newspaper, wrote of his support for the growing temperance movement and specific political candidates. In 1886, he was asked to speak to the New England Society at Delmonico's restaurant in New York City.[89]

In what became known as Grady's "New South" series of speeches, he opined on the current state of the region, telling the audience that the time for division was gone and that secession and slavery were part of the past.

Grady urged Northerners to support the region financially, bringing corporate investment and putting struggling Southerners back to work. But he also recommended allowing white people to continue to control Black citizens.[90] The speeches painted a rosy, if debatable, picture of life in the region between the races.

This 1890 photograph depicts Henry Grady, the editor of the *Atlanta Constitution*. *Library of Congress.*

Among the businessmen to arrive was the oft-cited "carpetbagger" Hannibal Kimball, who moved to Atlanta in 1867 while working for the Pullman rail car company.[91] The term unkindly applies to Northerners who came to the crumbling South to seek their fortunes, often with bags made of carpet. He quickly became involved in Reconstruction politics, becoming president of the Atlanta Cotton Factory and taking over one of the city's railroad companies.[92]

Atlanta became the capital of Georgia in 1877, moving from Milledgeville to the south, and the legislature set up shop in Kimball's newly constructed opera house until a proper capitol could be constructed.[93]

In 1845, as there was only one hotel in town, Kimball saw another opportunity to make his fortunes in Atlanta.[94] He opened the grand Kimball House Hotel in 1870 after a seven-month building period in today's Five Points, not far from the *Constitution*'s offices. With over three hundred rooms across six stories, boasting fine European carpets and walnut furniture, the hotel became the best place to stay in the city, especially for the International Cotton Exposition of 1881, which Kimball also had a hand in alongside Grady.[95] Originally envisioned as little more than a cotton industry trade show, the expo became a nationally recognized event that brought together the North and South that only a few years prior had been at war.[96]

The expo brought in an estimated 290,000 guests over three months in 1895, shuttled from downtown to Oglethorpe Park by the Western & Atlantic Railroad that had been so instrumental in the creation of Atlanta.[97] With the expo spread across dozens of buildings, different groups were responsible for showcasing their products, like art pieces and inventions. The Georgia Manufacturer's building had a whiskey bar, and several of the dining outposts slung pitchers of beer for attendees. Kimball was praised by the *Constitution* for his work to bring business to the region. The expo also

This 1880 photograph features the Kimball House Hotel and the city railroad depot. *New York Public Library Digital Collections.*

paved the way for other events Atlanta would host in the next 150 years, including the 1996 centennial Olympics.

The hotel business was booming, especially for traveling politicians. The Kimball House menu featured the most luxurious delicacies of the day, like caviar, prime rib and turtle stew with a variety of wines, like Amontillado, as well as Imperial punch and beer.[98] The hotel hosted big names, including Sherman, who attended the Cotton Expo despite the results of his last visit to the city, and Presidents Cleveland and McKinley.[99]

An 1884 fire at the hands of a careless tenant destroyed the famed hotel without loss of life thanks to the fast work of employees.[100] A then-new *Atlanta Journal* newspaper broke the story.[101] But Kimball quickly set to work rebuilding with the help of local businessmen like Grady. It was one story higher, with over one hundred additional rooms.[102]

Despite the state being under Prohibition from 1907 onward, the hotel was one of the largest sellers of alcohol at the time.[103] The Kimball House Hotel remained popular through the 1930s but was demolished in 1959 like so many early Atlanta landmarks to make room for another parking deck.[104]

In 2013, a fine dining seafood restaurant called Kimball House opened in Decatur as a nod to the hotel and its luxurious setting (see "The Mixology Era" section).[105] The James Beard–nominated restaurant offers classics like shrimp cocktail, caviar and oysters, which Kimball himself surely would have enjoyed. Teetotaling Grady, whose legacy has been reexamined in recent years, may not have.[106]

Behind the Pharmacist's Counter

If there's one drink immediately associated with Atlanta's past and present, it's Coca-Cola. But before pharmacist John Pemberton invented the now-iconic soda, he had something else in mind. And like so many classic drink ingredients, like Peychaud's and Angostura bitters, Coca-Cola's ingredients originated in medicine and the region's long history with folk medicine and self-treatment.

Born in 1831 in rural Knoxville, Georgia, Pemberton, also called "Doc," was wounded in the Civil War and treated himself with morphine for his ailment.[107] After studying medicine, he moved his family to the big city in 1869.[108] Only a few decades from its founding, Atlanta was still a rough-and-tumble place where the rail lines ended.

Once settled in town, Pemberton opened a drugstore at the Kimball House Hotel, the city's grandest, but his store went bankrupt.[109] But it didn't stop his experiments, as the Gilded Age crowd were constantly in search of miracle cures from their pharmacists, like Pemberton's formulas for cough syrup and "blood balm," which was believed to cure diseases of the blood and skin.[110] The city was also home to brands like Bradfield's Female Regulator and Swift's Sure Specific.[111]

One of Pemberton's successes was called "French coca wine," which he created in 1884 with wine and coca extract created from leaves from Peru.[112] Vin Mariani was a successful brand of the day that predated Pemberton's version of the drink, blending the extract from the coca leaves with Bordeaux wine, and it had fans that included Pope Leo and Thomas Edison.[113] The concoction featured 0.12 grains of cocaine per fluid ounce, using a process invented in 1863 to create *Erythroxylon coca*.[114] Cocaine was then also used as treatment for a variety of ailments.

Pemberton trademarked his French Wine Cola, which he claimed could battle depression, provide energy and make drinkers feel especially sexy as an aphrodisiac.[115] He told a local reporter that he sourced the finest wine, Peruvian coca and kola nuts for the invigorating beverage.[116] The drink became popular in Atlanta, but it wasn't long before Pemberton had to rethink his options.[117]

French wine was banned from import as the temperance movement took hold of the city.[118] Evangelist Reverend Sam Jones of Cartersville, Georgia, hosted Anti-Saloon League events around town, including at the Bijou Theater, an opera house that was demolished in 1921. The prohibitionist crowd was ultimately successful, passing legislation in 1885 that banned liquor in Fulton County.[119]

Left: Vin Mariani was the inspiration for Pemberton's "French coca wine." *New York Public Library Digital Collections.*

Right: Coca-Cola was originally sold for five cents and gained popularity through its advertisements. *Library of Congress.*

The pharmacist then turned his attention to a "temperance drink," swapping out his drink's wine with the kola nut extract, mixed in a large pot in his backyard with an oar, with the subsequent syrup stored in a spent whiskey barrel.[120] This method followed the model of other successful sodas like Dr Pepper, which had been created in Texas in 1885 and was also marketed as a hangover cure. Creating the drink as a syrup was also a cheaper option.[121] The drink was created using soda already available at pharmacies, which was often used to cover the taste of bitter medicine.[122]

Pemberton served the first drink, now called Coca-Cola for its two main ingredients, at Jacobs Pharmacy in downtown Atlanta in 1886 for only five cents. The pharmacy's owner, Dr. Joseph Jacobs, was also a pharmacist who studied under fellow Georgian Crawford Long, who is credited with the creation of anesthesia.[123] The following year, a portion of Pemberton's new company was purchased by Asa Candler, a fellow pharmacist and shrewd local businessman who later became mayor.[124] The drink was also offered for free to attendees of the 1887 Piedmont Exposition.[125]

Left: Asa G. Candler, as photographed in 1923, was the owner of Coca-Cola and, later, the mayor of Atlanta. *Library of Congress.*

Below: The World of Coca-Cola is a popular Atlanta attraction that showcases the brand's history with a replica soda fountain to honor its origins. *Photograph by the author.*

But Pemberton's success was sadly short-lived. He died in 1888 before he saw the major success of his creation. He gave away the bottling rights for a small fee, as he didn't expect people to drink Coca-Cola anywhere but a soda fountain. Candler ran the company until 1916, starting the advertisements that the company has been known for in the following decades and growing its national presence.[126] The reins were then passed to Robert Woodruff.

Today, Coca-Cola is not just a soda; it has become an integral part of bar culture, considered one of the essential drinks of the world, according to historian Tom Standage.[127] The company has ownership of dozens of brands, including mixers like Schweppes and Topo Chico.[128] It also owns an alcoholic Jack Daniel's and Coca-Cola mixed drink, a cocktail that was reportedly first created in 1907, likely in Chattanooga, site of the first Coca-Cola bottling operation and a short drive from the distillery, which opened in 1875.[129]

The men at the helm of the company also forever left their mark on Atlanta. Asa Candler's family is the namesake of the Candler Park neighborhood, and his $1 million contribution led to the development of Emory University. Emory's Goizueta Business School is named for Roberto Goizueta, another Coca-Cola CEO. Robert Woodruff's name was given to the Woodruff Center for the Arts and the library at the Atlanta University Center.

Jacobs Pharmacy no longer stands, but a giant neon sign and a historic marker show the site of the company's origins. Pemberton's handwritten "secret recipe" is now kept in a secured vault at the World of Coca-Cola, a tourist attraction created in honor of his famous beverage that sees over one million visitors every year.[130] The building sits alongside a statue in Pemberton's likeness in a park named for him.

The Massacre on Decatur Street

In the post–Civil War years, Atlanta's Black residents were able to carve out their own communities in the segregated city, especially as the population soared at the turn of the twentieth century, in part because rural Black people began moving to the city to find work beyond farm labor.[131] A Black elite formed, with many individuals becoming involved in local politics and running successful businesses. Alonzo Herndon grew his wealth with three barbershops and later became the city's first Black millionaire through his Atlanta Life Insurance Company.[132]

But the opportunities of the "New South" Grady spoke of in his famous speech didn't include Black Atlantans. In December 1905, a woman was allegedly assaulted by an unknown man, and a manhunt and vigilante violence followed. It was one of several alleged encounters that stirred up anti-Black sentiment, especially among the brothels and watering holes of Decatur Street that served whiskey and beer to mostly Black patrons, like the Laboring Men's Pleasure Club and Charles Mosely's saloon.[133]

Grady's protégé at the *Atlanta Constitution*, Clark Howell, used his platform to perpetuate racist ideas against rival politician Hoke Smith, formerly of

A local saloon features a sign banning Black customers in the early 1900s. *Stuart A. Rose Manuscript, Archives, and Rare Book Library, Emory University.*

the *Atlanta Journal*, at that year's governor's race.[134] Both noted that this type of violence from the Black men who frequented the downtown nightclubs of "Rusty Row" could be tied to vices like alcohol.

An assault on another woman led the newspapers to release sensationalized stories in extra editions in a further act of yellow journalism. The *Atlanta Evening News* followed the same lead, even calling for the reorganization of the Ku Klux Klan to protect Atlanta's white women from these would-be criminals. Editor John Temple Graves at the William Randolph Hearst–owned *Atlanta Georgian* was one of the worst offenders, using his white supremacist background to connect Black-owned saloons and businesses with unsubstantiated reports of violence against white women.[135]

More violence erupted on September 24, 1906, as white men, while leaving the saloons, attacked Black residents at random, marauding through the downtown business district.[136] People were pulled from the streetcar by the vigilantes. Victims were reportedly beaten, stabbed and shot, with men thrown from the windows of the Kimball House Hotel and bodies placed beneath the Henry Grady statue, which had been erected in 1891, a few years after his death.[137]

By the end, after four days of violence, much of the Black business district was in ruin, including one of Herndon's barbershops.[138] The massacre was only ended after the state militia stepped in. Herndon's employees were among the victims. Then-President Theodore Roosevelt was informed of the event but refused to interfere.[139]

At least twelve people died, but there could have been many more that were never recognized.[140] The event was covered in international news, damaging Atlanta's "New South" reputation.[141] Despite over one hundred

Left: Clark Howell was a protégé of Henry Grady and one of the figures that predated the Atlanta Race Massacre. *Library of Congress.*

Right: Hoke Smith perpetuated racist propaganda during his race for governor. *Library of Congress.*

individuals being indicted, only one person, a Jewish man, was charged in the massacre's aftermath.[142]

Following the massacre, the local government made a concerted effort to close Black gathering spaces or at least make it much more difficult for them to continue to operate. All bars had to reapply for their liquor licenses, and the number of Black-owned whiskey and beer saloons greatly decreased.[143] The general sentiment was that it was acceptable for the upper class to indulge in alcohol, but this was not permissible for working-class white people or people of color.[144]

At the time of the massacre, the city of Atlanta raked in around $50,000 in annual fees from liquor licenses.[145] The decision to not renew licenses to Black and immigrant businesses was considered an acceptable loss. After his win, Governor Hoke Smith even suggested that Black saloon owners be required to pass a test like those for voting, later instituting the grandfather clauses that disenfranchised Black Atlantans for generations.[146] Himself a bar owner of the Piedmont Hotel, Governor Smith didn't want to lose

Houses burned amid the
Atlanta Race Massacre.
*Stuart A. Rose Manuscript,
Archives, and Rare Book
Library, Emory University.*

money if the entire state enforced prohibitionist laws.[147] But other calls to
ban booze were stronger.

Atlanta experienced another race massacre in 1896, and it was not the
last, but it certainly left an impact on Atlanta's history.[148] In the wake of
2020's Black Lives Matter protests, the events of 1916 are rightfully being
reexamined by historians. Similar to the assessment of the Tulsa Race
Massacre, the language surrounding Atlanta's violent past is being shifted
from *riot* to *massacre* in interpretive materials. Memorial markers have also
been discussed to remember the events, and the removal of the Henry
Grady statue has been considered.

1907–1920

Prohibition Comes to Georgia

America's period of nationwide temperance may have started in 1920, but for Georgians, the laws against the consumption of alcohol started even earlier. The Georgia Temperance Society first met in 1828, before Atlanta even became a city, calling for moderation, not outright prohibition.[149] But within a few years, the message was for complete teetotaling, with claims that alcohol ruined families. In 1855, Atlanta hosted a Temperance Convention as interest in changing the city's laws around drinking rose.

When the ban on alcohol was announced in 1907, Atlanta was anything but dry. The city had twelve saloons offering beer, eighty-six with whiskey, one brewery and several wholesale operations. This proposed "experiment" would cost $131,000 per year in lost revenue from liquor licensing fees.[150] Atlanta also had one of the highest rates of alcohol-related arrests of any major U.S. city at the time.[151]

When the law was ultimately signed, bars put up signs signaling that it was the death of Atlanta.[152] In 1916, a "funeral procession" took place in town, with a barrel of moonshine and copper still fueling a bonfire.[153]

Big Bonanza owner John McMahon told a newspaper that his revenue had fallen from $100 to $5 per day in the wake of Prohibition, but he later stayed afloat thanks to domestic wines, which were then exempt from the legislation.[154]

Georgia Representative William D. Upshaw, who supported the "drys" in the prohibition movement, symbolically holds his umbrella over the dome of the U.S. Capitol building in 1926. *Library of Congress.*

But many of the counties of Georgia were already dry, especially those surrounding Atlanta, and many residents had already found ways around the rules.[155] While American Prohibition usually elicits images of jazz musicians and dancing, the experience in Atlanta was very different. The majority of illegal drinking took place in people's homes and private spaces at events like parties and social gatherings.[156]

The working classes sipped cheap corn liquor brought in from North Georgia (see "Fast Cars and Corn Whiskey" section) while the upper classes had their members' only clubs and hotels like the Kimball House Hotel, which remained one of the top sellers of alcohol during Prohibition.[157] The Ansley Hotel was popular with drunk legislators and call girls, as were the Winecoff and the Ritz.[158]

The rich also established locker clubs and rathskellers as loopholes at social clubs like the Capital City Club, but Black and Jewish residents weren't allowed to become members at many of these establishments.[159] Mail-order business was also allowed initially, with a maximum cap per month of two quarts of whiskey, one gallon of wine and six gallons of beer.[160]

But Prohibitionists pushed Governor John Slaton to close these allowances through a 1915 legislative session.

Breweries sprang up with "near beer," and doctors wrote prescriptions for medicinal alcohol for everything from cancer to diabetes.[161] In fact, these doctors are reported to have earned an astounding $40 million between 1921 to 1930 for these "medicines" nationwide.[162] Others survived by shifting their operations to making ice. Joseph Jacobs, who had come to prominence selling Coca-Cola and liquor at his pharmacies, leased his buildings to other businesses during Prohibition.[163] A 1916 raid found Atlanta's underground tunnels filled with bottled beer.[164]

The United States entered World War I, which ultimately added to the desire for nationwide prohibition, not to mention an anti-German sentiment for beer and the German American (and often Jewish) Atlantans who made it.[165]

When the United States was ready to sign the Volstead Act in 1918, Georgia was more than happy to join, becoming the thirteenth state to ratify the legislation it had already enacted over a decade before.[166]

It wasn't until 1935 that the state's prohibition would finally be repealed through the Alcoholic Beverage Control Act signed by Governor Eugene Talmage. In the end, it wasn't necessarily changing attitudes that pushed for this change but the desire for the tax revenue at the tail end of the Great Depression.[167]

Fast Cars and Corn Whiskey

Distilling in the United States traces its lineage back to the 1600s in Virginia, and it slowly made its way throughout the South. Georgia's distilling traditions can be traced back to the earliest days of its founding, thanks in part to the Scotch Irish settlers who moved to the mountainous northern towns after generations of crafting spirits back home.[168]

Corn whiskey was, of course, one of the most-sold spirits in the state because of the region's abundance of corn and distillers' ability to make it cheaply. In fact, the spirit was more valuable than the vegetable on its own. Distillers also created fruit brandies with excess produce. It was an easy way for farmers to avoid waste while earning extra money on the side, especially during difficult economic times in which jobs were scarce.[169] Even the poorest of the region could purchase a gallon or two with their wages.[170]

The term *moonshine* is often misapplied to what was created, usually unaged corn whiskey given nicknames like "white lightning." But legally speaking, it describes any homemade liquor that hasn't been taxed by the government.[171] It was usually made in a pot still with a copper coil set near a water source and protected by trees and the prying eyes of revenue agents.

The federal government attempted to collect taxes on bootleg spirits early as the 1790s, but it was the creation of the Internal Revenue Service during the Civil War that put a strain on these distillers.[172] Many refused to pay, while others gave up their operations.[173] In 1876, under President Ulysses S. Grant, several convicted moonshiners were granted clemency.[174] A few decades later, moonshiners were allowed to serve jail time, but they could also return to their farms to work.[175]

This 1903 drawing of a moonshiner is a caricature that would continue for many years to come. *Library of Congress.*

In the North Georgia counties like Dawson and Rabun, moonshiners set up creek-side stills, running their product into Atlanta to sell. Violence between the revenue officers and moonshiners was common, resulting in what's known as the Georgia Moonshine Wars in the 1870s. Gangs of vigilante moonshiners, called "whitecaps," fought against revenue agents and informants.[176]

Moonshiners developed a caricature-like status in the intervening years in television and film, like the namesake Discovery Channel show, the *Barney Google and Snuffy Smith* comic strip and Burt Reynolds's character in the film *White Lightning.*

Some had successful distilling operations, like Rufus Mathewson Rose, who established his Four Roses Whiskey distillery in 1867 in modern-day Vinings with no relation to the Kentucky brand. It became a destination, with trains running straight to the tasting room for day trippers, and it would stack up with any modern company.[177] When the state went dry, Rose moved the company to Tennessee, but his wealth allowed him to purchase an Atlanta mansion that still stands on Peachtree Street.[178]

Of course, Prohibition didn't put a stop to drinkers' ability to find moonshine in Atlanta, where whiskey was always available, especially in working-class neighborhoods like Cabbagetown.[179] Workers could get a

Cars like this one, on display at the Georgia Racing Hall of Fame in Dawsonville, were specially outfitted to run moonshine to Atlanta. *Photograph by the author.*

pint from a bootlegger after leaving a day's work at the mills.[180] Customers could also place orders from payphones, speaking in code, asking if "peaches were in stock."[181]

Getting the spirits to Atlanta was an operation unto itself. Henry Ford's Model T was released in 1908, and with it followed a series of affordable vehicles, which provided many the chance to own their first cars. The South's roads were also in the process of being repaved, like the creation of US-41, also known as "Dixie Highway," and State Highway 9 in the 1920s, two routes that became known as moonshine-running routes.[182]

The cars had to be outfitted to drive faster than those of the police and had to be able to carry special cargo, the millions of gallons of illegal spirits requested by Atlantans. Despite the danger of these chases, which often led to accidents and deaths, they led to the creation of stock car racing or, as it's known now, NASCAR.[183]

These "runners" made names for themselves in the process. Future stock car racer "Lightning" Lloyd Seay was said to have driven to Atlanta four times per day to "run shine." Forrest Turner spread his moonshine-running network while working for the Civilian Conservation Corps in the 1930s.[184] The liquor business also funded racing; store owner Raymond Parks contributed to several early racers, like his cousins Roy Hall and Seay.[185]

Above: Grandaddy Mimm's is one of Georgia's now-legal moonshine operations that stemmed from generations of illegal distilling. *Photograph by the author.*

Left: A sip from this jar of moonshine was offered to the author during a visit to a small Georgia town. *Photograph by the author.*

When Prohibition ended, bootlegging and the distilling of corn whiskey didn't end right away. In fact, the following decades made moonshine even more popular, especially in greater Atlanta.[186] A 1922 article cited that more illegal stills were destroyed in Georgia than anywhere else.[187] In 1968, Georgia had 3,169 stills seized, second only to neighboring Alabama.

But this wasn't done without incident.[188] In 1951, a local bootlegger named John "Fat" Hardy distilled a batch that led to the alcohol poisoning of over four hundred people, leading some to become permanently blinded.[189] It later inspired a blues song by Tommy Brown.[190]

Today, the distilling tradition continues in Atlanta and North Georgia, as modern interest in moonshine grows, including legal operations that were started by the relatives of original moonshiners. Grandaddy Mimm's Distilling Co. in Blairsville is named for Jack "Mimm" McClure.[191] The company uses his original recipe and is operated by his great-grandson. Ivy Mountain Distillery in Mt. Airy is also run by the family members of a former moonshiner.

1921–1960

Working-Class Beer Joints

The new decade was a difficult one for Georgians, especially in the many agricultural communities near Atlanta, as the boll weevil infestation struck cotton crops in 1915 and continued to impact farms for decades.[192] The war also came to the state's shores, as German U-boats set up along the Georgia coast in 1941.

But in the years between the Great Depression and the world wars, Atlanta redefined its relationship with alcohol, with citizens now able to drink in public spaces for the first time in nearly thirty years.

Prohibition was solidly in the past for most of the city, and the first liquor stores opened on county lines, where people could purchase booze for their enjoyment at home.[193] Fulton County, where Atlanta sits, passed laws allowing for alcohol sales with a slight majority. One store in the suburb of Marietta opened at 10:00 a.m. and was sold out of product within an hour.[194] Cheshire Bridge Road, which had previously thrived with moonshiners, became popular for now-legal alcohol sales.[195]

Working-class pubs also popped up around the city in places like the cotton mill worker's community of Cabbagetown, charming Poncey-Highlands and downtown, where Atlanta's drinking culture began. They had bar counters where customers could order a cheap meal with a beer.[196] Like the early Georgia taverns before them, these bars operated as social hubs, where information and opinions were passed among patrons.[197]

Top: Downtown Atlanta as photographed by John Vachon in 1938. This image includes a deli offering Pabst Blue Ribbon in the foreground. *Library of Congress.*

Bottom: This 1933 survey photograph shows the Cabbagetown neighborhood that surrounds a cotton mill. *Library of Congress.*

Grocery stores and delis also sold beer, wine, and some liquors.[198] While they typically offered national brands like Pabst Blue Ribbon and Schlitz, the few local breweries that survived Prohibition sold their offerings (see the "Rise of Craft Beer" section). The anti-German sentiment from World War I extended to the beer industry, with customers turning to American brands instead. Many of these watering holes have seen generations of patrons and remain relatively unchanged.

ATKINS PARK TAVERN (1922–PRESENT)

Called the oldest licensed bar in Atlanta, Atkins Park Tavern was opened in 1922, when Georgia was still under Prohibition, by cousins Morris Franco and Reuben Piha.[199] Taking its name from the planned streetcar suburb, it started as a delicatessen, selling beer and sandwiches.

It remained so until around 1983, when it was purchased by Warren Bruno, who owned several other local restaurants at the time, and he added a full bar. He kept features like the tile flooring and original ceilings from the 1920s, which are still visible today. The building was originally a home, but it was later lifted up, with the deli built underneath. The upstairs rooms still resemble a residence, and past employees have spoken of ghost sightings there.[200]

The bar adopted the phoenix as its logo, the icon of the city that appears on the official seal with the word *resurgens*, which means "to rise again" in Latin. It honors Atlanta's ability to "rise from the ashes," specifically following the devastation of the Civil War.

These days, Atkins Park is still a restaurant and bar, with its original location still standing along with another outpost in Smyrna.[201] Its menu has shifted from the classic beers it had when it opened to trendy drinks

Atkins Park Restaurant is considered Atlanta's oldest licensed bar; it was opened in 1922 as a deli. *Photograph courtesy of Atkins Park Restaurant.*

like frozen margaritas and Irish coffee, which it adopted in the 1980s.[202] Its offerings now sit somewhere in the middle, but it still leans into beer, with most of its brands now local to Atlanta.

RAY LEE'S BLUE LANTERN (1939–1986)

Long before Ponce de Leon Avenue was trendy, there was Ray Lee's Blue Lantern, a watering hole in what was then a rough neighborhood. Opened in 1939, it took its name from its owner, Ray Lee, who would go on to be nicknamed the "mayor of Ponce de Leon."[203]

Ray Lee's was just one of the city's many working-class dives at the time. Often called Atlanta's top redneck bar, it was where out-of-towners might come to see what the "South" looked like. Sitting under a portrait of Elvis Presley, the crowd of patrons at the bar on any given night might include travelers straight off the bus, off-duty policemen, construction workers or the occasional sex worker.[204] The bar also had a reputation for fights. Legendary blues performer Blind Willie McTell performed for cash all along Decatur Street and Ponce de Leon Avenue, including in the Ray Lee's parking lot and the Pig 'n Whistle, a restaurant he would use as a nickname to get competing record deals.[205]

Blind Willie McTell was often found along Ponce de Leon Avenue, including at Ray Lee's Blue Lantern. He's pictured here strumming his guitar in a local hotel room in 1940. *Library of Congress.*

Lee worked alongside his wife, Mildred, who he met while was the manager of Jennings Rose Room, a big band–style dance hall on Monroe Drive in modern Midtown in the 1940s.[206] He'd hitchhiked to Atlanta at the age of sixteen and never looked back, working for two decades in Atlanta's bars before opening his own.[207]

The bar usually opened at 6:00 a.m., with breakfast offerings and country music tunes filling the room, and finally closed for the night—or morning—at 4:00 a.m. Despite a 1966 fire, Ray Lee's had a loyal customer base who continued to turn up night after night. Even after Ray died of a stroke in 1983, Mildred carried on his legacy, running Ray Lee's and other clubs like the White Dot.[208]

She took no pushback from customers and was willing to toss them out, but she was also always happy to feed someone in need.[209]

But after Mildred ran the place by herself for a few years, the complaints from neighbors about fights and noise became too much. The lease expired, and over the years, the space became valuable to developers, so she shuttered the watering hole in 1986.[210]

For the past twenty years, the former Ray Lee's space has been occupied The Local, itself a popular dive bar. It also faces encroaching development in an ever-changing neighborhood that has already experienced the closure of many adjacent businesses.

Moe's and Joe's (1947–Present)

Opened in 1947 in Virginia-Highland, Moe's and Joe's was named for brothers Moe and Joe Krinsky and it gained popularity by serving cheap beer and hot dogs.[211] In the 1950s, the bar formed a partnership with Pabst Brewing, which has continued to this day, operating as a "tied house." The model from the Midwest was that a bar would exclusively serve one brewery's products.

Despite the bar no longer being under any official obligation, Pabst Blue Ribbon has continued to be the drink of choice of Moe's and Joe's ever since. The lore includes early neon signs, yellowed advertisements and framed checks from Pabst dating back to 1899 on the wall. One of the wildest stories from the bar's history is that the Krinskys once traded 1,700 pitchers of PBR for a 1947 Rolls Royce.[212]

The side of the building features a mural dedicated to a legendary former server, Horace McKennie, the first employee hired by the Krinskys in

Left: A 1984 photograph shows the Pabst Blue Ribbon that once hung outside Moe's and Joe's. It can now be found behind the bar. *Library of Congress.*

Opposite: The exterior mural honors McKinnie's legacy at the bar. *Photograph by the author.*

1949.[213] He wore his signature red jacket and bowtie, a holdover from his time working hotel banquets, and presented the beer on a platter, calling it the "finest beer served."

The neighborhood around it has changed over the years, but some things haven't. There's a regular crowd, especially on Tuesdays, when the bar offers $3.50 pitchers of the beer. The 1920s cash register still sits on the bar. The worn booths are frequented by old-timers who never left and a young crowd of college students.

Moe's and Joe's continues to serve some of the highest volume of Pabst Blue Ribbon in the nation, but this signature beer is now served alongside plenty of other brands of beer and liquor. The bar still has one of the best deals in town, its MoJo burger, which has been on the menu since 1947, costs only six dollars.[214] Wash it all down with a five-dollar pitcher of PBR, offered on Sundays, or the 1947 Mimosa, its recipe, found in the back of an old filing cabinet, dating back to the bar's founding year.

Manuel's Tavern (1956–Present)

Before there was Manuel's, there was the Tip Top Billiard Parlor, opened in the 1920s by Lebanese immigrant Gibran Maloof.[215] He didn't know that Georgia and the rest of the United States was under Prohibition and opened Tip Top as a bar, but he got around the rules by selling beer-

Above: Several regulars have brass placards at their favorite bar seats. *Photograph by the author.*

Opposite: A mural on the weathered brick features Manuel's logo. *Photograph by the author.*

making kits for at-home consumption. Located across the street from the Georgia State Capitol, Tip Top became a popular spot for the politician crowd for the next thirty years.[216]

It was followed across town with the opening of Manuel's Tavern, run by Maloof's sons Manuel and Robert, in Poncey-Highland in 1956. Before becoming Manuel's, the bar was operated as Harry's Delicatessen, a casual sandwich and beer spot. Inspired by their time in English pubs during World War II, the Maloofs installed eclectic décor, like the stools and the wooden bar from Tip Top, which had survived a fire, and wood paneling from

nearby houses that faced wrecking balls.[217] It became a popular hangout spot for students from Emory University and Agnes Scott College, who sipped on pints of Budweiser and Andeker, a Munich-style lager made by Pabst.[218] Only beer was served there until the 1970s.[219] The bar also quietly integrated in the 1960s, as sit-ins and protests were taking place at the other lunch counters and cafeterias around the city.[220]

Manuel wanted to keep things simple at his tavern, so he didn't have live music or a jukebox and instead let customers engage in conversation or the occasional political debate like they did in early taverns.[221] In fact, it's been an essential stop for campaigning Democrats, including Jimmy Carter, Al Gore, Bill Clinton and Barack Obama. Carter announced his bid for the governor's mansion inside the tavern in 1970. When Manuel Maloof himself ran for the DeKalb County Board of Commissioners in 1974, Robert kept the business going.[222] Maloof even became known as the "godfather of Georgia Democratic politics."

Over the years, the bar has become like a museum, each piece on its wall with a story of Atlanta's past. They include pennants from Atlanta's sports teams, hundreds of beer cans and portraits of Franklin Delano Roosevelt and John F. Kennedy.[223] The bar also has a rooftop chicken coop and assigned parking for members of the clergy.[224]

After Manuel's death in 2004, his ashes were added to a space behind Roosevelt's portrait, alongside those of his brother Robert, who died in

2013, and regular Calvin Fluellen, the first Black graduate of the Grady Memorial College of Radiology.[225] A bicycle that hangs from the ceiling in the Eagle's Nest room honors Manuel's son Tommy, who died in 2001 from complications of Crohn's disease. Brass nameplates at the bar also honor other regulars. Two attempts were made to franchise the tavern, but neither location had the magic of the original.[226]

Countless groups have met at the bar's wooden tables over the years, including the Atlanta Press Club through the 1980s and the Georgia Production Partnership Group, which laid the groundwork for Hollywood productions like *Anchorman 2* to be filmed inside the bar.[227] The Audubon Society and *Dungeons & Dragons* clubs still meet there.[228] A 1984 performance of *As You Like It* at the tavern led to the creation of Atlanta's Shakespeare Tavern, a long-running local theater organization that performs the works of the Bard and others.[229]

In 2015, the bar closed for a seven-month-long renovation that patrons feared would spell the end. But the artifacts on the walls were carefully removed, archived and cleaned before they were rehung. The updates adjusted the bar's dining spaces and also made improvements to the bar setup.[230]

The COVID-19 pandemic also hit the bar hard, and Manuel's faced closure, but the community rallied together for a fundraising effort to keep the doors open. It was subsequently added to the National Register of Historic Places, hopefully to preserve it for generations to come.[231]

Inevitably, no one could describe his bar quite like Manuel himself. He told *Atlanta* magazine, "This ain't no beer joint. It's a community center."[232]

1961–1980

Sweet Auburn and Black Atlanta

After the 1906 violence on Decatur Street (see "The Massacre on Decatur Street" section), little by little, a Black business district returned around Auburn Avenue, spared by the 1917 Great Atlanta Fire.[233] Originally named Wheat Street and changed in 1893, it gained the nickname "Sweet Auburn," and it was where a young Martin Luther King Jr. grew up.[234]

The first wave of the Great Migration saw Black Americans leave Southern cities like Atlanta for more opportunities in the North.[235] But for those who stayed, Sweet Auburn thrived. A 1956 issue of *Fortune* magazine called it the "richest Negro street in the world."[236]

Similar to what was happening in Harlem, nightclubs and entertainment venues popped up in Sweet Auburn to host Black performers, like the Roof Garden Dance Hall at the Odd Fellows building.[237] The Poinciana hosted small bands in its cocktail bar, along with big names like Louis Armstrong, Billie Holliday and Benny Goodman.[238] People came to the 81 Theatre to dance the Charleston.[239] The area's other venues included the Sunset Casino, the Crystal Theater and the Magnolia Ballroom.[240]

Dee's Birdcage was a twenty-four-hour Chitlin' Circuit bar in Castleberry Hill that hosted notable Black musicians like Isaac Hayes, Gladys Knight and Curtis Mayfield.[241] A fire would shutter the establishment for decades, but another bar took over in the new millennium (see "From Snakes to Castles" section).

The creation of the Martin Luther King Jr. National Historical Park in 1980 helped revive the neighborhood, returning Sweet Auburn to its status as the city's thriving Black business district.[242] The park includes King's birth home, church and several other historic landmarks.

While all of these bars and clubs are now long gone, a few have stood the test of time.

TOP HAT CLUB (1938–1949) AND ROYAL PEACOCK (1949–1973, 2010–PRESENT)

In 1938, local Black businessmen opened the Top Hat Club, a lively nightclub in Sweet Auburn with a house band and performances from Chitlin' Circuit performers Cab Calloway and Louis Armstrong.[243] By 1949, the club had been purchased by Carrie Cunningham, a former circus performer who also owned a nearby hotel that appeared in the *Green Book*, an essential resource for Black travelers in the segregated South.[244] Performers at her club could also stay there safely.

She renamed it the Royal Peacock and decorated it with an Egyptian motif. It's said that Cunningham set up her son, Red McAllister, to perform at the club, often referred to as "Club Beautiful," to keep him out of trouble.[245] She was also among the minority as a female bar owner in the country at that time.

The Royal Peacock drew comparisons to Harlem's Apollo Theater, as it became a place to see and be seen, especially in the 1950s and '60s.[246] Athletes Jackie Robinson and Muhammad Ali and civil rights leaders Martin Luther King Jr., Hosea Williams and Andrew Young were among the club's distinguished guests.[247]

It's much easier to note who did *not* perform at the Peacock rather than list who did, but the top acts included Georgians Ray Charles, Little Richard, Otis Redding, Glady Knight, Tina Turner and James Brown.[248] Sam Cooke held one of his last performances here before his untimely death in 1964.[249] The club also had a house band with floor shows from peacock-clad dancers and touring comedians like Timmie Rogers and Mantan Moreland. "Gorgeous George" was the emcee for the evening events.[250] Artists would come to entertain for one night or have multi-week appearances.

The end of segregation in the late 1960s and the assassination of Martin Luther King Jr. in 1968 led to a downturn on Auburn Avenue, as "white flight" moved many city residents out to the suburbs.[251] Highway construction

Left: The Royal Peacock during its heyday, with a neon showing off its nickname, "Club Beautiful." *Library of Congress.*

Below: Today, the Royal Peacock is a reggae and hip-hop club. *Photograph by the author.*

cut straight through the "Black Main Street" in the 1970s, as well as nearby Edgewood Avenue (see the "Edgewood Avenue Revival" section), further affecting the neighborhood.

Cunningham sold the club not long after to Henry Wynn, a local talent booker. Singer and pianist Ronnie Millsap frequented the space, both as a patron and a performer, describing it as a friendly place in a rough neighborhood.[252] Dionne Warwick also appeared at the club during this time, performing both original tunes and a Ray Charles cover.[253]

The Royal Peacock, as it was known, closed in 1973, the same year its matriarch died. It became a social club for The Men of Style, a cab drivers' group, in the late '70s, and by the mid-'80s, local musician Clay Harper had brought in acts like Hank Ballard and Thee Midnighters before a fire forced its closure in 1987.[254] In 1998, Atlanta's own OutKast featured the club in the music video for their song "Rosa Parks" from the hit *Aquemini* album, named in honor of the Civil Rights hero.[255] Never mind the fact that Parks didn't initially appreciate the mention.

After another change of hands in the mid-2000s, the Royal Peacock reopened in 2010 under the name Cunningham originally gave it.[256] But instead of Motown and soul, its soundtrack now skews toward reggae and hip-hop, but still, the Friday night crowd takes to the red and black checkered floor.

LA CAROUSEL LOUNGE (1960–1996)

Brothers Robert and James Paschal opened their first restaurant, Paschal Brothers Soda, on West Hunter Street in the historic West End in 1947.[257] Robert had previously worked at the soda fountain at Jacob's Pharmacy downtown, where Coca-Cola was first served.[258] The casual luncheonette started out serving sandwiches, but when the lunch menu took off, the brothers expanded the space and the menu.[259] They could no longer cook at home and bring in the food by taxi, as they had before.[260] Now operating the space as Paschal's Restaurant, the duo quickly found success serving their mother's secret fried chicken recipe, which remains a favorite of diners.[261]

The Paschals also opened the city's first Black-owned hotel, where politicians could come for essential rest and relaxation while they planned campaigns, like Reverend Jesse Jackson's 1984 and 1988 presidential runs. In late 1960, the brothers opened an adjacent jazz venue, La Carrousel Lounge, which served Black and white patrons, despite local segregation laws, as well as LGBTQ+ individuals.[262]

Inspired by the clubs James had visited in Europe, the lounge became an essential stop for touring jazz artists and Black musicians along the Chitlin' Circuit.[263] Over the years, the two-hundred-seat club welcomed Aretha Franklin, Dizzy Gillespie, Stevie Wonder, Quincy Jones and Lou Rawls, as well as local acts.[264] Billy Taylor penned his song "At La Carousel" for the club, and Jimmy Smith recorded an album here.[265] In fact, future Representative John Lewis hosted his wedding after-party here in 1968.[266]

The interior of Paschal's Restaurant. *Photograph by the author.*

Sadly, the former Paschal's Motor Hotel, home to La Carousel, has fallen into disrepair. *Photograph by the author.*

The restaurant and club were also hangouts for the neighboring students of Atlanta's historically Black colleges and universities, like Morehouse and Spelman.[267] In fact, many consider the Paschal's properties to be the unofficial headquarters of the civil rights movement, where Martin Luther King Jr. and his contemporaries planned the Poor People's Campaign over vegetable soup and peach cobbler.[268] After King's assassination, mourners came to Paschal's for comfort.

The hotel was sold in 1996, but it's now mostly abandoned, sitting next to another Atlanta dining institution, the Busy Bee Cafe, which has also been open since 1947. Clark Atlanta University purchased the building and used it as a dormitory for a time.[269] Paschal's opened a newer, larger restaurant location in Castleberry Hill in 2002, but it did so without its lounge.

Hotels, Motels and Holiday Inns

Atlanta's party scenes aren't limited to homes and bars. The hotels have played a large part in the city's nightlife from its the earliest days. Hotels like the Kimball House rose as alternatives to saloons. It continued to pour the booze straight through Prohibition, and the tradition certainly hasn't stopped. In the years that followed, the party continued at the Ansley's Rainbow Room, Aragon, Biltmore's Empire Room, Georgian Terrace, Henry Grady's Paradise Room and the Piedmont, among countless others.[270] Some even served as residences, especially for the bachelor crowd.

The Piedmont Hotel's reputation preceded it, with its lobby bar called a "cesspool of sin" within years of its 1903 opening. It was able to survive Prohibition by selling beer—and perhaps the stronger stuff if you knew who to ask—hosting presidents Theodore Roosevelt and Woodrow Wilson.[271] The Ansley's Rathskeller was intended to be reminiscent of the eating and drinking halls of Germany when it opened in 1913.[272]

The Imperial Hotel opened in 1911, advertising its "absolutely fireproof" design in Chicago-style architecture, with eight floors and original Otis elevators.[273] For a period, it was owned by Glenn and Lillian Loudermilk, who also owned the Clermont Hotel (see "Strip Club City" section).[274] During its heyday, The Imperial had several nightlife spots, like Joe Dale's Cellar Restaurant, a fine-dining restaurant in the 1950s; the Copa Caprice; and Whisk a Go Go.[275] But the best known was the Domino Lounge, a

The grand Georgian Terrace Hotel hosted celebrities and politicians over the years. *Photograph by the author.*

showplace with exotic dancers and cabaret performers.[276] Little Richard, Piano Red and Fats Domino were also said to have performed here.[277]

The hotel's party days ended in 1980, when it closed and became low-income housing. In 1990, it became the site of an occupation, as activists fought to have the abandoned hotel converted into much-needed space for the unhoused in the pricey leadup to the 1996 Olympics.[278] The group hung a banner from the top of the building with the words "House the Homeless Here." Their efforts were eventually successful, and the hotel now serves as affordable housing for those in need.

The Georgian Terrace opened in 1911, a Beaux-Arts beauty with ten stories that wouldn't look out of place in Paris.[279] It hosted such guests as Calvin Coolidge, F. Scott Fitzgerald, the Metropolitan Opera Company and the two stars of the film *Gone with the Wind*, Vivien Leigh and Clark Gable, who stayed during the 1939 premier at the nearby Loew's Grand Theater.[280] Each decade had its own nightlife spot inside the hotel, including The Purple Poodle in the 1960s, the Electric Ballroom in the 1970s (see "That Dive Bar Sound" section) and, later, the Agora Ballroom. The Purple Poodle was known for its live music, welcoming John Benedetto Jr., the younger brother of Tony Bennett. The Agora had a wide range of performers, from Joan Jett and the Blackhearts to Bow Wow Wow.

The hotel fell on hard times in the 1980s, with calls for its demolition.[281] After a 1991 renovation and a stint as apartments, the Georgian Terrace was reopened as a hotel. It still hosts the Hollywood set, including in its use as a filming location, and hosts performers from the Fox Theater across the street.[282] Its lower level is home to Edgar's Proof and Provision, a speakeasy-inspired cocktail bar.[283]

Opened in 1913, the Winecoff Hotel was among the finest in the city, also claiming fire resistance. It boasted 150 rooms spread across 15 floors and entertained a wide variety of customers.[284] Call girls would entertain legislators, and the Cotton Blossom Club was welcoming of the city's gay patrons.[285] In fact, the city's first gay-affirming church met at the hotel.[286]

Sadly, on December 7, 1946, the fully booked hotel caught fire, resulting in the deaths of 119 people, including several who jumped from windows to escape the flames. The hotel's original owners, William and Grace Winecoff, also perished, as the building had no fire escapes or sprinklers.[287] Photographer Arnold Hardy won a Pulitzer Prize for his images of the disaster. It remains one of the deadliest hotel fires in history and led to many changes in building safety requirements. Since 2007, the site has been occupied by the Ellis Hotel, where a historic marker memorializes the fire's victims.

The skyline may have noticeably changed over the past one hundred years with the loss of some hotels and the renovations of others. For better or worse, the revival of downtown's hotels, much at the hands of developers like John Portman, made Atlanta an international city, with watering holes popular with both the conventioneer crowd and locals.

PLAYBOY CLUB (1965–1975)

In 1913, the Ansley Hotel was built by Edwin P. Ansley, a local developer with a namesake neighborhood, on Forsyth Street downtown. It had a bar called the Owl Room, which became a popular hangout. In 1953, it was purchased by the Macon-based Dinkler Hotel group and renamed, memorably hosting the city's first biracial formal dinner when it held a reception for Dr. Martin Luther King Jr. after he won a Nobel Peace Prize in 1964.[288]

In 1965, at the center of the swinging '60s, the Playboy Club opened its Atlanta outpost at the Dinkler, marking the chain's fifteenth location to open in only five years.[289] Access was granted to only members and their guests, who were given physical keys they had to show at the door and pay

A mug from the Playboy Club is one of the souvenirs guests could enjoy their drinks in. *Photograph by the author.*

an annual fee for. A Bunny would come to greet them in the signature corset and ears and then take them up the stairs to the club. Of course, magazine creator Hugh Hefner was on hand for the Atlanta location's grand opening.[290]

The walls of the bar were adorned with framed images of the magazine's centerfolds. The Bunnies played bumper pool with guests and could flirt but were forbidden from dating patrons, one of the several rules found in the *Bunny Manual*. They also had to keep their appearance neat, wear three-inch heels, and be able to execute the perfect "Bunny dip," a careful pivot that allowed them to bend down and serve drinks in the tight costume.[291] And they couldn't go to work without first passing inspection.[292]

Much of the club's crowd were local businessmen or visiting conventioneers, who were required to wear a suit and tie, but it was also a celebrity hangout that brought in the occasional female patron. Another level above held the Penthouse, where four performers and comedians took the stage every weekend for a $2.50 cover charge.[293]

Tony Bennett, Dean Martin, George Burns, Lou Rawls, Roy Orbison, George Carlin, Steve Martin and Milton Berle made appearances.[294] The Paul Mitchell Trio even recorded a live album at the Playboy club.[295] Famous faces looking for a night out were also customers of the club. On any given night, you might see songwriter Johnny Mercer and actor Robert Mitchum sharing a table.[296]

Patrons could also get a fine meal from the buffet or order from the menu, with offerings like filet mignon, ribs and the "Bunny burger." The bar served the signature drink, Playmate Pink, made of gin and served in Playboy Club–branded glassware that featured a bunny holding a key.[297]

By the end of the 1960s, the Playboy Clubs faced financial setbacks, as other nightlife options opened, including strip clubs. The Atlanta location was affected by a fire and was shuttered in 1975.[298] The main hotel building was demolished in 1973, but the addition, where the club was located, is now operated as another hotel.[299]

Polaris (1967–2004, 2014–Present)

Portman is responsible for much of what makes up today's Atlanta skyline, including the then Regency-Hyatt House, which was opened in 1967.[300] It was the first new hotel to be opened in the city since 1924, and it then claimed the title of the tallest building in the city—but that didn't last long.[301] Portman's design included features like an open atrium to showcase the twenty-two stories accessible by sets of glass elevators and fountains in the lobby that pranksters would throw bubbles in.[302] The downstairs Le Parasol Lounge had an aviary with live exotic birds, and the Midnight Sun Restaurant was a tourist favorite.[303]

But it was the Polaris Lounge that gained the most notoriety, with its blue glass UFO-esque dome and unrivaled views of the city through the floor-to-ceiling windows 312 feet above street level.[304] It made a complete rotation over the course of forty-five minutes and frequently elicited gasps and expletives upon first glance.[305] Visitors would come for prime rib and $1.25 cocktails to share with the view. The drink of choice was the peach daiquiri, served in a branded cocktail glass with a Polaris-shaped swizzle stick.

The lounge attracted politicians and celebrities, including Jim Morrison, Sidney Poitier, Harry Belafonte, Gladys Knight and The Jackson 5.[306] The

Polaris offers incredible views of downtown Atlanta. *Photograph by the author.*

hotel also gained a reputation for its tolerance after offering Dr. Martin Luther King Jr. a meeting place for a luncheon after another hotel refused.[307]

Portman followed up the Hyatt with the Westin Peachtree Plaza Hotel in 1976, located on the site of the Henry Grady Hotel with its own revolving top-floor restaurant, The Sun Dial; and the Atlanta Marriott Marquis in 1985, which has a similarly open atrium.[308] The design would be replicated in countless hotels over the years.

Polaris closed in 2004; as the surrounding buildings overtook it, it could no longer boast the best view in town.[309] After the lounge spent a decade in the dark, Hyatt Hotels took part in a $65 million renovation that brought it back to life in 2014, complete with its signature cocktails and mid-century modern–style furnishings.[310] Over fourteen thousand locals came to see its grand reveal.[311]

One of the new additions to the revived Polaris is a rooftop hive of honeybees, which produce the bar's Blue Dome Honey, which is incorporated into dishes and drinks.[312] The menu also focuses on Black-owned businesses, including spirits and wine brands.

TRADER VIC'S (1976–PRESENT)

The Trader Vic's menu includes classics like the Mai Tai and Suffering Bastard (*pictured*), plus a signature drink made specially for the Atlanta location. *Photograph by the author.*

Atlanta may have been late to adopt the South Pacific–style watering holes, but it jumped in full force. Trader Eng's came first, opening in 1963 downtown at Peachtree Towers, serving Polynesian fare and tropical drinks before expanding to Cobb County.[313]

While the first location opened in Emeryville, California, Trader Vic's opened an outpost in Atlanta in 1976, and it is, as of this writing, only the second location left in the nation. It's also one of the few left that "Vic" himself, Victor Bergeron, worked on, and it is in its original location, a a result of an early partnership with Hilton Hotels.[314]

Set in the basement of the downtown hotel, the dimly lit space features bamboo-covered walls, rattan chairs and pufferfish that hang from the bar. In addition to Trader Vic's classics, like the Mai Tai, Fog Cutters and the Scorpion Bowl, the Peachtree

The basement-level Trader Vic's Atlanta is one of the few remaining bars that "Vic" himself worked on. *Photograph by the author.*

Punch was created as the Atlanta location's signature drink (see "The Drinks That Made Atlanta").[315] It's made with fresh peaches, rum, orange juice, peach liqueur and coconut syrup, blended and topped with grated nutmeg.

Today, Trader Vic's Atlanta is still wildly popular with conventioneers, especially attendees of DragonCon, an annual pop culture fan convention similar to ComicCon. It's also a draw for lovers of tiki culture who are in search of one of Trader Vic's original locations. The location previously hosted Hukilau, a tiki lover's weekend, in the early 2000s.[316] The bar now celebrates almost fifty years of operation.

Chattahoochee River

The state's boundaries follow the Chattahoochee River, which winds its way from the North Georgia Mountains through Atlanta and into a lake near the Florida border. Taking its name from the Muscogee word for "marked-rock river," the body of water is where Native tribes settled starting as early as 1000 BCE.[317]

Travelers and traders used the water way to get around in the 1820s, with steamboat operations running from the Gulf of Mexico to Columbus, south of Atlanta. It even inspired the work of Sidney Lanier, Georgia's poet laureate, in his poem "The Song of the Chattahoochee."[318]

Local business owners set up along the river to power their mills and established ferries to cross the water, usually near taverns.[319] Many of these ferries gave their names to Atlanta's modern roads, like Pace's Ferry and DeFoors Ferry. Hardy Pace, the former road's namesake, even had an inn and tavern he operated on the land he gained from a land lottery.[320]

Much the river's modern acreage is encompassed by the Chattahoochee River National Recreation Area, which includes forty-eight miles of river accessible by boat, all federally protected.[321] The river is also where the majority of Atlanta's drinking water comes from.[322]

Giving its name to the iconic 1992 Alan Jackson song, the river also becomes a playground for Atlantans during the summer months, as they are desperate for some reprieve from the humidity hundreds of miles from the coast. And nothing helps cool off locals quite like muddy river water and booze.

The Chattahoochee River is a large presence in Atlanta, forming the city's boundary to one side, running from North Georgia to Columbus. *Photo by the author.*

Ramblin' Raft Race (1969–1980)

In 1969, Larry Patrick and a group of Delta Sigma Chi fraternity brothers from Georgia Tech held the first of what would become a famous race down the Chattahoochee River, a floating party that would be talked about for generations to come.[323] Nicknamed "Woodstock on the Water," the revelry started as a rivalry between the students and the hosts of a local radio station.[324] It took its name from the "Ramblin' Wreck," the school's storied mascot Model A Ford, which appears at every football game.

The first race that occurred on the third Saturday of May was nearly thirty miles long, starting at Buford Dam on Lake Lanier, named for the poet.[325] But the following year, it was cut down to a ten-mile stretch from Morgan Falls Dam in Sandy Springs to Paces Ferry in Vinings.[326] Rafts were made with improvised or rented materials, including discarded beer cans and pool floats, and took the shapes of trains and animals. You might have seen a riverboat replica, a *Jaws*-sized shark, a piano or even a Volkswagen beetle where a live beaver had taken up residence floating down the water.[327] By 1972, there were six award divisions, including Showboats and the appropriately named Bikini Division, made up of scantily clad ladies.[328]

Revelers would stop for refills at the infamous Riverbend Apartments, or the "Party Spot," a clearing in the woods that, at that time was, accessible only by water. Many never made it to the finish line, and racers often had to be rescued along the way.[329]

But no matter what, the most common ingredient was a copious amount of alcohol, both brought along and picked up along the way on the banks of the river from spectators who brought supplies from the local liquor stores. Age was of little to no concern during the race, with plenty of people willing to sell beer to the underage set. The drinking age was lowered to eighteen in 1972, which allowed for more partiers. You could also find harder stuff, like speed and quaaludes, among the crowd.[330]

With every year, the event grew to include more people, some half a million at its peak, who came from all over the country. The race was covered in international media and earned a Guinness Book of World Records title for "biggest participation sports event." Live entertainment included

Opposite: A shirt from the 1976 Ramblin' Raft Race. *Photograph by the author.*

Above: The raft race paved the way for tubing, or "shooting the Hooch," a popular summer pastime. *Photograph by the author.*

appearances by the Charlie Daniels Band, Mother's Finest and Atlanta's famous names; then-Governor Jimmy Carter and CNN owner Ted Turner, also turned up. Playboy Playmate Candy Loving also caused a stir with her arrival as part of an appearance for Budweiser.[331]

Coca-Cola gave out free soda for the winners one year, and corporate sponsorships from Anheuser-Busch added to the annual budget.[332] People would park on the riverbanks to watch the debauchery, and some even took to hot air balloons to see it from above.[333]

Patrick was one of the creators of the American Rafting Association (ARA), formed in 1972 to help manage the race and protect the environment. But this didn't solve the race's problems, including traffic along the bridges from spectators and pollution in the river. A net was even placed to catch some of the trash, and the ARA banned Styrofoam during the race.[334]

In August 1978, after that year's event, Jimmy Carter (then in the Oval Office), alongisde Patrick, established the Chattahoochee River National Recreation Area under the National Park Service to permanently protect

Atlanta's river.[335] The final event took place in 1980. Other events were inspired by the Ramblin' Raft Race, with similar versions taking place in the following years along rivers in Florida and Oklahoma.[336]

The end of the Atlanta raft race didn't stop the party. On any given sunny weekend from May to September, you're sure to see flotillas of people making their way down the river in mismatched tubes with coolers full of beer. The national park, of course, keeps a close eye on river conditions and rafters' safety, adding life jackets to several put-ins and restricting glass on the water.

There's even an entire enterprise related to the summer pastime, with companies outfitting groups with tubes, life jackets and, most importantly, shuttles to and from the parking lots along the river. The unlikely raft race started a tradition that carries on for the generations too young to remember the party on the water.

HOTLANTA RIVER EXPO (1978–2003)

But the Ramblin' Raft Race wasn't the only party on the water to sweep the city. The gay community also had its version, the Hotlanta River Expo, which started in 1978. In its first year, it already had a large following, with three hundred gay men spending the day on the water in rented rafts instead of ramshackle floats.[337]

In the following years, people came from dozens of cities and even abroad to participate. It became a larger event, spanning four days, with corporate sponsorships, countless parties at clubs like The Armory, the Mr. and Miss Hot Atlanta pageants and a room block at the Colony Square Hotel, now The Starling Hotel.[338]

The day on the river was still the draw, with attendees piling into yellow school buses to make their way to the water. The outing in themed swimwear and accessories crawled for six hours from Johnson Ferry Road to US-41, with prizes handed out for the most creative outfits and rafts. Water fights were common, with water guns and buckets used to splash the other rafts. The event ironically took place in then-conservative Cobb County, which would make headlines in the leadup to the 1996 Olympics following a theater performance that depicted AIDS and gay individuals.[339] A boycott would follow called "Olympics Out of Cobb."

By 1989, the Hotlanta River Expo was known as one of the largest gay events in the Southeast, poised to continue for many years, like Aspen Gay

Ski Week and Dinah Shore Weekend in Palm Springs.[340] In the end, the debt of running the event caused it to fail, and it ended in the new millennium.[341]

RIVERBEND APARTMENTS (1970s–1980s)

In part because of its riverfront location in the heart of the Ramblin' Raft Race action, the Riverbend Apartments became Atlanta's party central. It signified a time when singles were now living on their own for the first time. And it had such an abundance of people like pilots and stewardesses coming in from elsewhere in the country, it became known as a "stew zoo."[342] It was one of many "singles-only" apartment complexes that opened around the country, with six hundred units overlooking the shoals of the Chattahoochee River.[343]

Until 1972, suburban Cobb County had strict liquor laws, but one of the loopholes was that it was legal to sell in private clubs, like the one at Riverbend, or on the river.[344] The complex hosted several wild parties per week that lasted well into the evening, with constantly flowing kegs of beer,

The former Riverbend Apartments clubhouse is now the leasing office and a coffee shop. *Photograph by the author.*

Attendees of the Ramblin' Raft Race could get out of the water right in front of the Riverbend Apartments to continue the party on land. *Photograph by the author.*

an estimated 126 in total at one event, and minimal clothing in the pool.[345] Men paid three dollars for admission, and women paid half.[346] Quaaludes were passed around freely as bands rocked out every weekend.[347] It even appeared as a plot point for 2002's *Catch Me if You Can*, where pilot and con man Frank Abagnale had his crash pad.

In 1972, *Playboy* magazine dubbed it "ground zero for the sexual revolution," while some locals called it, perhaps fairly, "Gonorrhea Gulch."[348] Residents talked about the sexual encounters between partygoers and topless women in the neighborhood pool.[349]

But by the next decade, the party had mostly died down as people moved to other suburbs. A lawsuit filed in 1989 targeted the apartments, citing the Fair Housing Act's recent amendments and eventually eliminating the option of "singles only" or "adults only" housing.[350]

The complex was sold in 2006 and renamed. The Riverbend Apartments clubhouse that hosted wild parties is the leasing office for the now-renamed Walton on the Chattahoochee apartments, which has held an outpost of the Chattahoochee Coffee Company since 2012, trading rowdy keg parties and topless swimming for coffee and coworking.[351]

The City Beneath the Streets

In the 1920s in the former Humbug Square area of downtown, city leaders faced a predicament.[352] The railroad tracks that had earned Atlanta its original name, Terminus, conflicted with the traffic of carriages and newly arrived automobiles. To ease the traffic, it was determined that the trains would remain in the viaducts below, and a new street-level city would be built above it.[353]

The first-level shops became basements, and especially during Prohibition, speakeasies were set up inside these now-underground spaces.[354] Blues singer Bessie Smith's 1927 song "Preachin' the Blues" described the city during that time, as she was inspired during her days performing at Decatur Street's 81 Theater: "Under the viaduct ev'ry day, drinkin' corn and holl'in' hooray, pianos playin' til the break of day."[355]

The streetlamps and cobbled streets were largely forgotten and difficult to access for the next few decades. In 1969, the city "rediscovered" the literal foundations of Atlanta and made plans to transform it into an entertainment district centered on the Zero Mile Post from Atlanta's railroad roots, now preserved inside the Atlanta History Center.[356]

Kenny's Alley was named for an early tavern owner and is home to The Masquerade music venue. *Photograph by the author.*

The cavernous space became Underground Atlanta, with bars and restaurants that became hotspots for young Atlantans, like The Blarney Stone and Mine Shaft. The Blackstone Inn was inspired by a classic British pub. The Bucket Shop was covered in Wall Stock memorabilia and became popular for its cheap burgers.[357] P.J. Kenney's took its name from an early Atlanta merchant.[358] The Mad Hatter offered penny draft beers.[359] Actor Dick Van Dyke got his start performing at Wit's End.[360]

At its peak, Underground Atlanta drew in 3.5 million visitors annually and was the city's answer to New Orleans's Bourbon Street.[361] But in 1975, the city's MARTA train line split the underground space, taking away some of the bar spaces, including Ruby Red's, The Blarney Stone and The Mine Shaft.[362] Bucket Shop closed its Underground location and moved to the up-and-coming Buckhead nightlife district (see the "Buckhead Meets Bourbon Street" section). The party stopped, at least temporarily, in 1982, when all of Underground closed.

The second reign of Underground started during the leadup to the 1996 centennial Olympic Games in Atlanta, with multimillion dollar upgrades and new bars, like Kenny's Alley, which opened in 1989.[363] Kenny's Alley took its name from early Atlanta tavern owner Michael E. Kenny, an immigrant from Ireland.[364]

Inspired by Baltimore's Harbor Place, the 1990s Underground was more family- and tourist-friendly, hosting the annual Peach Drop New Year's Eve festivities with plans for a railroad museum.[365] But it was still the one of the only places in town where you could get a drink until 4:00 a.m., so it continued to attract a nightlife crowd.

In the mid-2000s, new clubs and restaurants opened with the introduction of an open container zone, where people can move freely between bars with their drinks.[366] The drag performances from the then-shuttered club Backstreet moved over to Charlie Brown's Cabaret (see the "Dawn of Disco" section), and the nightclub Future brought the late-night dance crowd.

Drinks at La Pigalle, a burlesque club and speakeasy at Underground Atlanta. *Photograph by the author.*

Over the following decades, Underground Atlanta became a shell of its former self, becoming a constant point of discussion for every city election, with each prospective leader making big promises of what it could be. The area became associated with crime, including a fatal shooting in 2013.[367]

The City of Atlanta purchased the property in 2014 for $8.8 million, and there was interest from outside developers, including one who talked about opening a casino.[368] It was again purchased in 2020 by a young developer for over $30 million.

As of 2024, Underground Atlanta is open to the public and has seen another renaissance, this time from the arts community, who have moved in from increasingly expensive neighborhoods, like the Old Fourth Ward, East Atlanta and Edgewood. Developments in South Downtown, on the other side of the Gulch, including the area near Mercedes Benz Stadium, have also sparked renewed interest in Underground.

Future is still pulsing with tunes late into the night. The Masquerade, a longtime music venue, gave up its Old Fourth Ward former mill space in favor of three distinct venues at Kenny's Alley in 2016, mosh pits and all. It added Altar, another venue with dining, to host more intimate performances.

The MJQ nightclub (see the "Return of the Club Scene" section) moved from its longtime home on Ponce de Leon Avenue to the former Dante's space. There are also artist in residence galleries, a comedy club and a Parisian-inspired burlesque club to attract a new generation of revelers.

Ruby Red's Warehouse (1969–1975)

One of Underground's most influential bars and music venues was Ruby Red's Warehouse. Owner James Philip Ryan moved to Atlanta from New Orleans, where he co-owned another club on famous Bourbon Street. After a stint aboveground on Ellis Street, the club moved to the energetic new Underground Atlanta nightlife district in 1969.[369]

It was known for its Dixieland and jazz bands, and it was where patrons would come to watch, sip pints of draft beer and throw peanut shells on the ground. Tony Parenti and His All Stars recorded a live album at Ruby Red's, as did the house band, Ruby Red's Band, which continues to perform long after the original space closed.[370]

In 1975, the plans to run a rail line through part of Underground forced Ruby Red's to close. The club moved yet again, this time to Buckhead. It operated in the 1980s on Old Ivy Road before it became Hal's, a popular steakhouse that's been in operation since 1989.[371] An attempt was even made to revive the original Ruby Red's Warehouse in the 1990s in time for the Olympics, but it failed to capture the energy of the country-Western bar and closed within a year.

MUHLENBRINK'S SALOON (1969–1980)

Muhlenbrink's Saloon was a nod to the early drinkeries of the city, named for Hans Muhlenbrink, an early German American saloon owner and liquor merchant who brought in the city's first billiard table.[372] It was also said that the saloon was the site of an ill-fated duel between a stagecoach driver and a Civil War veteran.[373]

The modern version opened near its original spot with the rest of Underground. As the name implies, the design was an old-fashioned saloon, like one you might have seen in Atlanta's early days. It was also home to a drink called the Flaming Hurricane, served in a souvenir hurricane glass. It was opened by Jack Tarver Jr., who later owned the Great Southeast Music Hall, founded by Alex Cooley (see "That

A souvenir glass from Muhlenbrink's Saloon, a popular spot from Underground's heyday. *Photograph by the author.*

Dive Bar Sound" section).[374] Tarver also owned a Muhlenbrink's outpost in Austin, Texas.[375] The Allman Brothers Band shot the photographs for their album *Win, Lose or Draw* inside the Atlanta saloon, as did Waylon Jennings for *The Ramblin Man*.[376]

Locals certainly came for the drinks, but they also came to see William Lee Perryman, also known as "Piano Red," perform.[377] Born in Hampton in 1911, the self-taught Perryman became a fixture in the local music scene, performing with Blind Willie McTell.[378] He had an almost-residency at Muhlenbrink's between 1969 and 1979. His style was heavily influenced by the blues, but it also had a hint of rock and roll, often referred to as "barrelhouse."

In addition to the local crowd, big names became fans of Perryman, including Keith Richards, Gregg Allman and Eric Clapton, who would come to Muhlenbrink's to hear him play.[379] John Lennon recorded a cover of one of Piano Red's songs with The Beatles in 1964.

The bar closed with the rest of Underground in 1980.[380] Piano Red died in 1985, but his legacy, especially his songs and many fans at Muhlenbrink's Saloon, go on.

DANTE'S DOWN THE HATCH (1970–2013)

Another draw to Underground was Dante's Down the Hatch, whose eccentric owner was almost as well known as the bar itself. Dante Stephenson opened his namesake bar at Underground in 1970, during the entertainment district's heyday.[381] The thirty-something former Aspen ski bum's bar was located down a set of stairs, even farther below the city's original streets. He first discovered the space while exploring with a girl he met through the Atlanta Ski Club.[382]

The quirky dive attracted the likes of future President Jimmy Carter, civil rights leader Julian Bond and rock star Rod Stewart, with a series of rooms themed like a bordello and lighthouse, plus a crocodile named Pinocchio, the country's first non-zoo facility to hatch a live crocodile.[383] It housed the city's original well and an 1850s staircase from the former Palmer Hotel.

Rumors spread that Stephenson's uniquely kitschy style, including a barbershop imported from England, came from his travels in Europe during the war.[384] Diners could share pots of fondue and enjoy live music, perusing the menu with items listed in sixty-four languages, including Braille.[385] The wine list was just as detailed, with bottles ranging from $16 to $800.[386] Dante's also hosted countless jazz acts over the years, including the house bands the Paul Mitchell Trio and, later, the John Robertson Trio, as well as Isaac Hayes and Gladys Knight.[387]

In 1981, the Dante's location at Underground closed but moved to Buckhead shortly after, as the Bucket Shop had done before it.[388] Much of the décor came with to the converted 1914 home, including the wax figurine of Mark Twain, antique cars, clocks from the British insurance firm Lloyd's of London and church pews.[389] A ship even sat in the middle of the dining room with water in the moat beneath it.[390] Diners could pay a bit extra to sit inside the ship and admire its walls plastered with celebrity guest photographs.

Stephenson brought a revived version of the bar back to Underground in 1989, just in time for the Olympics, but it eventually closed in 1999.[391] But even Buckhead wasn't immune to change, having undergone many changes in the decades since Dante's set up shop.

The doors were shuttered for good in 2013 to make way for an apartment tower; this was done after a series of sales in which fans could purchase some of Stephenson's wildest antiques. Longtime employees were given commemorative T-shirts to remember their time with Dante.[392] Stephenson continued to live in a luxury railcar filled with treasures that was once owned by the Woolworth family until his death in 2020 after a battle with pancreatic cancer.[393] A room within the Fernbank Museum of Natural History was named in his honor for his visionary spirit.

That Dive Bar Sound

Modern Atlanta is recognized for its music legacy, especially when it comes to hip-hop and rock. But during the city's early days, its scene remained under the national radar, a place for artists to pass through on their way elsewhere. Radio stations played an integral part in artists finding success, but there was another factor. Before social media and the art of "going viral," many big-name acts got their start in the most unlikely places: bars.

The Indigo Girls, one of the most famous bands to come out of Atlanta, were discovered at a 1988 performance at the Little Five Points Pub.[394] The Black Crowes played several early shows at venues around town, including Dark Horse Tavern in Virginia Highland. Several of these watering holes still host live music five nights a week, with both big names and up-and-comers participating.

Blind Willie's was opened in 1986 in Virginia Highland and has fostered generations of blues artists alongside Northside Tavern and Fat Matt's Rib Shack. For years, artists like Rufus Thomas, Tommy Brown and Mose Allison have performed there alongside The Shadows, the house band.[395] Mick Jagger also stopped by when The Rolling Stones passed through town.[396]

Eric King and Roger Gregory, also a bassist for the band The Shadows, founded the bar, which has been recognized by the Blues Foundation for its commitment to preserving the genre. It takes its name, of course, from the iconic performer who spent years playing around the city. A wall of photographs represents the noted musicians who have taken the bar's stage. The bar is so important to the people who come here that several have even asked the owner to have their ashes spread here.[397]

The Blind Willie's neon sign depicts an alligator playing tunes. *Photograph by the author.*

Memorial Drive had Lenny's Food and Spirits, nicknamed the "CBGB of Atlanta," to bring in local artists during the 2000s. Its dive status dated back to the decades when the Cabbagetown cotton mill was still operational. From the '90s onward, the smokey space would welcome artists Cat Power, the Black Lips, Deerhunter, Killer Mike and Janelle Monae.[398] They'd usually be paid with a pitcher of beer, typically Pabst Blue Ribbon, and the theft of equipment during load-in was a constant plague. The bar was closed in 2010 after encroaching development forced a move and a tornado damaged the building.[399]

The Star Community Bar is another dive bar that was opened in a former Little Five Points bank on Halloween night 1991 by David Heany and Marty Nolan.[400] It soon attracted an alternative crowd, with its Christmas lights and Elvis shrine, plus cheap drinks.[401] The bar is still renowned for its diverse programming, including a weekly comedy show and live music from local and national bands five nights a week, like past performances from the Drive-By Truckers. Despite threats of closure in 2019, it reopened under new owners in 2021, thanks in part to patron support.[402] There's even the pint-sized Little Vinyl Lounge inside the bar with craft beer and cocktails.

East Atlanta has long welcomed musicians, especially at The Earl, which was opened in 1999 by John Searson. The bare bones space is covered in graffiti but has been the unlikely setting for early performances by Band of Horses and The Get Up Kids.[403] The bar and restaurant, which is named for East Atlanta Restaurant and Lounge, also has one of the city's best burgers.

If it wasn't for Atlanta's bar scene, you might not have heard of some of the world's most iconic artists.

Alex Cooley's Electric Ballroom (1974–1979)

If there is one figure that helped put Atlanta's music scene on the map, it's Alex Cooley, who brought the top artists of the time to his clubs and events. In 1970, he brought in Jimi Hendrix as the headliner for the second Atlanta International Pop Festival in Byron. The festival hosted the Black musician in a still-divided South, where he performed his famous version of the "Star-Spangled Banner."[404] Janis Joplin, The Allman Brothers Band (the hometown favorites and opening act) and Led Zeppelin also appeared to crowds of over three hundred thousand.[405] The festivals introduced a generation to the music of the region, just as another event, Freaknik, would do decades later. Despite these legendary performances, much of the discourse following the event was about the use of LSD and marijuana, nudity and other aspects of the counterculture.[406]

In 1974, Cooley opened the Electric Ballroom in the ballroom of the historic Georgian Terrace Hotel with two bars and big crowds (see "Hotels, Motels and Holiday Inns" section). The first to perform at the rock hall was Grand Funk Railroad, with the show promoted through flyers Cooley

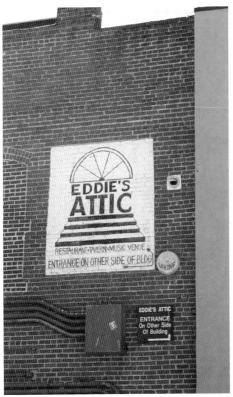

Above: The hotel was also the site of Alex Cooley's Electric Ballroom, a popular rock venue. *Photograph by the author.*

Left: Eddie's Attic was co-owned, for a time, by Alex Cooley and is considered one of the region's most important venues for singer-songwriters. *Photograph by the author.*

himself tacked up around the city.[407] The acts who later passed through the bar's doors are considered a who's who of modern music and include KISS, Bruce Springsteen, Patti Smith, The Ramones, Prince and Fleetwood Mac.[408] It closed after a fire damaged the building and it was slated for demolition, but Cooley wasn't done establishing Atlanta's rock presence.[409]

The Great Southeast Music Hall opened a few years later near Lindbergh, and Cooley had a hand in its opening as the talent booker for the first American show of the Sex Pistols. The band made quite a first impression, as fans lined up around the block and extra police were called in.[410] There was an after-party at the Sweet Gum Head (see "The Great Gay Way" chapter), and Sid Vicious ended the night at a local hospital for a self-inflicted slash to his wrist.[411] The Great Southeast Music Hall gained a reputation for its rock pedigree, with appearances from Willie Nelson and Jerry Lee Lewis, not to mention comedian Steve Martin and cheap beer sold by the bucket.[412] But it ultimately closed in 1978.[413]

Champagne Jam was another one of Cooley's festivals that year, and it hosted Mother's Finest at the Georgia Tech football stadium. He also brought major acts, like the Rolling Stones, Waylon Jennings, Madonna and Frank Sinatra, to other spaces around the city, including the Fox and the Omni (a since-demolished space downtown) and the Capri Ballroom in Buckhead (which closed around 1979 but whose building continues as a venue, now known as the Buckhead Theatre).[414]

Cooley went on to cofound Music Midtown in 1994 with fellow promoter Peter Conlon. It's an annual music festival that still brings thousands of attendees to Piedmont Park (see the "Party in the Park" section) every year.[415]

In 2011, he became one of the owners of Eddie's Attic, founded in 1991 as one of the city's premier listening rooms. The listening room launched countless careers from its open mic nights and played host to a noted live album from The Civil Wars.[416]

Northside Tavern (1972–Present)

Built in the 1930s, Northside Tavern is a piece of Atlanta history that feels like it's captured in amber. The area that surrounds it was the site of former stockyards and is one of the only buildings that survived a fire.

After functioning as a grocery store and gas station for a period, the structure became known as Northside Package but has operated as a blues club since 1972.[417] In the club's early days, its crowd was mostly composed

Northside Tavern started as a working-class bar and pool hall before it became a beloved blues institution. *Photograph by the author.*

of workers from the nearby mills who'd come for a post-shift beer, canned snacks and a round of pool.[418]

For most of its existence, the "urban juke joint" of sorts was owned by the Webb family. The family's patriarch, Butler, bought the bar from a friend and ran it from 1964 to 1989, when his daughter Ellyn took over. Her tenure marked its shift toward focusing on music, from both local and touring acts.

Musician Danny "Mudcat" Dudeck approached Ellyn about hosting blues artists, and a collaboration was formed between the tavern and the blues community. Dudeck brought his talents over from Fat Matt's Rib Shack, another retro space that hosted artists from the music genre. He and his fellow musicians were fairly paid, establishing Northside as a favorite venue for both locals and touring acts.[419]

The smoky interior is dimly lit, with breweriana covering the walls. A "wall of fame" honors the local and national heroes of the blues genre, with portraits by artist Drew Galloway of Blind Willie, Sean Costello and Piano Red Perryman (see "City Beneath the Streets" section). The ramshackle exterior has made it popular with the Hollywood crowd, who have used the tavern in productions like *Ozark*, the *MacGyver* reboot series and *Stomp the Yard*.

Ellyn's brother Tommy joined the team in 2015, and he began running the tavern following Ellyn's death in 2017.[420] The Webbs have fought off plenty of offers to buy them out over the years, as the neighborhood has now been overtaken by skyscrapers and apartment complexes.[421] But, for now, Northside Tavern remains a top blues venue and one of the top dive bars in the country.[422]

688 Club (1980–1986)

While not a dive bar, the 688 Club, named for its Spring Street address, could certainly be described as a dive. Located in a white cinderblock building in Midtown, the club became nationally known for being the early incubation space for bands that would hit it big, especially in the punk and new wave scenes that were imported from England.[423] Steve May, who previously mixed at Alex Cooley's Great Southern Music Hall, created the club alongside Tony Evans and Sheila Browning.[424] Despite being called a "rancid dump" by the late Black Flag roadie Joe Cole, the 688 was legendary.[425]

The black room, with plentiful graffiti covering its walls, was the site of one of RuPaul's early performances in Atlanta, as well as that of a then-unknown group called the Red Hot Chili Peppers.[426] Other acts, like The Ramones, Iggy Pop (who played a week of shows), George Clinton, Bad Brains, The Go-Gos and R.E.M., also took to the stage.[427] Local performer Jeff Calder saw Prince at a show at the 688 after his own show at the Agora, the space that followed the Electric Ballroom. Music lovers, including the young fans who, at the age of eighteen, could then drink, would come to dance on the 688's crowded floor and sip canned beer.

The club closed in 1986 and changed names and owners several times over the years, effectively ending the 688 as it had been known. But the community was still there. When May fell on hard times a few years ago, the music-loving crowd started a fundraiser to help him get back on his feet.[428] The space is now a medical building.

Smith's Olde Bar (1994–Present)

Set in Atlanta's first strip mall in Virginia Highland, Smith's Olde Bar has cemented its legacy as an essential stop for musicians, including then-unknowns like Zack Brown and John Mayer.[429] Jason Isbell, Chris

Smith's Olde Bar is considered an essential stop for touring musicians. *Photograph by the author.*

Stapleton, Janelle Monae, The Indigo Girls and The Revivalists have also performed on the bar's stages.[430] David Bowie even made a memorable appearance with a local radio station, and several live albums have been recorded inside the bar.[431]

Opened by Dan Nolen and Mike Reeves in 1994, the bar's logo features the image of a man in a derby hat with a cigar, nicknamed Smitty.[432] In addition to the big names who've shared the stage among the bar's two performance spaces, Smith's hosts weekly open mic nights, jazz jams and DJs.

With its curved red booths and posters from the artists who have appeared there, Smith's is a popular spot for a round of pool and a pint of local beer, even when there are no tunes playing.

Dawn of Disco

The counterculture made its way into Atlanta in the 1960s, especially in an area of Midtown called The Strip, set on Peachtree Street between Eighth and Fourteenth Streets.[433] Often compared to gay-friendly boroughs like Greenwich Village in New York or Haight-Ashbury in San Francisco, The

Strip had clubs like Catacombs and Twelfth Gate, which hosted bands, and *The Great Speckled Bird*, the city's alternative newspaper, had its offices nearby.

A few years later, the hippie scene morphed into disco fever, which had recently swept the nation, and Atlanta wasn't immune. The term *disco*, coming from the French word *discotheque*, came to define both the clubs where people went to dance and the musical genre that featured high-energy beats.[434] The release of the film *Saturday Night Fever* in 1977 only cemented the genre's nationwide impact.

Nightclubs opened all over the city, where DJs would spin the latest tunes from artists like Gloria Gaynor, KC and the Sunshine Band and Van McCoy. The clubs promoted primarily Black artists in a time barely beyond segregation. The clubs seemed to one-up each other with their over-the-top features, like live animals, flashy décor and celebrity appearances.

Pogo's was a chain of nightclubs with locations in the Midwest and two in Atlanta, one in Brookhaven on the northside and another on the southside. Its mascot was a kangaroo, which appeared on its branded glassware that held beer from the weekly nickel pitcher special. Flanigan's attracted the suburban crowd off Powers Ferry Road, an, as the name implies, Club Anytime allowed partygoers to dance all night long.[435] Even actor Burt Reynolds had a disco, named Burt's Place after himself, that operated briefly at the Omni complex downtown.[436]

The so-called Disco Demolition Night of 1979 at Chicago's Comiskey Park was a publicity stunt put on by a local radio DJ. A crowd of around fifty thousand (mostly white men) showed up to destroy disco records. But along with disco, with its many female artists and heavily gay and Latino fanbase, records from Black artists were also destroyed.[437]

But despite the buzz this event drew, disco wasn't dead in Chicago, Atlanta or other places around the country. Instead, several of Atlanta's disco clubs adapted, and some even survived for decades to come, long after the mirror balls had been put away.

Backstreet (1977–2004)

For a time, Atlanta's party scene couldn't be stopped, culminating with the opening of Backstreet, the city's most famous twenty-four-hour nightclub. The club described itself as "gay bar that accepts everyone but no bad attitudes wanted."[438] It debuted in 1971 as Peaches Back Door behind Joe's Disco in a former furniture warehouse on Peachtree Street.[439]

The only reminder of Backstreet's heyday is the disco ball, now on display at the Atlanta History Center. *Photograph by the author.*

After another stint as Encore, it was renamed Backstreet in 1975 and welcomed all types: gay, straight, male and female from every background. Spread across three floors, the ten-thousand-square-foot club was decorated with decadence in mind, and included red wall-to-wall carpeting, a shiny DJ booth, a rooftop aviary and couches where patrons could cozy up together.[440] You could play a round of pool, take part in a round of blackjack (for no prize due to Georgia's gambling laws), belly up to the circular bar or take your spot on the crowded dance floor.[441]

Vending machines sold anything partygoers might need over the course of the night, including snacks and condoms.[442] There were a few rules, including no cameras inside and shoes required. Patrons were asked to pay a quarterly membership fee, only ten dollars, plus a weekend cover charge for access to the debauchery.

Backstreet quickly earned a title as the South's Studio 54, even though it opened before the famed New York City club and lasted much longer. It attracted a celebrity clientele, including Cher, Gladys Knight, Farrah Fawcett, Liza Minelli, Elton John, Madonna and Janet Jackson.[443] The disco also appeared in the movies *Dragtime* and *For Ladies Only*, as well as episodes of the 2000s series *Insomniac with Dave Attell* and MTV's *ElimiDate*.[444]

The club was owned by Carmine and Janice Vara, but by the club's heyday in the early 1980s, their children Vicki and Henry had taken over, just in time for the bar to get its famed twenty-four-hour license.[445] Hits of the day spun from the bar's booth as dancers moved under the glow of the disco ball. Backstreet was particularly known for its DJs, following the progression from disco to techno to electronic over the decades.[446]

The staff donned shirts that said, "Always Open & Always Pouring," a nod to the all-night spot. Charlie Brown's Cabaret was an upstairs drag show that lasted for over a decade, and it was where its namesake fostered a local drag community that continues decades later. The Armorettes, a local drag troupe, and DJ George Greenlee also performed there.[447] During the AIDS epidemic in the late '80s, when much of Backstreet's clientele were suffering, the club put up memorials and formed a sort of support group.[448]

But by the new millennium, Midtown had changed, no longer the bohemian haven it had been when Backstreet opened. Neighbors of the club complained about the noise and crime. In 2001, Atlanta ended its twenty-four-hour licensing, forcing Backstreet to close at 4:00 a.m.[449] The club also lost its liquor license and tried to keep its customers, despite the continued series of obstacles.[450] Backstreet's attempt to keep its private club status was denied in court, along with those of fellow bars Club 112 and Riviera.[451]

On July 17, 2004, Backstreet shut its doors for the final time. Other gay bars had popped up by that time, especially in the Cheshire Bridge Road area, and the crowd went elsewhere. After a stint at Underground Atlanta, Charlie Brown moved his cabaret to Lips on Buford Highway.

The building was demolished to make room for yet another condominium complex. Its last reminder is its disco ball, which hung in The Jungle, another dance club, for another thirteen years before that club's closure in 2018.[452] It was then donated by the Vara family and is now on display at the Atlanta History Center, where it continues to cast light on the galleries.[453]

Johnny's Hideaway (1979–Present)

Time stands still at the so-called cougar bar in a Buckhead strip mall, so much so that it says so on the club's water bottles. But the ages of its clientele actually range from twenty to eighty. The charm of Johnny's Hideaway comes from its stubbornness, with very few changes during its decades-long run.[454] At the bar, opened by Johnny Esposito, its namesake, guests enter the unassuming door into the strip mall club, lit by the glow of the disco ball. A crowd gathers around the long bar and the postage stamp–sized dance floor.

The rules are abundant, from the dress code (no backward hats, men must wear sleeves) to "no drinks on the dance floor," and they are strictly enforced by security.[455] The walls are covered with photographs of celebrities, and the tunes are strictly from the '50s and '60s big-band era, despite the frequent patron requests.[456]

In years past, the bar has hosted prime rib and spaghetti dinners, plus customer talent contests. Ladies' night is still held every Wednesday. Celebrities like golfer Arnold Palmer and actors Steve Martin, George Clooney and Robert Duvall have appeared there.[457] Hollywood has even used the bar as a setting for several movies, including 2011's *Hall Pass*. Stars Christina Applegate, Owen Wilson and Jenna Fischer returned after work to join the locals on the dance floor.[458]

Johnny's Hideaway has been a staple of Buckhead since it opened in 1979. *Photograph by the author.*

The Sinatra Room pays homage to "Ol' Blue Eyes," and another corner is a nod to Elvis. The best seats in the house are the closely placed round tables around the dance floor with red stained-glass lights and matching upholstered swivel chairs, which are ideal for people watching. But don't miss your chance to take a spin on the floor. Just don't forget to wear your best attire and bring five dollars in cash for the door.

LIMELIGHT (1980–1985)

Before the Limelight's New York City location was made famous decades later, nightlife impresario Peter Gatien opened his Limelight nightclub in a Buckhead strip mall that previously held a theater in 1980.[459] This followed his time in Miami, where he'd opened another club.

From the beginning, the Limelight gained a wild reputation for its over-the-top décor, like a giant lit King Tut's head, an indoor slip 'n' slide, tigers and a panther, caged dancers and a clear glass dance floor that revealed live sharks, taken from a Florida aquarium, swimming beneath.[460] The club also had a movie theater and private rooms, where even more debauchery took place away from prying eyes.[461] There was even a dress as "bare as you dare" night.[462]

Over six thousand invitations were sent ahead of the official opening, where crowds imbibed at six bars spread across the space.[463] Travelers made it an important stop for any visit to Atlanta, where drag queens mingled with frat boys. The party kept going until 4:00 a.m., and revelers could pop into the grocery store next door to get snacks to help counteract whatever substances they might have ingested.[464]

The celebrities also followed, including a who's who of the day, like Rod Stewart, Andy Warhol, Tina Turner, Eartha Kitt, Isaac Hayes, Farrah Fawcett, Burt Reynolds, Neil Simon and Grace Jones.[465] Tom Cruise and Ali McGraw also came together.

In 1981, conservative speaker and Florida orange juice spokesperson Anita Bryant, who campaigned against the "gay lifestyle," was famously photographed dancing at the club.[466] Her photograph made the covers of dozens of magazines and newspapers, giving the club publicity while tarnishing Bryant's reputation.[467] In 1979, she spoke to the Southern Baptist Convention in Atlanta, drawing over two thousand protestors and causing many bars to start making cocktails with apple juice in protest.[468]

A mural once recognized the grocery store's nickname, "Disco Kroger," given for its location next to the former Limelight. *Photograph by the author.*

The eyepatch-donning Gatien himself didn't relish the spotlight; he was hesitant to pose with celebrities for photographs and could usually be found in his office with a book and a glass of wine instead of on the dance floor.[469] But the bright lights of the disco ball fizzled within a few years, especially when Gatien moved to New York City to open another Limelight in 1983, the same one that would later become associated with the "Party Monster" murder in 1996.[470] Gatien left his brother Maurice in charge of the Atlanta club, but he couldn't keep up with the operations and closed the club's doors in 1985.

Gatien's bad luck didn't end there. He opened another club, Petrus, in Midtown in 1989, but it didn't last long.[471] His New York club Tunnel was raided, and in 1996, he was arrested by the DEA for the distribution of MDMA. He had been invited to build the "official disco" of the Athlete's Village by the Atlanta Olympics Committee and worried the news would affect his plans.[472]

In 1999, Gatien was convicted for tax fraud and, millions of dollars in debt, was finally deported back to his native Canada in 2003.[473] The club became Rupert's, which continued to be popular with the celebrity set for its house band, operating until the '90s.[474]

Despite no longer being the site of a nightclub, the grocery store in the shopping center that once held the Limelight was nicknamed "Disco Kroger" by generations of Atlantans. The shopping center was redeveloped in 2022, but locals continue to use the name to describe the area.

1981–1999

The Great Gay Way and Beyond

When Atlanta was named one of United States' top gay cities by the *Advocate* in 2010, other cities may have turned their heads in surprise.[475] But the city's gay community dates back to the turn of the twentieth century, of course it existed less openly then than it does today. In fact, the first drag performer in the city made a name for himself way back in 1913.[476]

In the 1930s, The Lounge was where the gay men gathered in privacy, but in the decades that followed, there was an increased police presence in the community. In 1953, the police performed a stakeout of the men's restroom of the Carnegie Library to charge patrons with sodomy.[477] Many had their names published by the newspapers, outing them to friends, family and employers.[478]

Six weeks after New York's Stonewall Riots of 1969, the Atlanta police raided the Ansley Mall cinema screening of Andy Warhol's *Lonesome Cowboys*, a satire of Hollywood westerns featuring several of his muses. The police operated based on an obscenity law because of the film's depictions of gay sex. Patrons and theater staff were harassed, photographed and arrested.[479] This event is considered Atlanta's Stonewall and was a turning point for the gay community that led to the founding of the Georgia Gay Liberation Front.

But despite these challenges, gay businesses began to thrive, especially around Cheshire Bridge Road, which was nicknamed the "Great Gay

Way." The Tick Tock Grill, Five O'Clock Supper Club, the Blue Room at Americana Motel and the Wonder Club all operated as welcoming but unofficial gay bars that predated the Stonewall Riots of 1969.[480] In fact, the Americana was Atlanta's first integrated hotel, and it played a role in the Milwaukee Braves moving to Atlanta.[481] Mrs. P's, Chick's and Joy Lounge followed, and within five years, the number of gay bars in Atlanta had tripled.[482] Tower Lounge was a popular spot for the lesbian crowd.[483]

City leaders denied a permit for Atlanta's first Gay Pride March in 1971, but that didn't stop over one hundred attendees from marching through the city's downtown streets.[484] It expanded to include lesbian and transgender individuals in 1980 and is now one of the country's largest Pride celebrations, now held in October (see the "Party in the Park" section).

Many drag performers have made their names in Atlanta, including RuPaul, who moved to the city in 1975 and saw his first drag show at a Cheshire Bridge club, along with Diamond Lil, Charlie Brown and Savannah's Lady Chablis, famously featured in John Berendt's novel *Midnight in the Garden of Good and Evil*.[485] Phyllis Killer debuted at Joy Lounge in the late 1960s.[486]

The AIDS epidemic hit Atlanta hard as the welcoming gay nightlife spaces became memorials to lives lost and places where those left behind could come together as a community.[487] AID Atlanta was founded in 1982 to care for the HIV positive. The Armory, a popular gay nightclub between 1971 and 2004, even raised funds for the medical, living and funeral expenses of those with HIV and AIDS.[488] The club's drag troupe, the Armorettes, is now the longest running in America, with monthly performances at the Heretic.[489]

Around the same time, then-Councilman John Lewis was fighting to end discrimination based on race, sexual orientation, gender, religion, age and ability. The expansion of the Civil Rights Act in 1986 made Atlanta one of the first cities in the region to protect gay rights.[490]

Atlanta is still a destination for the LGBTQ+ community, especially those who come from all over the rural South. The gay nightlife scene now spreads across the city, but the hub is still Midtown, now with its iconic rainbow crosswalk.

The city has several important gay bars, including Lips on Buford Highway, which hosts drag shows, following in the footsteps of the late performer Charlie Brown; Mary's, which has operated in East Atlanta since 1998; and Blake's on the Park in Midtown, which has been in continuous operation since 1988. The Heretic still shows off its moves with weekly line

My Sister's Room remains the city's only lesbian bar. *Photograph by the author.*

dancing classes under the disco ball after over two decades of operation on Cheshire Bridge Road.[491]

My Sister's Room opened in 1996 and has moved four times, most recently to Crescent Avenue in Midtown. It's also one of only thirty-three lesbian bars in America, according to the Lesbian Bar Project, an award-winning documentary film project that highlights inclusive spaces.[492] The owners of My Sister's Room also run Sexacola, an annual queer gathering that is held in Florida over Memorial Day Weekend.

Bulldogs is another Atlanta classic, opened in 1978 by Michael Clutter and Jerry Psyzka, and it is still in its original Midtown location.[493] It once had a trucker theme and a real-life bulldog mascot named Winston. The bar remains popular in the Black gay community.

While many other gay bars have come and gone, they are still a significant part of Atlanta's LGBTQ+ history.

Mrs. P's Cafe (1956–1991)

By the time the Stonewall riot occurred in New York in 1969, Atlanta had only three "official" gay bars.[494] Among them was Mrs. P's Cafe, which was opened in 1956 in the residential Ponce de Leon Hotel by local restaurateurs Hubert and Vera Smith.[495] It had been operated as a hotel since the 1920s and became a safe space for LGBTQ+ Atlantans over the following decades.

Vera had previously owned Piedmont Tavern, a lesbian-friendly bar in Midtown that was opened in 1944; this space is now home to The Nook.[496] In the 1960s, Mrs. P's was purchased by Bill Copeland, followed by Chuck Cain, the owner of Chuck's Rathskeller, a former Midtown juke joint.[497]

A key from the former Ponce de Leon Hotel, where Mrs. P's and MJQ became part of Atlanta's nightlife scene. *Photograph by the author.*

Mrs. P's became a popular venue for drag shows, hosting the first in the city, thanks to a working relationship Cain had with the local police. Performer Diamond Lil would put on shows there and then enjoy the filet mignon dinner special afterward.[498] Tea dances were also popular in the city's early days, as they allowed gay men to meet under the premise of drinking "tea" instead of alcohol.[499]

In 1971, it was taken over by Bill Norton and Bernice Bright, who rebranded the space to become a cruise bar, swapping out the lace curtains and chandeliers for wooden stools and Western décor. It was big with the leather crowd, long before the Atlanta Eagle took the reigns as the resident leather bar.[500]

On September 25, 1980, P's, as it was by then known, was raided by the police, fracturing the relationship between business owners and law enforcement.[501] The community formed ties with city council and met with police for sensitivity training for LGBTQ+ businesses.[502]

After the bar's closure in 1991, its building fell into disrepair, but from 1994 to 1997, it was the first home of MJQ Concourse, a gay-friendly club that still welcomes revelers.[503] In 2021, the building was reopened as the Wylie Hotel, calling its restaurant Mrs. P's Bar & Kitchen in honor of its history, even hosting tea dances for Pride.

Sweet Gum Head (1971–1981)

One of the staples of the Great Gay Way was the Sweet Gum Head, named for the tree found throughout the South. It was opened in 1971 in a former grocery store by Frank Powell, who operated several gay bars in the city for over thirty years, like Joy Lounge and the Cove.[504] The building had held a series of clubs beforehand, including the Cheshire Cat, which hosted Sonny and Cher, and Soul City, named in honor—but without any association with—Georgia music legend James Brown.[505]

From the beginning, the Sweet Gum Head was called the "Show Place of the South," known for its drag performers like Rachel Wells and Satyn Deville.[506] For a time, it was the site of the Miss Gay Atlanta pageant, taking over from Chuck's Rathskeller and, later, the Biltmore Hotel.

Patrons could also drink seventy-five-cent cocktails late into the evening, as the city allowed clubs to stay open until 4:00 a.m. in 1973, especially in the unincorporated stretch of Cheshire Bridge. People came from neighboring states, not to mention Georgia's dry counties, to dance to disco tunes. Gloria Gaynor and Freda Payne partied there, and Burt Reynolds, a fixture in the city throughout the '70s, was a fan of Rachel Wells. But it never had the star power of fellow disco palaces like the Limelight and Backstreet.

The Sweet Gum Head has the honor of being the site of the city's first gay marriage ceremony. Another important event took place at the Sweet Gum Head; according to RuPaul's memoir, it was here that he heard local drag performer Lakesha Lucky recite what has become his catchphrase: "You're born naked, and the rest is drag."[507]

The club suffered financially as other gay-friendly spots opened around it, and it ultimately closed in 1981. Another bar came, Illusions, after it, carrying over many of the previous bar's performances with a similar crowd.[508] It's now Allure, a gentleman's club.

Atlanta Eagle (1987–Present)

The Ponce de Leon Avenue space was well known long before the Eagle took up residence there. It was originally built in 1889 as a nine-room home for the former Atlanta mayor's daughter Lula Belle Hemphill Quinby.[509] After serving a period as an Italian restaurant, the building became the Celebrity Club in the 1980s, and it was here that RuPaul has his early performances, along with Drivin N Cryin.[510] It was later called Renegade's Saloon.

But in 1987, the building, under an aging Kodak sign, became the Atlanta Eagle, a destination for those in the LGBTQ+ leather community. Its popularity rose as the city's other gay bars, like Mrs. P's and Texas Drilling Co., closed.[511] The Atlanta Eagle got its name from the Eagles Nest, a bar in New York City, and the term *eagle* became associated with the leather community worldwide.[512]

The darkest period of the club's history came in 2009, when a police raid brought in members of the VICE squad right before midnight. In search of alleged acts of public sex and drug use, the squad assaulted patrons and used homophobic language.[513] The city alleged that there was "adult entertainment," meaning nude dancing, going on at the club without proper licensing, which patrons say wasn't true.[514]

What resulted were eight plaintiffs filing an unlawful arrest lawsuit that resulted in an over $1 million settlement. The Atlanta Police Department (APD) fired several of the officers involved and disbanded the Red Dog Unit, the antidrug strike force formed in 1987 that had a reputation for brutality.[515] Then-Mayor Kasim Reed issued an apology and made promises to enact important reforms to the city's police force, but the raid broke the trust between police and the community.[516] The APD also responded by hiring a LGBTQ+ community liaison to address the remaining concerns.

When the bar was closed during the COVID-19 pandemic, as so many others did, there were fears that it wouldn't come back.[517] But in 2020, the space was listed in the Georgia Trust for Historic Preservation's Places in Peril list because of the building's condition and development along Ponce

The former site of the Atlanta Eagle has fallen on hard times after experiencing two fires. *Photograph by the author.*

de Leon Avenue.[518] It was later approved to become an official historic landmark, Atlanta's first dedicated to the city's extensive LGBTQ+ history.[519]

In 2022, the Atlanta Eagle moved to the former Burkhart's space in Midtown, just across the street from the Piedmont and Monroe section of Piedmont Park, where Pride festivities take place, and it is now surrounded by other gay bars like Felix's and Mixx.[520] Sadly, the original building caught fire twice in 2024, but law enforcement says they aren't pursuing arson charges.[521] Owner Richard Ramey hopes to be able to rebuild the original space in the future, despite its current derelict status.

OTHERSIDE LOUNGE (1990–1999)

The Otherside Lounge lesbian bar, opened by Beverly McMahon and Dana Ford in 1990, enjoyed half a decade of success, attracting the likes of Ellen DeGeneres, comedian Steve Martin and tennis champion Martina Navratilova.[522] The humble spot off Cheshire Bridge Road was surrounded by strip clubs and adult entertainment venues. McMahon had successfully operated a location in Fort Lauderdale before expanding into Georgia.

At twelve thousand square feet, the sprawling club pulsed with all types of music, bringing in a diverse crowd along racial and sexuality lines for themed nights like Cruise Ship Sundays and country music events, as well as an annual transgender convention. It was a hangout for Atlanta's own Indigo Girls, who performed there before they hit it big.[523]

It would have been just like any other night, but on February 21, 1997, two bombs exploded at the club around 9:45 p.m., shattering the windows and scattering long nails and shrapnel across the dance floor. Patrons ran for cover, away from a place they'd considered—until that moment—a safe haven. Another bomb was later discovered by law enforcement. It had been seven months since bombs exploded amid Atlanta's centennial Olympics. And even more time passed before authorities determined that both attacks were the work of Eric Robert Rudolph, a Christian Identity movement extremist.

There were no casualties at the Otherside, but the fallout was great. Survivors of the bombing were outed on television, with one woman losing her job. McMahon spent years trying to receive money from the insurance company that covered the bar, and two years after the bombing, Otherside closed its doors. After another attack on a Birmingham abortion clinic and a multiyear manhunt, Rudolph was captured and given four life sentences without the possibility of parole, to be served at a supermax prison in Colorado.

The violent event was returned to memory after the 2016 Pulse nightclub massacre, and it surfaced again in 2021, when a gunman killed employees and patrons at a spa next door to where the Otherside once stood.[524] The building is now part of an office complex.

Strip Club City

Atlanta is constantly cited as one of the top cities for adult entertainment in America.[525] Far more than just spots for the bachelor party crowd, these clubs are a big part of the city's nightlife scene. Many have had an impact on pop culture, including music, television, film and even food.

You'll find at least one of these establishments in just about every part of town, especially on the stretch along Piedmont Road in the upper part of Midtown and Cheshire Bridge Road. The Cheetah has been open since 1977 in a former Chrysler dealership, with an award-winning restaurant on site.[526] The likes of 2 Chainz and Jack Harlow have been known to hang out there to enjoy the craft cocktails and, of course, the dancers.

The Blue Flame was the site of early playings of Lil Jon's 2003 chart-topper "Get Low," thanks to DJ Will, who had previously made a name at places like Club 112, featured in the song "Welcome to Atlanta."[527] The Pink Pony and Tattletale Lounge are other popular strip clubs. And for even more hedonism, Trapeze is a decades-old swingers club.

And none of this would have been possible without a Broadway performance. In 1971, a touring production of the controversial show *Hair* was set to come to Atlanta's Civic Center. The play has a scene with nudity, which ruffled feathers locally. The case went to the federal level, where a judge ruled that nudity fell under free speech. After this ruling, Atlanta's strip clubs could use this loophole to offer full nudity, not just the "go go" shows of the past.[528]

Clermont Lounge (1968–Present)

Set in the lower level of the Hotel Clermont, the Clermont Lounge is likely the oldest of Atlanta's adult entertainment venues still in operation, famously "alive since '65."[529] For most of the building's history, the hotel and lounge have operated separately. Until its renovation in 2018, at the hands of a boutique hotel group, the upstairs area was an aging flophouse with transitory residents and sex workers, not to mention punk rocker G.G. Allin, who lived in the hotel and recorded his single "Hotel Clermont" based on his stay there.[530]

Called the Bonaventure Arms Apartments when it opened in 1924, the seven-story building took its current name in 1940.[531] While the Clermont Lounge was born in 1968, the basement club had held several nightlife

The Clermont Lounge is an Atlanta icon, known for hosting dancers like Blondie. *Photograph by the author.*

spots since its founding, including the Gypsy Club and the Playboy Club, which was unaffiliated with Hugh Hefner's operation and resulted in a cease and desist order (see "Hotels, Motels and Holiday Inns" section).[532] The Continental Room was opened in 1955 as a chic cocktail lounge, but five years later it became known as Anchorage Supper Club, offering dinner and burlesque.[533]

The bar shifted to nudity in the late 1960s to compete with the increasingly adult clubs that were opening around town. To call it a strip club requires further explanation, because although the Clermont Lounge does feature scantily clad dancers like its Atlanta comrades, its dancers are not like any others you've seen.

The star of the show is "Blondie," one of the longtime dancers who was born Anita Rae Strange.[534] The blonde performer is best known for crushing cans of Pabst Blue Ribbon and Budweiser, the patron drinks of choice, between her breasts while on stage.[535] Her tenure at the lounge extends to 1978, and she's seen all manner of people pass through the doors, becoming a celebrity in her own right and mentoring younger dancers. She's also appeared in documentaries, art shows and the *Sally Jessy Raphael Show* and has her own collection of poetry and a comic book series.[536]

In addition to the random crowd of out-of-town frat boys and tallboy-sipping hipsters who pass their dollar bills to the stage, no shortage of celebrities have been attracted to the Clermont Lounge. Jon Stewart, Kid

Rock and Margaret Cho are past customers. Anthony Bourdain filmed a memorable episode of his show *The Layover* here, buying a lap dance for food host and Atlantan Alton Brown. But the biggest rule of the lounge—no photographs—was broken by members of the band Mumford and Sons, leading to their immediate removal.[537]

The bar itself is a duct-taped disaster, but it surrounds one of the stages where performers strip down among the crowd sipping strong drinks out of plastic cups. There's also a small dance floor that hosts themed music nights. Blondie no longer appears on the pole, but you'll see her colleagues showing off their moves most nights. The dancers usually pick the tunes, with quarters slipped into the jukebox.

The swag the lounge sells includes beer koozies and T-shirts with the logo and the phrase "I saw your mama dancing at the Clermont Lounge," the ultimate souvenir from a night without photographs as reminders.

MAGIC CITY (1985–PRESENT)

The crown jewel of Atlanta's strip club scene is Magic City, which was opened in 1985 by Michael Barney, a Duke University graduate, former Kansas City Chiefs player and a printer cartridge salesman.[538] He'd been given the name "Magic" and assigned it to his new club, set in a building on Forsyth Street.[539]

Called America's most important club by *GQ*, the establishment set itself apart with luxury food items like lobster and steak for patrons, plus top-shelf bottle service of champagne and cognac.[540] It quickly developed a cult-like following for its chicken wings, specifically the lemon pepper variety the city is known for. Rapper Rick Ross is a fan, among many others.[541] Producer Jermaine Dupri called it "hip-hop adult Cirque du Soleil," and it earned the title of "America's most important strip club" from rapper Jeezy.[542]

Since its founding, Magic City has become *the* place to celebrate for local musicians and sports teams, attracting the likes of MC Hammer, Shaquille O'Neal, Rihanna, Magic Johnson and Michael Jordan, among countless others.[543] Drake allegedly had $100,000 delivered by armored car to spend at the club for friend Future's birthday.[544] The Atlanta United soccer team celebrated their MLS win at the club, bringing the trophy with them. Kevin Hart celebrated his engagement here.[545]

The club and its contemporaries have also had connections to the music industry from the beginning, playing the work of up-and-coming artists. In

Magic City is by far the most famous strip club in Atlanta. *Photograph by the author.*

1992, the group Tag Team's single "Whoomp! (There It Is)" debuted at Magic City.[546] Dancers from Magic City appeared in a video for the group Migos.[547] The sayings "make it rain," which appears in the lyrics of several rap songs, and "asshole naked" are also tied to the locale.[548] Magic City even influenced the Starz show *P-Valley*.

But of course, Magic City's tenure hasn't been without drama. It survived a 1995 fire, and the year before, Barney was convicted on federal drug conspiracy charges after accusations arose concerning a cocaine ring existing within the club.[549] He received a ten-year sentence. During the COVID-19 pandemic, Clippers player Lou Williams famously broke his "team bubble" for a night out at the club, as captured by Jack Harlow.[550] He allegedly went to the club for its famed lemon pepper wings, not the entertainment.

These days, Magic City is still deeply entrenched in Atlanta's nightlife scene, now under the second-generation management of Barney's son, Michael "Lil Magic," who briefly appeared on an MTV show called *Buckhead Shore* about well-to-do young Atlantans.[551] And if you want to get a taste of the famous wings without the nudity, like Williams, you can get them delivered from the attached Magic City Kitchen.

Gold Club (1994–2001, 2014–Present…Sort Of)

While Magic City still reigns supreme, for a time, the place to be was a concrete building near Lindbergh called the Gold Club. Opened in 1994, it was first more of a cabaret, but under the ownership of Steve Kaplan, it was where decadence really came to play in Atlanta.[552] The five-thousand-square-foot club cost $4 million to build, with Art Deco accents like mirrored walls and red velvet curtains.[553]

It was where one might come to see and be seen and, most importantly, spend lavishly. Kaplan brought the Vegas club experience, including bottle service of Cristal and VIP rooms for "private encounters" with dancers. Dennis Rodman, Patrick Ewing, Bill Maher, Wesley Snipes, Bruce Willis, Mick Jagger, Jim Belushi, Charles Barkley, Magic Johnson, Keanu Reeves, Madonna and Dikembe Mutombo were all known to frequent the spot.[554] Donald Trump was spotted there, but a spokesperson later denied it, of course. The King of Sweden came by during the 1996 Olympics. The club even hosted a celebration for the acquittal of Ray Lewis, who was accused of murder following a night out with friends at the Cobalt Lounge in Buckhead in 2000 (see "The End of All Night Bars" section).

Big spending was a requirement, as tips were expected from waitresses, dancers and even bathroom attendants, most of whom were clad in tuxedos—if they were dressed at all.[555] And that doesn't even include the cover charge to get into the club or the price of drinks, all served at a significant markup.

"Gold Bucks" were the club's form of currency, traded for cash to pay for the VIP rooms.[556] Patrons could enjoy sushi, steaks and whatever else they wanted during their night out. Gold Club membership was available for $1,000 per year, which included a minimum champagne charge of $300 plus tips.

Of course, more than one guest complained about being overcharged or fraudulently charged while at the club, not so unlike what was happening at Scores in New York City.[557] Both were allegedly connected to the Gambino crime family, something straight out of an episode of *The Sopranos*.[558] One customer testified that he was charged over $6,000 for a two-hour Gold Club visit, and another was said to have been so drunk that a dancer signed his check for him, with a hefty tip included.[559] It's no wonder the club raked in an estimated $25 million per year.[560]

The fun came to a halt in 1999, when the feds busted into the club, seizing all assets in sight. Revelers didn't stop partying until the doors were officially locked. Kaplan was arrested for a laundry list of charges, including money

The Gold Club, now known as the Gold Room, a standard nightclub. *Photograph by the author.*

laundering for the Gambinos and running a prostitution ring within the club.[561] He was also charged under the Racketeer Influenced and Corrupt Organizations (RICO) Act, which has since been used locally against rapper Young Thug and President Donald Trump.

Despite the charges being mostly financial in nature, the months-long trial brought many revelations, including the testimonies from professional athletes like the Atlanta Braves' Andruw Jones and Dennis Rodman about what really happened behind the club's closed doors, including live sex shows and sex acts performed on customers. An ex-dancer described her R-rated exploits with Mutombo and an ex–Georgia Bulldog on the witness stand.[562] Another described a trip to South Carolina, during which Gold Club employees were brought along to "entertain" players from the New York Knicks.[563] Locals tuned into the news to hear the sordid details. Ultimately, Kaplan was sentenced to sixteen months in prison.[564]

After the raid, the Gold Club's building was sold by the government for a cool $5 million, but it sat vacant for two years.[565] Following a six-month stint as the campus of Christian Church Buckhead in 2004, nicknamed "God's Club," the space was reopened in 2009 as the Gold Room, a run-of-the-mill 2000s nightlife spot under the reign of Alex Gidewon (see "The Gidewon Mega-Clubs" section), now sans strippers.[566] It's still a popular nightlife spot for hip-hop royalty, including Cardi B, Jermaine Dupri and Meek Mill, with equally over-the-top décor, like a colorful chandelier and long, studded leather couches.[567]

And in 2017, another Atlanta strip club, The Cheetah, faced similar accusations of racketeering and prostitution. It was none other than attorney Steve Sadow, who defended the Gold Club, who took The Cheetah's case[568]. It was settled in 2019.[569]

Atlanta's strip clubs fell on hard times long before the COVID-19 pandemic closed doors for months, as fewer licenses for "adult entertainment" were issued and neighborhoods turned residential. Follies, the only strip club in the city of Chamblee, closed in late 2020, as the city banned fully nude clubs and pulled the club's liquor permit.[570] The Pink Pony in Brookhaven, at the time of this writing, is facing similar difficulties, as it has filed for bankruptcy and local officials claim it's behind on liquor taxes.[571] Sandy Springs has closed at least four clubs in the past decade.[572]

Onyx, a strip club not to be confused with an earlier drag bar of the same name, was recently the victim of a burglary. The future of Oasis Goodtime Emporium in Doraville is uncertain, as the city has banned "sexually oriented" establishments from selling alcohol.[573] Even Swinging Richards, Atlanta's first male strip club, ended its twenty-six-year run in 2022 to make room for more apartments.[574] At least for now, the clubs inside Atlanta's city limits seem to be safe.

Party in the Park

Before it was Atlanta's largest park, Piedmont Park was the pioneer home of the Walker family, later passed down to their son. A series of events took place in the park, namely, the 1887 Piedmont Exhibition, which gave the park its name. Next came the Cotton States and International Exhibition of 1895, which hosted Black spokesman Booker T. Washington's famous speech, "Atlanta Compromise," despite the fact that the event was segregated.[575] Both events followed the format of the International Cotton Exposition of 1881, with agricultural exhibits and the Cotton Queen pageant. Buffalo Bill and the Liberty Bell were among the attractions that drew attendees to these events.[576]

After the expo events were over, little of the Walker family's home remained, apart from a set of stone stairs and Lake Clara Meer, which

This photograph shows the Cotton States and International Exposition at Piedmont Park. *Library of Congress.*

Piedmont Park hosts many of Atlanta's large annual events. *Photograph by the author.*

Right: Park Tavern is the park's former stable complex and a longtime watering hole. *Photograph by the author.*

Below: The Peachtree Road Race is America's largest 10K race and ends with a party in Piedmont Park. *Photograph by the author.*

are visible today. The park's owners tried to sell it to the city, which wasn't initially interested but finally agreed in 1904.[577] In 1909, the city hired the Olmsted brothers, sons of famed landscape architect Frederick Law Olmsted, to create a plan for the run-down fairgrounds. Their vision was completed in 1912, but due to the cost to enact it, only some of the features were put into place. It wasn't until 1995, under the founding of the Piedmont Park Conservancy, that their plan was revisited.

Now spanning over two hundred acres, Atlanta's answer to Central Park has been the setting for several important events, including annual festivals like the Dogwood Festival, the Atlanta Jazz Festival, Piedmont Park Arts Festival and the Peachtree Road Race, the world's largest 10K race, which ends in the park. The race attracts both locals and visitors, with sixty thousand participants and twice as many spectators, who party on the streets and spill out of bars across Buckhead and Midtown.[578] The park also hosted an early football game between the University of Georgia and Auburn University, now a drinking tradition in itself.

The park has also been the setting for several music festivals, including Music Midtown, with appearances from artists ranging from the Allman Brothers Band and Notorious BIG to the Village People and Willie Nelson.[579] Duane Allman even named Piedmont Park as his favorite place the Allman Brothers Band performed.[580]

Park Tavern, a bar in the park's former horse stables, also has a legacy of live music, welcoming Collective Soul and Bon Jovi.[581] The tavern hosts a lively annual post–Peachtree Road Race celebration. It originally opened in 1996 as a franchised location of Mill Brewery, but it took its current name in 2000.[582] It still serves English-style beer, including house-brewed options, and has a promotion where drafts are sold for only one dollar when it rains.

The park also connects to the Atlanta Beltline, a former rail line that now serves as a pedestrian and bike trail through the city, with several bars, restaurants and breweries along the way. The ever-expanding path is planned to loop the city in its entirety but currently extends through the West End, Old Fourth Ward and Buckhead.

Atlanta Pride (1971–Present)

From the earliest days of Piedmont Park, it's been tied to the queer community. In fact, the 1895 Cotton Exposition featured two female impersonators, Dick Harlow and Mr. Stewart.[583] It was also a meeting place for cruising in

Held annually in the fall, the Peachtree Road Race takes place mainly in Midtown, including at Piedmont Park. *Photograph by the author.*

the 1950s, despite raids and antigay legislation in 1956.[584] And it was the site of counterculture events in the 1960s.

Following the police raid at the Ansley Mall Mini Cinema (see "The Great Gay Way" chapter), the Georgia Gay Liberation Front was formed, one of the first local groups to push for a Pride event. The first event in 1971 brought out around one hundred participants, who brought signs to march through Midtown, ending at a rally in Piedmont Park.[585] The city refused organizers a permit, but it became an official march the following year.[586] In 1976, Mayor Maynard Jackson named June 26 Gay Pride Day, but after backlash from conservative groups, the next year featured a "Civil Liberties Day."[587]

The 1979 Pride event was a strong reaction to the earlier appearance of Anita Bryant and her antigay rhetoric in Atlanta (see "Limelight" section), bringing in four thousand participants.[588] The Dyke March was added to the programming in 1983, as was a Stop AIDS banner to recognize the growing epidemic.[589] Within the decade, it had become the nation's fifth-largest Pride celebration.[590] A trans march was added in 2009.[591]

In 2000, Atlanta Pride turned thirty, and this anniversary was rung in in style with a free concert in Piedmont Park from the Georgia-grown and majority queer band The B-52s.[592] The Indigo Girls, another of Georgia's gay musical groups, headlined to over three hundred thousand in 2005.[593] Past grand marshals include the late Representative John Lewis, who was instrumental in the passage of gay rights legislation in Georgia; the Armorettes, the drag troupe originally formed at the Armory bar; and Anita Rae Strange, also known as "Blondie," from the Clermont Lounge.[594]

Today, Atlanta Pride has been celebrated for over fifty years and is now held in October in accordance with National Coming Out Day. The weekend-long celebration includes the parade, performances and vendors in Piedmont Park and parties all over the city. There's also a Black Pride event, held every year since 1996.

Freaknik (1983–1999)

There may have been spring breaks before and the tradition will continue long after, but for nearly two decades, Atlanta was known for Freaknik, or as it was called by one author, the "Big Bang for Atlanta rap."[595]

It started humbly enough, as a picnic organized by students of the Atlanta University Center from the Washington, D.C. area who weren't going home for the break.[596] The group of no more than sixty got together in Piedmont Park for beer and barbecue, to listen to music and enjoy the spring weather.[597]

The next year, the event grew bigger, as word of mouth spread on the campuses of America's historically Black colleges and universities, and it earned the name Freaknik. The name comes from the dance for Chic's "Le Freak," combining *freak* and *picnic*, and it was brainstormed by student Rico Brown.[598] But it still remained fairly tame, with rounds of flag football and pajama parties.[599]

As the event grew, the timeframe switched from the March weeks of spring break to the week before final exams in April. It moved to other parks around town, like Washington Park and Adams Park, before it went back to Piedmont Park. Partygoers still showed up with coolers full of drinks and boomboxes. Promoters later got involved, with handwritten fliers turning to sponsorships.[600]

It also introduced people from around the country to Atlanta, where many settled after attending the festival, as well as the city's music. The after-parties at places like Club 112 showcased up-and-coming artists from LaFace

Records, and acts like Snoop Dogg and Queen Latifah performed.[601] Videos for Luther Campbell's 1993 "Work It Out" and Playa Poncho's "Whatz Up, Whatz Up" also included footage from the event. The then-teenage duo OutKast gained popularity by passing out cassettes of their song "Player's Ball" to the crowds, bundled with dice and incense.[602] Even Notorious BIG performed in Piedmont Park one year.[603]

Freaknik was featured in Morehouse alum Spike Lee's *School Daze* and the sitcom *A Different World*. The event reached a fever pitch in 1994, as two hundred thousand attendees flocked to the city, with a $15 million impact on the city over a single weekend.[604] There was, of course, drinking, like there is at any college-focused event, but getting drunk wasn't the point of Freaknik like it was at other spring break events.[605]

But not all of Atlanta was welcoming to the Freaknik crowd. Commuters got stuck in traffic through Midtown and Buckhead alongside gridlocked revelers, who would get out of their vehicles or hang from their sunroofs, late into the night.[606] The 1994 event had reports of theft and assaults, and arrests were on the rise for drugs and weapons charges. After the 1995 event, there were ten reported rapes, over five hundred arrests and multiple lootings at local malls.[607] Students were greeted by police in riot gear, with malls and roads shut to them and hotels refusing to rent rooms to them.[608]

What the local newspaper called "Freaknikaphobia" was believed by some to be a reaction against Blackness and sexuality, an affront to the patriarchal views on female decorum, with nudity captured on camcorders, a new technology.[609] It wasn't as if Atlanta was a puritanical city—it was one that, even then, was nationally known for its strip clubs.

Mayor Bill Campbell, called "the mayor who killed Freaknik," finally dropped the hammer on the event with mounting pressure from community groups and an overextended police department.[610] But many locals believed Freaknik wasn't any worse than what was happening at mostly white spring break gatherings in Florida or Texas.[611]

There were several attempts to revive the Freaknik name, with inspired events, parties (including one held by 21 Savage), reunions and even a cartoon musical, but none quite captured the energy of the original.[612]

These days, there are several other HBCU spring break events held throughout the country, including Orange Crush, which has been held on Tybee Island outside of Savannah since 1988.[613] Since the event severed ties with Savannah State University in 1991, the festivities have continued independently.[614] It hasn't yet gained the national recognition Freaknik did.

Rise of Craft Beer

After Georgia's first brewery was established on colonial Jekyll Island, the state's taste for beer only grew. Atlanta's brewing tradition started before the city was even named, with German-born men crafting lagers and "steam beer" using recipes from the homeland with hops sourced from Europe and beyond.

By the 1870s, Atlanta City Brewery and Fulton Brewery were operating in different parts of the city, both through distribution and tied houses, bars that exclusively sold one brewery's products. Atlanta City Brewery was owned by Albert Steiner, a Jewish immigrant, and in 1900, he joined the chamber of commerce's fundraising committee alongside pharmacist Joseph Jacobs, who owned the place where Coca-Cola was first sold.[615]

At its peak, Atlanta City Brewery filled 2,500 bottles each day and was able to compete with big-name companies in St. Louis.[616] Even during Prohibition, breweries stayed afloat by selling soft drinks, ice and low-alcohol beer. Atlanta City Brewery also remained one of the top retailers of alcohol during this period.[617] Atlanta City Brewery finally closed in 1955, starting a dark period for local brewing that wouldn't improve for decades.

Egidius Fechter was another figure of the period, called the "godfather of Atlanta brewing," running a competing brewery from his brother Dionis in the 1850s.[618] After Dionis's death, Egidius inherited his stake.

Governor—and later president—Jimmy Carter is considered a champion of the homebrewing movement. *Photographer Karl Schumacher, Library of Congress.*

Jimmy Carter passed legislation that allowed for homebrewing nationally in 1978, but homebrewing wouldn't find a foothold in Georgia until 1995, officially kicking off the craft beer industry in Atlanta.[619] There are now dozens of beer operations, ranging from humble brewpubs to nationally recognized breweries with massive distribution and several taprooms, many claiming top awards. But breweries still face legal challenges through Georgia's tier system that dates to Prohibition and requires sales to go through distributors.[620]

In the 1990s, craft beer exploded within the state, with new breweries opening in just about every suburb and small town in the greater Atlanta metropolitan area from Fairburn to Senoia and Peachtree Corners to Woodstock.

In 2015, breweries were required to sell "tour tickets" in order to serve their beer in a taproom. Two years later, they could sell directly to consumers, but only in limited quantities.[621] High-gravity beer wasn't legalized until 2004, and this allowed for an increase in alcohol by volume percentage from 6 to 14 percent.[622]

In 2023, the Georgia Craft Brewers Guild came together in the hopes of passing what they called the FOAM Act, or the Fair and Open Access in Market Act. They wanted to be able to sell directly to businesses without going through a distributor. The act unfortunately failed, but thankfully, Atlanta's breweries persevere.[623]

ATLANTA BREWING COMPANY (1993–2022)

Atlanta Brewing Company was the city's first modern craft brewery, opened in 1993 in a warehouse on Atlanta's Westside. Founder Greg Kelly, formerly of Irish beer giant Guinness, brought over brewing equipment from England.[624]

Due to a highway widening project, the brewery moved to Defoor Hills.[625] It gained recognition for its wide range of beers, including Laughing Skull, created in collaboration with the Vortex Bar and Grill, a popular bar and comedy club. It won a gold medal in the "English-Style Bitter" category at the 2016 European Beer Star Awards, stacking up against the continent's best.[626]

One of Atlanta Brewing's most popular beers was Laughing Skull, made for The Vortex Bar & Grill. *Photograph by the author.*

In 2010, the brewery changed its name to Red Brick Brewing, a nod to the building it inhabited for decades, before it returned to its original branding in 2018.[627] Over the years, the brewery became a popular spot for trivia and live music, with beers inspired by the city like the Hartsfield IPA and Sea Otter Stout, a brew created for the Georgia Aquarium.

Sadly, the company reached an uncertain future, as the Atlanta beer market and the Westside neighborhood became more saturated. In 2022, the longtime Defoor Hills tasting room was closed for good, with discussions of plans to move to Underground Atlanta and contract brew with other companies.[628] However, as of this publication, the brewery's earlier lease was terminated without further announcement.[629]

SweetWater Brewing Company (1997–Present)

While Atlanta Brewing Company got its start first, SweetWater Brewing was close behind and has since gone on to become the nation's tenth-largest craft brewery.[630] A pair of college roommates founded the brand after working in breweries all over Colorado, and they gave it the name of a local creek that flows into the Chattahoochee River.

The once-humble taproom has grown to include a full-service restaurant and barrel aging facility. Over the years, its brews have racked up dozens of awards from the Great American Beer Festival and the World Beer Festival.[631] The company has also expanded to produce hard seltzers and canned cocktails.

SweetWater Brewing may have opened only recently, but it has become Georgia's most successful brewery. *Photograph by the author.*

Acquired by Tilray Brands in 2020, the company behind Breckenridge and Redhook Breweries, SweetWater now boasts an additional brewery in Fort Collins, Colorado, plus licensed restaurants in the Atlanta and Denver Airports.[632] As of 2024, Tilray has picked up another Georgia Brewery, Terrapin Beer Company from Athens.

Throughout its history, SweetWater has been connected to the outdoors, and its music festival, SweetWater 420 Fest, is an annual Earth Day gathering that benefits the Waterkeeper Alliance. Past acts have included Snoop Dogg, Widespread Panic and the Avett Brothers.

West Atlanta Brewery Boom

Atlanta Brewing and Sweetwater may have kicked things off, but the city's craft beer scene exploded in the following two decades, especially in West Midtown and the West End, where the city's drinking had begun.

Monday Night Brewing was started in 2006 by friends who met during a Bible study and started homebrewing.[633] The operation now has taprooms in Atlanta's West Midtown and West End, Knoxville, Charlotte, Nashville and Birmingham, and the company now also makes spirits and canned cocktails under its Sneaky Pete brand.

Wild Heaven was founded in 2010 in Avondale Estates and has since expanded to additional locations in Toco Hills and on the West End. It was only the fifth brewery to open in the state, and the company set up in the brewhouse that was originally purchased by the founders of SweetWater in 1997.[634]

Hippin' Hops Brewing was opened in 2021 in a former pharmacy building in East Atlanta, making it the city's first Black-owned brewery. The menu includes IPAs and Louisiana-inspired fare like fresh oysters and po' boys.[635]

West Midtown's Bold Monk, Firemaker, Round Trip and Scofflaw; Castleberry Hill's Atlantucky; Grant Park's Eventide; Three Taverns in Decatur; New Realm in the Old Fourth Ward; Summerhill's Halfway Crooks; and LaGrange-based Wild Leap's downtown taproom are among what makes the Atlanta beer scene what it is today, despite rapid changes (see the "Where to Next" chapter).

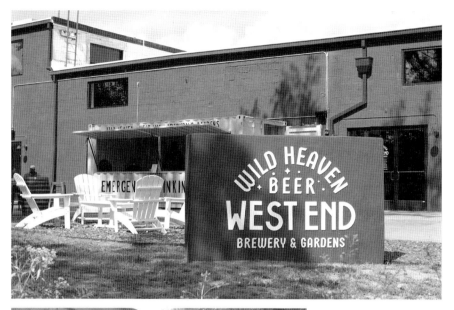

Above: Wild Heaven was started in Avondale Estates but opened a second location on the West End. *Photograph by the author.*

Left: Hippin' Hops is Atlanta's first Black-owned brewery. *Photograph by the author.*

Opposite: Steady Hand was one of several breweries in the corridor along Howell Mill Road. *Photograph by the author.*

Return of the Club Scene

In the remaining decades of the last millennium, Atlanta's nightlife scenes shifted from being solely in the downtown core and Midtown area to surrounding neighborhoods like Buckhead and Sandy Springs. Several bars and clubs also opened to appeal to the thousands of travelers who came for the 1996 Olympics.

Club Esso (or ESSO) was among them, opened in 1996 by New Yorker Kenneth Flynn.[636] The club joined the World Club and House of Blues, which popped up near the Olympic Village. The three-story club on Courtland Street featured five bars, two dance floors and a rooftop patio, plus a VIP lounge with a menu of top-shelf cognac and cigars.[637] Flynn even teamed up with an associate of Peter Gatien, who, despite interest, didn't open a club in time for the games due to his pending indictment with the feds in New York. But the club didn't last, and it is now a vacant lot. Chili Pepper opened a second location based on the site in Miami just in time, with three stories and walls covered in comic strips.

Club Kaya was both a restaurant and venue in Midtown that brought both locals and transplants in for its themed nights, like '80s hip-hop events.[638] DJs made names for themselves by spinning tunes from up-and-coming local artists. It didn't have booths, like many clubs in the following years; it was mostly a bar and dance floor, attracting the likes of Jay-Z and Ludacris.[639] It later became a club called Vision, run by the Gidewon brothers (see "The Gidewon Mega-Clubs" chapter), but was inevitably bulldozed in 2006 to make way for yet another condo building.

The Olympic boom was short-lived, as many clubs closed in the years after the games. The House of Blues closed in 1997 and became The Tabernacle, a long-running music venue in a former 1911 church, the following year. Several of the hot spots that had opened additional locations in town also moved along. But Atlanta's club scene was far from over, as young blood reinvigorated the nightlife.

THE KROHNGOLD EMPIRE (1988–PRESENT)

While Peter Gatien's reign as Atlanta's nightlife king came to a close after his arrest and prosecution, Michael Krohngold was there to take the reins, starting his hot spot empire with its own celebrity following.

After serving stints as a bartender and a worker at a PR agency, Krohngold worked as a manager at Club Rio, a 1980s hotspot in the converted vault of the former Columbia Pictures film distribution warehouse.[640] Set in the club was the beating heart of downtown, lauded by the *Village Voice* as being worth a trip from New York.[641] As the creative director, Krohngold set the aesthetic of the club, which attracted an eclectic crowd from the punk and new wave scenes. On the club's first night, David Bowie and his crew showed up after his performances at the Omni Coliseum and danced until closing.[642]

The club gained infamy as the site of a Ted Turner–hosted after-party the 1988 Democratic National Convention. It was here that a young Rob Lowe danced alongside fellow Brat Packers Judd Nelson and Ally Sheedy and players from the Atlanta Braves.

But the night didn't end when the bar closed; it instead ended when Lowe left the club, bound for the nearby Atlanta Hilton and Towers with two girls, including one who was underage, who later appeared in a sex tape.[643] It would become the event most tied with the club and Lowe's time in the city. The club is now a parking lot that surrounds SkyView, a Ferris wheel that overlooks Centennial Olympic Park.

Tongue and Groove is still a popular nightclub at Lindbergh, originally opened in Buckhead by Michael Krohngold. *Photograph by the author.*

Next came Colorbox, which opened in 1987 in Virginia Highland, where a young performer named RuPaul Andre Charles, subsequently known by only his first name, took the stage alongside Lady Bunny, a fellow drag performer and later roommate.[644]

Velvet came in the 1990s in another downtown warehouse attracting finance bros, dancers from The Cheetah strip club and celebrities alike.[645] Madonna appeared there, dancing with producer Dallas Austin, as did Lisa "Left Eye" Lopes and Jermaine Dupri. Bjork even hosted her album debut party there.[646] It's now the site of a stone wall that surrounds Woodruff Park, named for the Coca-Cola CEO.

Perhaps the best known of Krohngold's businesses is Tongue and Groove, which opened in 1994 and remains the city's longest running nightclub. The upscale atmosphere was popular with athletes and artists, with different types of music for every night of the week, including Latin, EDM, and hip-hop.[647] Partygoers could "groove" to the music or get bottle service and sushi from one of the booths. Janet Jackson, Mick Jagger, Jennifer Lopez, the Backstreet Boys, TLC and Naomi Campbell have partied there, and most recently, Jamie Foxx filmed a new movie at the club.[648]

It was a stronghold of Buckhead Village (see "Buckhead Meets Bourbon Street" section) until its closure in 2007, when it relocated to the Lindbergh area, also known as the Uptown development, where it remains today.

MJQ Concourse (1994–Present)

In 1994, a club opened in the basement of the then-ramshackle Ponce de Leon Hotel behind an unmarked door.[649] The Euro-inspired lounge took the name MJQ for founder George Chang's favorite band, Modern Jazz Quartet.[650]

With its mismatched furniture and a giant astronaut picture, the club attracted an eclectic crowd with a wide variety of music like retro-soul and dub. The artsy intellectual set could sip canned beer and eat snacks while they caught a show from a relatively unknown performer, a fashion show or even an art exhibition.

In 1997, the club moved a few doors down on Ponce de Leon Avenue to an underground space previously home to Lou's Blues Revue, but not before it took a sledgehammer to the old club, taking it down to the studs.[651]

Much of the crowd moved to the new spot, including the celebrity set. Janet Jackson and Flava Flav made appearances, and Atlanta royalty, like

Ludacris, Cee Lo Green and Andre 3000, could hang out there without being bothered. According to Buzzfeed, the club was so beloved by the cast and crew of *The Hunger Games* that its former address made an appearance on the set: PDL-736 for 736 Ponce de Leon Avenue.[652]

When Michael Payne took over the reins, there were appearances from bands like Deerhunter, Peaches and the Black Lips. DJs like Gnosis and Sinceelay also made names for themselves at the club, amid the glow of the neon "no requests y'all" sign. It's also cash-only and has no guest list, making it the antithesis of other clubs operating in the era.

In 2004, MJQ took over the former Cajun restaurant next door and christened it the Drunken Unicorn, its sister club.[653] Since there was no bar here, the eighteen-and-over and student crowd could now also come and dance for the DJ nights, displaying the previous night's photographs all over the scenester MySpace.

Throughout its tenure, MJQ has been a welcoming space for people from all backgrounds and interests, where you might find a young college student or an older regular who has spent years at the Ponce de Leon spot.

As apartments and hotels popped around Ponce City Market, a retail district and dining hub, developers announced in 2022 that MJQ's stretch of Ponce de Leon Avenue was set to be demolished to make way for new structures.[654]

In 2025, MJQ reopened in the former Dante's Down the Hatch space, which had remained untouched since its closure in 1999, at Underground Atlanta, continuing its legacy for future generations.[655]

Buckhead Meets Bourbon Street

In the 1990s, the best place for partying in Atlanta was in Buckhead. The neighborhood took its name from an early tavern that had a mounted buck's head that served as a marker for travelers. With comparisons to Bourbon Street—just like Underground Atlanta in the '70s—the handful of blocks around Peachtree and East Paces Ferry Roads were packed to the rafters with nightlife spots. In fact, in 1996, the eight-acre area had one hundred businesses with liquor licenses.[656]

There was the original location of Tongue & Groove, which moved after over a decade in Buckhead Village.[657] Mike 'n Angelo's had an aesthetic that could best be described as "eclectic," with mounted faux animal heads,

The Andrews Entertainment District was a complex with multiple bars and entertainment venues. *Photograph by the author.*

neon beer signs, rugby trophies, a stained-glass image of Jerry Garcia and pool tables with cheap beer.[658] The college crowd flocked to CJ's Landing for beer pong and live music on the patio, which had a large tree in the middle of it.[659] Lulu's Bait Shack was known for its grain alcohol fishbowl drinks topped with plastic alligators.[660]

You could start with a meal at Café Tu Tu Tango, a Miami import that slung artist-inspired cocktails, or Steamhouse Lounge, a bar and seafood shack that called itself the "best little dump in Buckhead."[661] Then you might dance into the night at Frequency, Club Uranus, Mako's Cantina and the Cobalt Lounge.[662]

A few blocks away, the multilevel thirty-thousand-square-foot Andrews Entertainment District operated from 1990 to the 2000s, home to eight separate bars.[663] It included Prohibition, a speakeasy and cigar bar; Stout, a fraternity-favorite sports bar with beer pong and dart leagues; Czar Ice Bar, a vodka ice bar with hundreds of bottles; and Andrews Upstairs, a dance club. The complex was closed suddenly in 2015.[664] Across the street, Buckhead Saloon operated from 1995 to 2000 in a cavernous former Mexican restaurant, closing and reopening multiple times in the decade.[665]

Unfortunately, the events of Super Bowl 2000 (see "The End of All Night Bars" section) were the final straw for a neighborhood that had seen rising crime and several complaints from neighbors concerning drug dealing, underage drinking and even prostitution.[666] The Buckhead Coalition was founded and worked alongside Mayor Shirley Franklin to crack down on the party zone.[667] Bars and nightclubs were forced to close by 2:30 a.m. instead of 4:00 a.m., as they had previously in the post-Olympics years.

Crime decreased significantly, but so did business, especially nightlife. Then came the developers, who bought up every block they could. By August 2007, Buckhead Village as it had been was bulldozed to make way for retail spaces and apartments.

After a stint called of being called, oddly, the "Streets of Buckhead," the area is now known as the Buckhead Village District, reviving its former name with luxury shopping, a dog park and several restaurants, plus Fado, a longtime Irish pub that has witnessed the many eras of the neighborhood.[668] It's now drawing comparisons to Rodeo Drive, where you're more likely to see Real Housewives and professional athletes than revelers with neon-hued drinks.

That's not to say that Buckhead doesn't still have its party scene—it just looks different now than it did in years past. The dueling piano bar Park Bench Tavern remained in Buckhead for thirty years before it was closed and a new version was opened at The Battery at Truist Park's burgeoning nightlife district in 2020.[669] After its move from Underground Atlanta in 1982, The Bucket Shop Cafe has remained a Buckhead staple, especially for fans of the Auburn Tigers and Carolina Panthers.

The college and post-college crowds still frequent dives like Five Paces Inn, Red Door Tavern and Moondogs, a complex with four bars in one that has somehow survived the area's changes since 1993.[670] Buckhead's nightlife continues to thrive with rooftop bars like St. Julep and Tesserae; speakeasies Red Phone Booth (around the corner from the old Limelight) and The Blind Pig Parlour Bar; and Lucian Books and Wine, a popular bookstore and bar.

There was even a 2023 attempt to make Buckhead its own city, but it didn't get enough votes for passage, so it remains part of Atlanta—at least for now.

2000–2020

The End of All-Night Bars

The new millennium didn't bring the end of the world like the Y2K crowd predicted, but the year 2000 did bring an important shift to the Atlanta nightlife scene after a violent end to Super Bowl night.

After a scuffle inside the Cobalt Lounge in Buckhead, a broken champagne bottle led to all-out mayhem. Richard Lollar and Jacinth "Shorty" Baker were left stabbed to death, allegedly at the hands of Baltimore Ravens player Ray Lewis and two members of his entourage. Lewis wasn't playing in the game at the Georgia Dome between the Titans and Rams, but he came to enjoy the city's nightlife before the night took a tragic turn.

The subsequent court case rattled the city, and the Cobalt Lounge closed a few months after the incident.[671] It's now an unassuming shopping center. While Lewis was found not guilty, the events of that night are still up for debate, and as of this writing, no one has been held responsible for the murders. Important pieces of evidence also disappeared before the trial.[672]

The fateful night at the Cobalt Lounge is commonly cited as the reason for the end of the Buckhead party scene—and that of Atlanta overall. The twenty-four-hour licenses at afterhours clubs like Backstreet in Midtown were not renewed, and most bars inside the city limits were forced to close by 2:00 a.m. Buckhead Village's days as Bourbon Street East were also numbered. A few spots were able to skate by if they offered food or were grandfathered into a 3:00 a.m. closure time, like Northside Tavern.

A 2005 smoking ban further hurt Atlanta's bars and restaurants, as they had to choose between allowing smoking and operating as only a bar with no one under twenty-one allowed or being smoke free and welcoming all ages.

But the "blue laws" that had long plagued the South, including many parts of Atlanta, started to finally lift in 2011. Then-Governor Nathan Deal signed a bill that allowed communities to choose if they would allow for the Sunday sale of alcohol at liquor stores, just like the local option for prohibition a century before.[673] The majority of the state passed the law, but nine Georgia counties decided to remain dry, where you can't buy alcohol or operate a liquor store.[674]

A so-called brunch bill in 2018 finally allowed restaurants to serve alcohol before the previously mandated 12:30 p.m. time, lifting one of the remaining holdovers from the religious temperance crowd.

From Snakes to Castles

Nightlife was nothing new for Castleberry Hill, a downtown neighborhood settled on the ashes of former Snake Nation, which had been torched by vigilantes around the Civil War. Around the turn of the nineteenth century, merchant Daniel Castleberry opened a store at Peters and Fair Streets, formerly Whitehall Road, which had been named for the tavern. He gave his name, along with a nod to the area's high ground, to the up-and-coming borough.[675]

It became inhabited by warehouses, where the city's tradesmen and women kept the city going, especially after the devastation of the Civil War, and little by little, residents moved in. In fact, Atlanta's first horse-drawn trolley line connected Castleberry Hill to the rest of downtown, allowing people to commute easily long before buses and trains.[676]

In 1985, the formerly industrial neighborhood was added to the National Register of Historic Places, as the intact warehouses were converted to lofts, restaurants and retail spaces. Many of the residents of the redeveloped area were artists, similar to residents of New York's Chelsea, and the neighborhood had space for galleries and living.[677] In recent decades, the monthly art strolls, when these spaces open their doors to show off their work on the second Friday of every month, have continued to attract attention.

By the 1990s, Castleberry Hill was in rough condition, with its crumbling exteriors standing in for the postapocalyptic setting for *Freejack* and the serial

Modern Castleberry Hill sits on the former site of Snake Nation. *Photograph by the author.*

killer landmarks in *Kalifornia*.[678] The neighborhood would later embrace Hollywood, as it was captured in *The Walking Dead, Driving Miss Daisy* and *Captain America: Civil War.*

Throughout the 2000s, Peters Street blossomed as a Black business district, especially for nightlife. Paschal's Restaurant took its current space in 2002, moving from its former site in the West End.

Celebrities' restaurants and bars have also left their mark on the neighborhood's food and beverage scene, including Cam Newton's Fellaship, Kandi Burruss's Old Lady Gang and 2 Chainz's Esco Restaurant and Lounge, which now has locations across the city and nationwide. Esco Restaurant and Lounge is known for its cocktails and fish bowls, including The Castleberry, a delicious concoction of vodka and fresh fruit named for its neighborhood.

FamFam is a cozy karaoke bar. It's the kind of place you'd expect to find on Buford Highway, but it is actually tucked inside a brick building in Castleberry Hill, where it moved after relocating from Grant Park in 2021.[679] It offers private suites where you can belt out your favorite tunes until the wee hours of the night or play a round of ping-pong. It's BYOB and only ten dollars per person, so you don't have to worry about overspending on your night out. Parlor serves pre-Prohibition cocktails, named for figures in Black history.[680] Founded by Boston native James Hamelburg, Match Lounge offers tropical cocktails, hookah and pizza.

Bottle Rocket and No Mas Cantina have each been neighborhood haunts for decades. The former offers sushi and tropical cocktails and typically hosts viewings of Atlanta United games, which take place a few blocks away, and an urban regatta–themed bike parade not unlike the Ramblin' Raft Race. No Mas is a sprawling restaurant and store that sells wares from Mexico and sizable margaritas with the best selection of tequila, including a barrel pick chosen especially for the space.

Castleberry Hill also has its own breweries. Atlantucky Brewing was opened by members of the rap group Nappy Roots and Wild Leap, a brewery from LaGrange that has a second taproom in the former Norfolk Southern building, just across the bridge from Mercedes-Benz stadium.

In 2017, the Georgia Dome stadium, which had previously hosted two Super Bowls, was demolished to make way for Mercedes-Benz Stadium, home to the Atlanta Falcons football and Atlanta United soccer teams. The stadium was the host of the 2019 Super Bowl, which brought even more development to the neighborhood.

The area will next host the FIFA World Cup in 2026, which promises to bring even more changes to the formerly rowdy 'hood, as celebrants will come from around the world to watch.

Elliot Street Pub & Deli (2006–2022)

The former carriage house at Elliott and Mitchell Streets has stood since the 1870s and operated as a bar for much of the time that followed.[681] In 1916, amid Prohibition, it was raided by the police, who found two unlicensed stills and another one hundred gallons of whiskey.[682]

By the 1950s, the building was known as Dee's Bird Cage, which lasted until a fire swept through the building three or so decades later.[683] It remained in this dilapidated condition until the late 1990s, when former contractors and brothers Michael and Peter Jakob saw the building on a late night jaunt.

The Jakobs opened their bar in 2006 and lived above it, and they hung a leftover Budweiser sign from Dee's in the pub.[684] The red-hued bar was an island unto itself, waiting for the area's development. It became a popular spot for people who went to Falcons games or got off work from nearby CNN, both bikers and hipsters. The bar had live music in the basement, The 51 and an iron foundry, where it'd do regular iron pours.

Long before it was Elliot Street Pub, the building was the site of an illegal booze raid. *Photograph by the author.*

The interior was covered in dollar bills and various ephemera, including a velvet painting of Willie Nelson and a MARTA bus stop sign, and it had a jukebox the brothers loaded with classics from Sam Cooke.[685]

The bar fit only ten or so patrons, and the tables couldn't manage many more, especially once staff was added.[686] It had no menu to speak of; instead, it had whatever bottles and taps you could see, plus a selection of tasty sandwiches.[687]

Once Mercedes-Benz Stadium was built in 2017 and development followed, the bar seemed to run on borrowed time. In 2022, the Jakobs sold the pub, which they'd bought for around $300,000, to athlete Cam Newton for over $3 million, expanding his empire in the neighborhood.[688] As of 2024, the bar is set to open as The N Zone, a sports bar.[689]

Fellaship (2019–Present)

Speaking of Newton, the football player and Atlanta native opened Fellaship, a cigar bar and lounge with upscale cocktails and DJs, with his brother C.J. in 2019, just in time for the city to host the Super Bowl for the third time.

Set steps away from Mercedes Benz Stadium, Fellaship is reminiscent of a sleek library, with walls of books, cool toned décor and televisions to catch a football game, especially when Newton's Carolina Panthers are playing. Artwork collected by Newton hangs on the walls as a nod to Castleberry Hill's history as an arts district.[690]

Fellaship has been praised by *Cigar Aficionado* for its selection of Cohiba, Ashton and Montecristo cigars.[691] The Newtons are whiskey fans, so the menu includes top-shelf bottles from Glenlivet and Bulleit. The house cocktail, A Whiskey Kind of Night, is made with Uncle Nearest 1884, orange and lemon juices and hibiscus brown sugar pink peppercorn syrup, smoked to perfection.

The best time to experience the bar's ambiance is at its lively jazz and juice brunch held every Sunday. Cam Newton also hosts a video series for BET, *Sip N' Smoke*, from the bar, where he interviews notable individuals, like Magic City's Michael Barney, Da Brat and Steve Harvey, over drinks and cigars.

THE SOBER SOCIAL (2022–PRESENT)

Atlanta nightlife isn't all about the booze. As interest in low- or nonalcoholic drinks continues to rise, so do the places where guests can enjoy them. The Sober Social opened in 2022 in Castleberry Hill as an alternative to the usual bar scene.

The Black-owned business not only offers nonalcoholic cocktails, crafted with the same care you'd expect from an upscale cocktail bar; it also has other menu items, including coffee and drinks with adaptogens and natural ingredients like Delta 8, a legal compound found in the cannabis plant. Guests can also drink kava kava, a traditional ceremonial beverage from the islands of the South Pacific known for its calming effects.

The cozy space has plush chairs and is a social atmosphere where nondrinkers or the sober curious can mingle. The bar also makes its own plant-based elixirs to use at home.

The Gidewon Mega-Clubs

At the same time DJs were becoming household names for their electronic music at mega-clubs in New York City and Las Vegas, Atlanta was developing its own scene. Michael Gidewon and his family cofounded a series of early

2000s nightclubs around the city, including the Velvet Room, Compound and Vision, set in the former Kaya space. It was popular with visiting celebrities like Britney Spears and Jay Z, plus locals Big Boi and T.I., whose album release party, along with Ciara's twenty-second birthday, were both hosted at the club.[692] Vanquish and Reign followed, arriving on the scene in 2011.[693]

Michael started as a party promoter at Velvet, owned by Michael Krohngold (see "The Krohngold Empire" section), before he started his own empire with his siblings Alex, Simon, Rachel and Gebriel. Rachel had worked the door at Kaya, which had helped make the Midtown party scene, along with Petrus, owned by Peter Gatien (see "Limelight" chapter), which later became Opera. The family came from Eritrea and fled during the nation's civil war, eventually settling in Atlanta.[694]

Despite being in the middle of the recession, these Midtown clubs were booming, with an excess of marble bars, flat-screen televisions and plush leather couches in the VIP lounges. No expense was spared, from top-tier bottle service to the attractive servers dressed to the nines, ready to pour them.

But as the years passed, the neighborhoods that housed these clubs, specifically the Westside and Midtown, became increasingly residential. A series of high-profile shootings at the clubs, including shootings in 2007 and 2020 at Compound and in 2014 at the Velvet Room, further affected public opinion of the region.[695]

Atlanta as a party scene also changed, as new spots opened further afield, hurting the family's empire. Patrons sought a more laid-back vibe, without the flashiness of bottle service and velvet ropes. Community groups became vocal opponents of the Gidewons' clubs, as they feared Midtown would become the new Buckhead Village.

Vanquish and Reign sat vacant by 2014, as Michael filed for bankruptcy, and Vision and Compound were torn down to make way for condominiums.[696] Sadly, Michael was fatally shot outside of Republic Lounge, another of his clubs, in 2023, and it subsequently closed.[697] As of 2024, a suspect has been identified but has not been prosecuted for the crime.

The Mixology Era

The first decade of the 2000s brought a greater focus on what we actually drink, not just where we drink. Nationwide, bartenders now called themselves mixologists, as an emphasis was placed on the actual craft of the

Leon's Full Service is a former auto shop; it is now one of the city's best restaurants and cocktail bars. *Photograph by the author.*

cocktail. It became a career, not just a job. Places like Milk & Honey, Employees Only and Death & Co. in New York; Bourbon & Branch in San Francisco; and The Violet Hour in Chicago became synonymous with an elevated drinking experience.[698]

Drinkers became aware of what exactly they were sipping, from the types of ice, house-made shrubs and mixers to the artisan glassware, with the attention similar to the farm-to-table movement going on in restaurants. But some also brought an air of pretension, with dress codes, secret passwords, rules (like those famously of Milk & Honey: "no name dropping, no star fucking") and high prices.[699]

Atlanta also had its turn in the craft cocktail movement, perhaps less nationally recognized but just as deserving. The bartenders who made names for themselves and their bars still play a role in the drinking culture today, especially in Decatur.

Paul Calvert gained a following during his time behind the bar at Pura Vida, Victory Sandwich Bar and Sound Table, later partnering with Ian Jones for Paper Plane, a mid-century-inspired cocktail bar behind Victory.[700] Jones later went on to open Little Trouble and S.O.S. Tiki Bar, while Calvert moved on to open his own space. Andy Minchow's Ration & Dram, now called Dead End Drinks, opened in Kirkwood after his time at Holeman & Finch.

Leon's Full Service, another Decatur restaurant, was opened in 2009 by the team behind Brick Store Pub. The former service station is known for its cocktail program, started by Miles Macquarrie, who went on to work at several high-profile cocktail bars in the city.[701] The menu changes seasonally, with unique ingredients, like roasted carrot mezcal and yuzu.

And in the most unlikely of places, One Flew South grew to prominence, opening in 2009 in an unused ticket counter in the E terminal of Atlanta's Hartsfield-Jackson International Airport.[702] It quickly picked up James Beard Award nominations along the way for its menu and service. Alongside offering upscale sushi, the menu takes inspiration from the world's busiest airport and the places its passengers fly. Chefs Todd Richards, Reggie Washington and Duane Nutter, alongside bar manager Jerry Slater, have gone on to found other spots around Atlanta, including Southern National, Soul: Food and Culture at Krog Street Market and The Expat in Athens.

HOLEMAN & FINCH PUBLIC HOUSE (2008–2020, 2023–PRESENT)

After a successful run at Restaurant Eugene, Chef Linton Hopkins opened Holeman & Finch in Buckhead in 2008, combining Southern classics with gastropub fare.[703] His wife and business partner, Gina, served as the sommelier and assembled a high-quality wine list, which helped the restaurant quickly top local lists of must-try spots.[704]

Following the success of its burgers, which were served only at brunch and late night, the restaurant spun off into a casual chain, H+F Burger, with locations at Ponce City Market and Truist Park, the Atlanta Braves baseball stadium.

Holeman and Finch contributed to Atlanta's growing cocktail scene. *Photograph by the author.*

With as much acclaim as the food at Holeman & Finch received, the cocktail menu was equally lauded thanks to the longtime beverage manager Greg Best, even after his departure in 2013. The restaurant was one of the first to adopt the "craft cocktail" trend that was taking off nationwide, with Regan Smith and Andy Minchow later taking over the reins.[705]

In 2023, the restaurant reopened in Colony Square in Midtown after a three-year absence with a new and improved menu. The burger returned to the new and improved public house, now without time restrictions. The cocktails pair with the farm-to-table style, with Benton's bacon fat–washed whiskey.

Another spinoff is the H+F Bottle Shop, a Buckhead liquor store that sells the spirits and wines the restaurant became known for. The shop sells cocktail kits with all the ingredients you need to make your own drinks at home, plus hard-to-find bottles and house-made syrups and cordials.

KIMBALL HOUSE (2013–PRESENT)

Taking its name from Hannibal Kimball's landmark hotel, Kimball House was opened in 2013 in a former train depot in Decatur. Inspired by the decadence of the period in which the original hotel operated, the restaurant features a long wooden bar and shelves carefully stacked with vintage glassware. Diners enjoy steak and seafood, along with champagne and oysters that would make Kimball himself proud.

The cocktails at Kimball House are among the best in the city. *Photograph by the author.*

But it's the drinks that earned it a James Beard Award for Outstanding Bar Program in 2019. The bar is led by beverage director Miles Macquarrie, previously of Leon's Full Service. The namesake cocktail, the Kimball House, is in the vein of a martini (see "The Drinks That Made Atlanta" chapter), while the bottled old fashioned is made with cola bitters and serves a group of four.

In 2019, Macquarrie helped found Tip Top Proper Cocktails, a line of miniature canned cocktails with all the quality you'd expect from a bartender of his stature, including mini full-strength versions of the old fashioned, espresso martini and margarita.[706] They're now served in flight aboard Atlanta-based Delta Airlines and sold at liquor stores throughout the city, racking up praise from several publications as the best canned cocktail around.

Ticonderoga Club (2015–Present)

Despite Ticonderoga Club's pedigree of being founded by the city's best bartenders, Greg Best, Paul Calvert and Regan Smith, there is perhaps no other Atlanta cocktail bar that takes itself less seriously. And that's a good thing. The name comes from the site of an eighteenth-century French fort not far from where Best and Smith both grew up.[707] The trio first met while working at Emeril Lagasse's since-shuttered Atlanta restaurant.[708]

Located inside a quiet corner of Krog Street Market, an 1800s stove and iron pan factory turned food hall, the bar is certainly playful, with nautical touches like the wooden shingles on the wall. The Captain's Chair may just

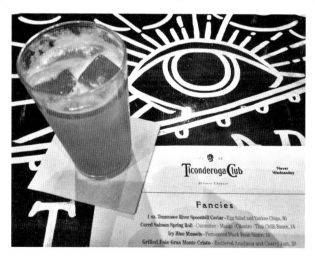

Ticonderoga Club is a playful drinkery inside Krog Street Market. *Photograph by the author.*

be another seat at the bar, but it's also a captain's seat from a boat—not a standard stool—and it is a highly sought-after spot.[709]

Despite the bar's name, it's welcome to all adults looking for a great night out. The food menu skews toward seafood, but there's a late-night bacon, egg and cheese sandwich straight from your favorite New York City bodega to soak up the booze. The sandwich is available only after 10:00 p.m., when the kitchen closes.

In terms of drinks, there's plenty of wine and a handful of beers, but most come for the cocktails. The "house cups" are the club's signature cocktails with aged spirits, but you'll also find spins on the classics, like the espresso martini and old fashioned. Some drinks must be sipped to be understood. The menu even has several increasingly popular nonalcoholic drinks.

The bar was honored by the James Beard Foundation with a 2019 nomination for Outstanding Bar Program and another in 2022 for Outstanding Hospitality.[710] After the COVID-19 pandemic closures, Ticonderoga Club faced another hit, as a burst pipe led to its closure for nearly a year. But as of this writing, the club's Christmas lights are once again twinkling, ready to accept new "members."

Edgewood Avenue Revival

For much of Atlanta's history, Edgewood Avenue was the main thoroughfare of the Old Fourth Ward, a neighborhood whose name is a holdover from the city's former ward system. The area was originally considered part of the suburbs, developed along the streetcar route between 1890 and 1930.[711] In its early days, its residents were mixed in terms of racial makeup, mostly separated on each side of Boulevard. Little by little, the area became more commercial, home to corner stores, groceries and liquor stores, at least after Prohibition.

After starting at a house on Grant Street, the Great Atlanta Fire of 1917 spread quickly through the city's cotton warehouses, homes and buildings, including much of Edgewood Avenue.[712] All told, three hundred acres burned throughout the city.[713] The fire left ten thousand people homeless, and many residents couldn't rebuild and had to settle elsewhere as the rebuilding efforts also became segregated.

White flight had already begun, taking businesses and residents to the west side and beyond.[714] But in 1962, the construction of the downtown

Edgewood Avenue is located in the historic Old Fourth Ward neighborhood. *Photograph by the author.*

connector brought Interstates 85 and 75 straight through Edgewood, causing business to grind to a halt and dividing Sweet Auburn in two. Since then, the aforementioned neighborhood where Martin Luther King Jr. grew up and Edgewood have seen similar ebbs and flows.

The first decade of the 2000s brought the renaissance of Edgewood Avenue, with a variety of bars and restaurants attracting a wide variety of Atlantans, drawing comparisons to parts of Brooklyn.[715] In 2014, a modern streetcar line was added to serve a nearly three-mile loop route, once again connecting the neighborhood to downtown as it had been until the 1930s.

Noni's served as an Italian restaurant by day, but by dusk, it shifted its tables to make room for a DJ. Georgia Beer Garden sat inside a historic brick building, with plentiful craft beer options from the city and beyond. The Music Room hosted up-and-coming bands, and crowds could grab a late-night slice at Pizzeria Vesuvius or visit the Edgewood Speakeasy beneath it. Folks could experience the smooth jazz tunes at Cafe Circa, the dive bar scene at Corner Tavern or dance into the night at Mother.

Several of the spots that made Edgewood into the nightlife spot it is have since come and gone, especially in the past few years, but their reputations carry on.

Sister Louisa's Church of the Ping Pong Emporium (2010–Present)

Just like Ticonderoga Club, the name of Sister Louisa's Church of the Ping Pong Emporium can be misleading. Often nicknamed "Church," the bar was opened in 2010 by artist Grant Henry and mostly defies explanation. Sister Louisa is the name for Henry's alter (or perhaps *altar*) ego, a nod to his time studying for a master of divinity degree from Columbia and Princeton Universities.[716]

The two-story space highlights much of Henry's artwork, typically thrifted religious artwork covered in quotes and sometimes sacrilegious statements (much of it available for sale), alongside vintage velvet paintings of Elvis Presley, Jesus and Martin Luther King Jr., who grew up nearby.

It attracts an expectedly artistic crowd, including the likes of Lady Gaga, who is said to have wanted to buy the bar.[717] Will Forte and Ben Stiller have also been spotted there over the years.[718] Patrons can don choir robes and play a round of ping-pong upstairs, if they can get a spot, or they can wait their turn from a vintage pew. Other popular weekly events include trivia, comedy shows and community karaoke, accompanied by, of course, a church organ.

The church is decorated in several of the owner's art pieces. *Photograph by the author.*

It's not exactly a gay bar, either, but is welcoming to all, with a Pride flag flying out front and regular drag shows on the calendar. It's a place where those from a religious background can rediscover the traditions so prevalent in the South with a twist of kitsch and openness, like DJ Vicki Powell's "Sunday Service." Patrons can take in the music while sipping on tall boys of Pabst Blue Ribbon or the "Blood of Christ," a slushie-like concoction of rum and Cheerwine soda.

The building is one of the historic spaces on Edgewood and, despite a 2015 fire, it survives with a series of murals that depict Kamala Harris, Stacey Abrams, Jimmy Carter and Puddles Pity Party, a local clown who appeared on *America's Got Talent*.[719] Following the Edgewood bar's success, a second location opened in 2014 in Athens, home of the University of Georgia, bringing with it its signature artwork and religious garb.

THE SOUND TABLE (2010–2020)

In 2010, The Sound Table was opened on Edgewood Avenue by husband and wife owners, Karl Injex and Muona Essa, after their successful run at Top Flr in Midtown. The dimly lit exposed brick space glowed under the narrow Edison bulbs, and a DJ booth was backlit to focus patrons' attention there.[720] The menu featured dishes from Southeast Asia and beyond, plus pop-ups from chefs who have since opened their own spaces, like Asha Gomez, Hector Santiago and Jarrett Stieber.[721]

But as much as patrons came to enjoy the food, they also came to take in the Sound Table's drinks and DJ-spun tunes, which provided a backing track to dinner and dancing. Paul Calvert, later of Ticonderoga Club, was among the bartenders who made the Sound Table so popular.[722] The menu was broken up into four categories based on flavors: sours and citrus, flips and fizz, bright and dry, and strong, rich and strange.[723]

Sadly, the lounge closed during the COVID-19 pandemic and never reopened.[724] Edgewood Dynasty was set to follow in its footsteps, operated by a pair of Sound Table regulars, but in late 2020, an exterior wall collapsed, exposing the interior of the restaurant to the elements and destroying a memorial mural for Breonna Taylor.[725] Edgewood Dynasty closed, and as of 2024, local DJ Ree de la Vega opened the space as Pisces, a music-driven space in the vein of its predecessors.

Our Bar (2020–Present)

Reminiscent of Edgewood's version of *Cheers*, Our Bar was opened by a group of thirteen friends and co-owners who have backgrounds in the bar industry. In fact, they met at the Department Store bar, a locale farther down Edgewood that shuttered in 2016.[726] Despite Our Bar's debut in March 2020, with no idea of what was to come to the once-bustling nightlife district, the gathering place has endured where many did not.

With its "DIS ATL HOE" red neon sign out front, this bar is full of local pride, with exposed brick walls and a popular photo booth. Patrons enjoy restaurant pop-ups, game nights, live music and karaoke and gather around the hookahs just about every day of the week. The DJs spin tunes during their residencies, and the bar has even hosted events for political campaigns.

The bar team also takes part in community events for its neighborhood, including hot meals and haircuts for members of Atlanta's unhoused population. Our Bar also participates in harm reduction training, teaching patrons how to use Narcan to prevent opioid overdoses for neighbors in need.

Our Bar's signature "DIS ATL HOE" neon sign. *Photograph by the author.*

2020–2024

The Pandemic Shuts Doors

The events of March 2020 permanently affected the drinking scene of Atlanta and the world, shuttering countless longtime favorites in its immediate aftermath and the years that followed. All restaurants and bars had to close their doors entirely for one month, and many operated in a limited capacity long after, with caps on the number of patrons allowed inside and mask requirements.

When businesses started to reopen in the summer of 2020 under strict guidelines, bars had to figure out a way to keep going, offering to-go drinks and takeout food. They leaned heavily on outdoor spaces, where people could safely gather. Some sold cocktail kits so patrons could make their own drinks at home.

The working-class tavern Elliot Street Pub, Buford Highway's beloved fifty-year-old The Rusty Nail, the *Night Rider*–themed Little Trouble, the longtime Midtown gay bar Henry's and the retro-inspired Golden Eagle were among the many shuttered bars of the period.

The city's craft beer bubble also seems to have burst in the few years before this writing, with the end of breweries like Second Self, Atlanta Brewing, Orpheus, Biggerstaff and Anderby, plus the beloved Georgia Beer Garden on Edgewood Avenue. Even nonalcoholic brewery Rightside wasn't immune. In addition to being hit hard by the pandemic, these establishments faced an uphill battle to brew profitably because they were unable to independently distribute their product.

Reading these chapters, especially this one, it's easy to think Atlanta's best drinking days are behind it. But that's far from the case. There's never been a better time to drink in the city.

Atlanta's restaurants are putting as much effort into the drink menus as they are into food menus. The wine programs at Miller Union and Lyla Lila in particular have been honored by the James Beard Foundation. More and more Georgia-made wines are appearing on fine dining menus, including those at Holeman & Finch, which carry wines from the Dahlonega Plateau American viticultural area. This viticultural area was established in 2018 in its namesake town north of Atlanta.[727] It certainly took long enough, considering Georgia's wine industry was founded almost as soon as the British landed here and the fact that it has four distinct climate zones and was home to the first modern winery (meaning it was opened after Prohibition), Chateau Elan, opened in 1981 just outside Atlanta.[728]

Distilling finally took off (also over a century after the start of Prohibition). Old Fourth Distilling became the first distiller in Atlanta, opening in 2014 in its namesake neighborhood. It now has plans to open a restaurant inside the airport. Independent Distilling and American Spirits Works followed, as did the award-winning Distillery of Modern Art and Murrell's Row Spirits.

Several breweries also started their own distilling operations, including Sneaky Pete from Monday Night, Atlanta Hard Cider & Distillery and Lost Druid. The city's first soju distillery, Minhwa Spirits, was opened in Doraville in 2023. It's honoring the Korean community of Atlanta with plans to open a *jumak*, or a Korean tavern.

The bar scene of Atlanta is alive and well with an atmosphere for every personality. Bar Margot at the Four Seasons in Buckhead honors the legacy of Atlanta's hotel bars, named for the seminal character in Wes Anderson's 2001 film *The Royal Tenenbaums*. It was opened in 2015 as a collaboration between Chef Ford Fry and bar professionals Greg Best and Paul Calvert, serving funky cocktails and zero-proof options.[729] The colorful St. Julep at the Kimpton Sylvan offers the best views of Buckhead. The St. Regis Bar, as well as the greenery-covered Garden Room, remain places to see and be seen. The lobby bar at Hotel Clermont, with its moody corners to cozy up in, has upscale cocktails you certainly won't find in its basement lounge.

The old-school steakhouses, like Chops Lobster Bar and Bones, elicit a Rat Pack atmosphere that just can't be duplicated by newer spots, with their dress codes, sommelier-selected wines and prices to match. Ray's on

Above: 12 Cocktail Bar is tucked behind a staircase in the tower at Ponce City Market. *Photograph by the author.*

Right: The disco vibes continue at Jojo's Beloved, a speakeasy at Colony Square. *Photograph by the author.*

the River, located, of course, on the Chattahoochee, has a regular happy hour crowd of folks who remember the Riverbend's heyday and now seek martinis and views.

Speakeasies can still be found in the city if you know where to look—they just exist in a different form now than they did in the past. Red Phone Booth was opened in Buckhead by the creators of Prohibition at East Andrews; it has a similar atmosphere and 1920s inspiration.

Jojo's Beloved harkens back to Atlanta's disco heyday in its secretive space in Colony Square in Midtown. If you can find 12 Cocktail Bar at Ponce City Market, you won't soon forget its incredible drinks and view. Himitsu is a celebrity favorite, tucked behind an upscale sushi restaurant. And while it's not exactly hidden, Ranger Station in the upstairs area of Ladybird offers an après-ski vibe, even in the middle of a Georgia summer. In fact, it was recently named one of *Esquire*'s Best Bars in America.[730]

Formerly industrial spaces like auto garages became places like Westside Motor Lounge, a sprawling courtyard with games, live music and drinks. Battle and Brew has been an OTP ("outside the perimeter," for the uninitiated) favorite since it opened in Sandy Springs in 2005. The sprawling bar offers plenty of video games along with themed trivia nights for several fanbases. A second location opened at The Battery in time for baseball season. My Parent's Basement in Avondale Estates has been popular with the comic book crowd since 2015.

Decatur is still the best borough for creative drinks, bar none. (See what I did there?) SOS Tiki Bar in Decatur has brought a modern twist to Atlanta's tiki scene since 2015, with restaurant pop-ups and classic tiki drinks alongside new spins in its space behind Victory Sandwich Bar. Brick Store Pub, just down the street, is still one of the best beer bars anywhere, showcasing the best beers from around the globe—but especially those from Belgium—since 1997, long before the words *craft* and *beer* were used together.[731]

James Beard–nominated Talat Market brings the flavors of Southeast Asia, with appropriate ingredients like Thai basil and pineapple skins. Bon Ton offers a Mardi Gras vibe year round with its "Fancy Service" neon sign and pink furry booth, plus its popular frozen Vietnamese Irish coffee and seafood by the plateful.

Righteous Room is a twenty-five-plus-year-old dive bar, but it somehow feels older, tucked into a narrow space near the Plaza Theatre, offering cheap pints and bites. Vesper in Glenwood Park, opened in 2020 by alums of Polaris and named for the iconic martini style, feels like a place where James Bond might feel at home. Its drink menu leans into the film series with

Above: Brick Store Pub is a Decatur staple with an unrivaled beer selection. *Photograph by the author.*

Left: Ladybird Mess Hall inspires summer camp vibes, as does the upstairs bar, Ranger Station. *Photograph by the author.*

its names. As of this writing, the same team has just opened Spectre, another Bond-inspired bar, next door.

Whoopsie's, opened in a beloved former coffee shop in Reynoldstown, offers cafeteria-style dishes served on the iconic divided trays with secondhand décor and classic cocktails, plus a daily concoction created by the bar staff. Mambo Zombi is a spooky spot in the former Georgia Beer Garden space on Edgewood with a Day of the Dead atmosphere with Caribbean and South American flavors in its cocktails. Floridaman brings the playful spirit of the Sunshine State above Breaker Breaker, a trucker-themed spot on the Eastside Beltline.

Pinky Cole of Slutty Vegan fame opened the Bar Vegan at Ponce City Market using only vegan ingredients in its theatrical cocktails, including one served in a fire extinguisher. Patrons can sip as they browse the shops, as the retail and dining complex is within an open-container district.

Making its debut in 2018 in East Atlanta, Banshee takes its name from the folklore character. With another one of the city's James Beard–nominated chefs, Banshee offers cocktails and local beers, and its dining room transforms into a dance floor on weekends with rotating DJs. Patrons can also soak up the drinks with Screamin' Weenies, the late-night hot dog menu.

But thankfully, it's not all new. Little Five Points has remained solidly local and independent for over forty years. Euclid Avenue Yacht Club has been steering us in the right direction since 1987 with its bric-à-brac covered walls and boozy slushies. Star Community Bar, known for its Elvis shrine, and The Vortex Bar & Grill, with its skull-shaped entrance, have been kicking since 1991 and 1992, respectively.[732] The Brewhouse Cafe followed in 1997 and still welcomes sports fans, especially during the big soccer matches of Atlanta United. And after a two-year period of uncertainty, the Porter Beer Bar (2008) reopened with many menu favorites, just a short walk from the legendary Wrecking Bar Brewpub (2011), set in a former antique store. Both showcase the world's best beers, including those brewed in house for the latter.

As of this writing, Underground Atlanta has been in the middle of another renaissance, hopefully one that will last, since it was purchased in 2020. On any given weekend, the subterranean space is pulsing with music and energy, with art gallery openings and concerts.

Farther afield, the nightlife scenes of Buford Highway and Gwinnett County are on another level; you can sing karaoke as late as 4:00 a.m. at Cafe Some Karaoke & Pocha, Mics Karaoke and Happy Karaoke while sipping soju and snacking on fried chicken.

Of course, this wouldn't be a book about Atlanta drinking without a special mention of the city's late-night eats. R. Thomas in Buckhead serves breakfast twenty-four hours a day, with a tent-like dining room and its famous parrots parked outside. Open since 1929, Majestic Diner (or Majestic Food Shop for the old-timers) in Poncey-Highland has a throwback vibe and what they call "food that pleases" until 2:30 a.m.

Metro Diner and Bar downtown hosts its lively late-night karaoke and bites that are popular with the convention crowd until the eye-watering 5:30

a.m. on the weekends. Hae Woon Dae on Buford Highway serves Korean barbecue until 2:00 a.m. on most nights, and chef-favorite Octopus Bar in East Atlanta boasts oysters and bulgogi alongside craft cocktails, sake, wine and beer until 2:30 a.m., as it has since 2011.

But there's nothing quite as iconic as the dozens of locations of Waffle House, the fluorescent-hued haven for residents of all walks of life, ideal for soaking up booze with greasy hashbrowns and pecan waffles. The local chain that started in Avondale Estates has been feeding hungry residents at all times of day and night since 1955. The Southern diner has a legacy all its own, inspiring books and a scale to determine the seriousness of a natural disaster, referred to as the Waffle House Index.

WHERE TO NEXT?

So, what's next? If I were to get out my crystal ball, I'd safely say that the city will continue to have a great drinking scene for years to come.

We've had virtual reality bars, bars where you can play all manner of childhood games (bocce! darts! ping-pong!) and bars with every theme, from Tulum and après ski to '90s cafeteria. We've got cat cafés, like The Frisky Whisker at Underground Atlanta, and dog park bars, like the Fetch franchise that has popped up around the city after finding success in the Old Fourth Ward. They're located in former mansions, horse stables, gas stations, plant stores, bookstores, airport terminals and, of course, underneath your feet if you know where to look.

Hopefully the gimmicks like robot bartenders and TikTok trends (i.e., charcoal, unnecessary garnishes and hard-to-drink-from glassware) are on their way out. I think we'll continue to draw inspiration from the past with different themed bars in unexpected places like this.

Bars will expand inclusivity in their spaces, appealing to different communities while still being welcoming to all. Following the lead of Woofs, the city's first LGBTQ+ sports bar, I've seen efforts to open a bar that follows women's sports called Jolene Jolene, which successfully met its goal on Kickstarter. It started by hosting watch parties for soccer, basketball and rugby at local breweries and will hopefully, one day soon, be its own brick and mortar bar.

The trends of mixed-use spaces like listening rooms are sure to continue, where it's as much about the atmosphere as the drinks themselves, inspired by those popularized in Japan. Commune in Avondale Estates has high shelves stacked with vinyl records and DJs spinning tunes throughout the evening. Stereo in Inman Park operates as a coffee shop by day, but come evening, the lights dim and the menu switches to serve wine and cocktails. Another is already in the works in Chamblee called Block + Drum.[733]

The West End has exploded with breweries, with three in one complex along with a kombucha bar and a distillery. A logical next step would be an urban winery, rounding out all of the drink options in one spot, or perhaps an in-town tasting room for one of the North Georgia wineries. This industry will certainly continue to grow, especially around that section of the Beltline, as the converted rail line expands its Westside Trail and it becomes as popular as its eastside counterpart.

The wine bar is alive and well, especially as an extension of a restaurant's wine program. Stem opened in 2013 in Marietta after the success of Seed, a modern American restaurant. Lucian Books and Wine brings the vibes with shelves of upscale design books, plentiful varieties of wine and delicious bites. Larakin offers coffee and pastries by day and wine at night, including weekly residencies from Loire Bar, which highlights winemakers from around France. Murphy's has been a Virginia Highland mainstay since 1979.

James Beard Award–winning Chef Terry Koval is set to open Fawn steps away from his Decatur restaurant, which focuses on wine and amaro from Italy and Spain.[734] Madeira Park Wine Bar is another spot that is set to arrive at Poncey-Highland's new apartment hotel complex in the former Highland Inn space from Steven Satterfield and Neal McCarthy of Miller Union and Tom Willard of Dive Wine, a wine pop-up. And that's not to even mention Vine Fine Wine, a Decatur shop that specializes in Georgia-grown wines.

As the city continues to expand (now with a population of five million and counting), I expect that Atlantans will be more willing to cross "outside the perimeter" in search of cool concept bars like '80s-style Okay Anny's in Dunwoody, The Third Door with its Prohibition setting in Marietta, Eleanor's at Muss and Turner's in Smyrna, The Chapter Room in Sandy Springs and Roaring Social in Alpharetta.[735] Austin's at Serenbe is bringing creativity to the New Urbanism community.

The city's neighborhoods are also rapidly changing. The formerly abandoned railyard used for countless movies, Pullman Yards, now hosts interactive events like its experiential AlcoHall, a food hall with drinks and bar games.

South Downtown is seeing new development, which will help connect communities like Castleberry Hill to downtown and Underground, especially as Atlanta continues to host large-scale events like the FIFA World Cup. The Cobb Galleria is poised to transform as well as the greater Truist Park area continues to expand.

I hope to see others follow in the footsteps of Minhwa Spirits, which launched its own native drinks like sake, rice wine, *aguardiente* and the low-proof beer popularized in Vietnam, representative of the city's diverse cultural makeup. The brewing scene is slowly becoming more varied but still has a long way to go. After all, beer is found in just about every part of the world.

Bars will continue to add nonalcoholic and low-proof options that allow for patrons to enjoy an outing without the buzz, especially as younger members of gen Z come of age. The Sober Social in Castleberry Hill has paved the way, as have nonalcoholic spirits stores Soberish in Kirkwood and The Zero Co. in Virginia-Highland. Zilch Market has hosted pop-ups, and many bars featured in the latter half of this book have added zero-proof cocktails that are as good as those with booze. I'd also like to see Atlanta's breweries add more nonalcoholic beer options. So far, only four have at least one nonalcoholic beer option. A local company, 18.21 Bitters, crafts bitters, tonics, syrups and shrubs for professional and home bartenders to make boozy and booze-free drinks.

In the same vein, an added emphasis on accessibility would benefit the city's bars. Some of Atlanta's old buildings have been grandfathered into the Americans with Disabilities Act, meaning their historic status precludes them from adding in features like ramps, elevators and wide clearance spaces for wheelchairs in hallways and restrooms. Design features like a sloped back bar could make wheelchair users feel more welcome, as they could sit at eye level with the bar staff. Accessibility also applies to those with neurodivergence, dementia and other needs, keeping in mind how reflecting sounds and flashing lights affect people inside these spaces.

Bar takeovers and pop-up bars will continue to appear—and not just those of the holiday variety—as a way for bar professionals to test out ideas before they take the leap to open a permanent space. T. Will offers pop-ups in the wine bar space like the previously mentioned Loire Bar. Girl Bar is a femme-forward pop-up with playfully feminine drinks, and it can usually be found at Banshee. Altered States emphasizes nonalcoholic options, especially mushroom- and plant-based drinks.

In a period that has seen several longtime gay bars close, new ones appear to be opening. 4West Lounge is a Black-owned LGBTQ+ bar that opened in East Atlanta after the success of its original space in Harlem.[736]

I also expect a further loosening of the alcohol-related laws that was started during the COVID-19 pandemic, including the creation of more open-container districts and more options for to-go drinks. Open-container districts already cover Atlanta, especially within food halls and entertainment districts in the city limits and beyond. To-go drinks are already commonplace in other states and provide a revenue stream for bars and restaurants that are still bouncing back after the pandemic.

I hope to see more landmark designations to protect these important places, like those we've seen for the Atlanta Eagle and Manuel's Tavern, with interpretive markers to describe what makes these locations so important. The Wylie Hotel, formerly Mrs. P's; the former site of the Otherside Lounge; and the Royal Peacock would make worthy additions. Perhaps Freaknik deserves a marker in Piedmont Park for its role in the city's music legacy, as it was the "big bang" for rap and hip-hop.

It's easy to take for granted the fact that our favorite watering holes will always be there, but as we've seen in the past few years, that's far from true. The bar as a concept even seems under threat, as we have spent the better part of two years drinking at home. Things are changing quickly, even as I type these words, with openings and closures occurring almost daily. But I think the bar as a gathering place is as secure as any part of American society, just as it has been since Oglethorpe's crew landed on the Georgia coast.

All I can say is, what are we drinking and who's paying?

THE DRINKS THAT MADE ATLANTA

As mentioned throughout this book, Atlanta isn't exactly known for its famous drinks, like the Manhattan or Ramos Gin Fizz from the "cocktail destination" cities of New Orleans, San Francisco and New York City. If anything, its earliest drinks were basic and straight to the point, including mixtures with beer, like the Mother-in-Law, made with "old ale" and "bitter ale," and pharmacy concoctions.[737] But the drinks that have been created here in the past few decades are certainly worth a mention.

Each of these cocktails was chosen because it represents a different chapter from this book and part of the city's culture. Some are still on the menus of local bars, where you can enjoy them in their intended surroundings. Others take inspiration from bygone places and now serve as recreations.

Most of the spirits mentioned in the following recipes are made locally, as noted, but any brand will do, and all are appropriate for beginner mixologists. The recipes were created by the listed parties, unless otherwise noted, in which case they were concocted by the author. And unless otherwise noted, all you'll need to create these drinks is a cocktail shaker (either Boston or cobbler) with a strainer, a jigger and a bar spoon, the basics of any bartending setup.

The Anita Bryant

After antigay speaker and Florida orange juice spokesperson Anita Bryant fought against a 1977 referendum in Miami that would ban discrimination based on sexual orientation, gay and lesbian organizers in San Francisco and beyond called for a boycott of orange juice.[738] Many bars joined in and created a new version of the Screwdriver, swapping out orange juice for apple juice. Bryant brought her hateful rhetoric with her when she appeared at the 1979 Southern Baptist Convention in Atlanta, but she couldn't keep the city's gay community from thriving, even inspiring drag performers.[739]

This is simple as far as cocktails go, but it's particularly tasty with fresh-pressed apple juice from North Georgia. I recommend pairing with the Atlanta vodka from the Distillery of Modern Art in Chamblee. Serve with a slice of cream pie like the one famously thrown at Bryant and toast to the city's queer legacy.

1½ ounces vodka
Fill the rest with apple juice

Build in a drinking glass, like a Tom Collins, over ice. Simply stir and enjoy.

Castleberry Smash

This drink was created by Danielle Williams, lead bartender of Paschal's Restaurant, and reprinted with permission.

Castleberry Hill has been a part of Atlanta's drinking history since the days when it was called Snake Nation. While Paschal's Restaurant started out on the West End in 1947, home to its La Carousel Lounge, it has fully embraced its new home, surrounded by history.

One nod to the borough is the restaurant's Castleberry Smash, a bourbon smash with blackberries for tartness and color. You can enjoy locally grown berries in the summer months, so stop by the market for this drink. Pick your favorite bourbon to round it out.

2 to 3 fresh blackberries	½ ounce simple syrup
2 lime wedges	1½ ounces bourbon
1 sprig mint	Club soda to top

Start by muddling your blackberries and lime in a shaker. Slap the mint against the palm of your hand to express the aroma and add to the shaker. Make the simple syrup by mixing one part each of hot water and sugar, mixing until dissolved. Add in your bourbon and simple syrup with ice. Shake well, straining over ice into a cocktail glass. Top with club soda and garnish with blackberries on a cocktail pick.

Champ-Ale

This drink was created by the bar staff of Ticonderoga Club and reprinted with permission.

The bar is known for its "Suppressors," which are lower alcohol drinks that pair well with food—and daylight. In fact, it has an entire section on its menu dedicated to these crisp, refreshing, slow-rolling beauties.

The "Champ-Ale" is one of the bar's favorites and one most requested by guests. It's also very easy to make at home and scales up nicely for parties. The recipe calls for a high-quality Italian vermouth, and the bar prefers Carpano Classico or Alessio Chinato, which you can find at some local liquor stores or online.

2 dashes Angostura bitters
Approximately $\frac{1}{3}$ ounces 2:1 cane sugar syrup
$\frac{3}{4}$ ounce fresh lemon juice
$1\frac{1}{2}$ ounces good Italian vermouth
$1\frac{1}{2}$ ounces dry sparkling wine, to top
$1\frac{1}{2}$ ounces cold lager, to top
Lemon twist, for garnish

Build the ingredients in a cocktail shaker over ice. Short shake and strain into a twelve-ounce tumbler glass over fresh ice. Top with $1\frac{1}{2}$ ounces of a good, cold, dry sparkling wine and $1\frac{1}{2}$ ounces of cold lager. Ticonderoga Club uses Narragansett Lager for this drink. Stir briefly to combine and garnish with a lemon twist.

Don't Care

According to *Soda and Fizzy Drinks*, a popular drink during inventor John Pemberton's day was called a "Don't Care." This was taken quite literally, as the pharmacist would add every syrup available, which could be delicious, like raspberry or peppermint, or less so, like celery. Each pharmacist had their own recipe.[740] It was then mixed with a splash of liquor and topped with soda water. It was also used to get rid of whatever was behind the bar that was no longer needed or to cover a medicinal taste.

It's reminiscent of the later childhood drink called a Suicide in my memory, in which you'd mix every flavor of soda from the Coca-Cola fountain with ice, usually a disgusting concoction that would get thrown away after a few sips. This low ABV drink gives plenty of flavor without too much of a buzz. It's far from the official version that would have been enjoyed back then, but it is a modern approximation. A local company, 18.21 Bitters, makes ingredients that can go into this drink, like a lemon basil simple syrup and blood orange and ginger shrub, a type of drinking vinegar. You can also make your own syrup by mixing fruit with equal parts sugar and water, letting it cook down and then straining any big pieces out.

½ ounce whiskey, or spirit of your choosing
2 to 3 ounces shrub or fruit syrup of your choosing
Club soda, to top

Mix your liquor and syrup into a glass filled with ice. Top with club soda and mix with a spoon.

Fly By Night

This recipe was created by One Flew South and is reprinted with permission.

Since opening in 1925 on a former racetrack, Hartsfield-Jackson Atlanta International Airport has slowly grown to be considered an international hub, called the world's busiest airport since 1999. It also welcomes over one million passengers per year from a wide range of places and cultures and gives these visitors their first taste of Southern hospitality inside its walls.

One Flew South (OFS) was one of the first upscale eateries to open within the airport, racking up awards for its upscale sushi and sandwiches upon opening in 2008. It even claimed a James Beard Award for its outstanding service, something you don't usually find in airports. The airport had previously been a place to grab an overpriced beer after another delay, but this restaurant's cocktail program is unmatched. It is a destination in its own right. OFS uses Four Roses, but any bourbon will do.

1 ounce bourbon
¾ ounce Montenegro Amaro
½ ounce Cynar
¾ ounce fresh lemon juice

1 bar spoon orange fig preserve
Bourbon-preserved fig, for garnish
  (optional)
Yuzu, for garnish (optional)

Combine all the ingredients to a shaker and dry shake (without ice) to break up the fig preserve. Add ice and shake once again. Fine strain into a coupe glass and garnish with a yuzu and bourbon–preserved fig.

Kimball House Martini

This recipe was created by Kimball House and is reprinted with permission.

The Kimball House Hotel was all about opulence. It was where people came to see and be seen and show off their wealth in the postwar South. Even Prohibition couldn't stop the party, as the hotel remained one of the top alcohol retailers in town, with its customers drinking fancy punches and champagne. The modern restaurant with the same name takes its inspiration from this period. Its bar program has also featured the city's best professionals who have had a permanent impact on Atlanta's drinking scene.

This spin on the martini fits in with the rebuilt hotel's operational period, as the drink is said to have been invented in the mid-1800s.[741] The Kimball House team recommends locally made Murrell's Row Gin Gin, a small-batch juniper-forward spirit with celery seed, coriander, lemon and angelica root notes. But another high-quality 94-proof London dry–style gin will also work in a pinch.

2 ounces Murrell's Row Gin Gin
½ ounce Dolin dry vermouth
½ ounce Cocchi Americano
2 dashes orange bitters

Lemon, for garnish (optional)
Olives, for garnish (optional)
Green Chartreuse, for garnish
  (optional)

Stir all the ingredients into a chilled mixing glass with ice until it reaches 26 degrees Fahrenheit (-3 degrees Celsius) on a digital food thermometer. Strain into a chilled cocktail glass. Express the oil of a lemon peel over the surface of the drink. Place the lemon peel on an iced side car, with 2 Castelvetrano olives as optional garnishes. Finish by placing 6 drops of Green Chartreuse on the surface of the drink if you'd like.

Moral and Rowdy

This Boilermaker is inspired by and embraces the spirit of the political parties that dominated Atlanta's early history, the Moral and the Free and Rowdy Parties. The two were constantly at odds over saloons and alcohol, with the Rowdies passing out booze as a bribe for votes and shooting off a cannon toward their opponent's building.

The drink uses moonshine or corn whiskey, whichever you can get your hands on—legal or otherwise—and nonalcoholic beer. I recommend Hellbender Corn Whiskey from Independent Distilling in Decatur and one of the handful of nonalcoholic beers made locally, like Decatur's Near Wild Heaven nonalcoholic IPA or Summerhill's Halfway Crooks Brevet Pils.

1 ounce corn whiskey or moonshine
1 pint nonalcoholic beer

Drop the shot in the beer or enjoy separately. After all, being a Rowdy is all about having personal choice.

Mrs. P's Tea

Georgia may be known for its tea, from the yaupon- or holly-based tea Native people called "black drink" and the English tea of colonists to modern sweet tea, but for the LGBTQ+ community, *tea* took on a different meaning. In the pre-Stonewall years in New York City and beyond, bars were not allowed to serve liquor to openly gay individuals. Instead, they'd host what were called "tea dances" as covers for open mingling. The tradition is believed to have started in 1966 on Fire Island.[742]

Mrs. P's bar in the Old Fourth Ward was one of the places in Atlanta that held them. Lady Bunny, a drag queen formerly of Atlanta, hosts one of the longest-running tea dances in New York, and the tea dance has also become a part of Atlanta Pride's programming.[743]

This drink takes inspiration from the literal and metaphorical, relying on some of the best local ingredients, including, of course, peaches. I recommend Earl Grey or another black tea from Just Add Honey, a tea shop in the Old Fourth Ward, but really, any kind of tea will do. In terms of bourbon, local brands include Doc Brown Bourbon, out of Senoia to the south, and Atlanta's American Spirit Works Fiddler Bourbon.

1 ounce peach purée, strained
1½ ounces brown sugar simple syrup, more or less to taste
1½ ounces black tea, chilled
1½ ounces bourbon
½ ounce fresh squeezed lemon juice

Add fresh (or canned, if you must) peaches to a blender until they form a purée. Then cook this down in a pan over low heat until most of the lumps are gone. To make the brown sugar simple syrup, add one part brown sugar and one part boiling water until it's fully blended, just as you would a traditional simple syrup. I also pre-make my black tea and refrigerate it so it can be ready to be mixed in without melting the ice. Combine all your ingredients in a shaker with ice and strain over a cocktail glass. This drink can be served hot or cold, but this boozy sweet tea is most refreshing in the summertime.

Peachtree Punch

This recipe was created by Trader Vic's and is reprinted with permission.

In April 1976, Trader Vic's opened its Atlanta outpost in the lower level of the Hyatt Regency Hotel downtown, a design from architect John Portman. It was a bar that founder Victor "Trader Vic" Bergeron had a hand in creating.

Inspired by the bar's Peach State location, not to mention the city's abundance of "Peachtree Streets," this tiki-style drink combines fresh peaches with a light rum and a hint of coconut. Incorporate local peaches into this drink for the best experience. They are typically sold from late spring to the end of the summer.

1 ounce Trader Vic's Koko Kreme

2 ounces peach halves

3 ounces orange juice

1½ ounces Trader Vic's Light Rum

¼ ounce peach brandy

Mint, for garnish (optional)

Nutmeg, for garnish (optional)

Blend all the ingredients with half crushed ice and half cubed ice to create a slushy-type texture. Once mixed, pour into a large Burgundy-style wine glass. To garnish, add a peach slice with mint and top with grated nutmeg to taste.

Playmate Pink

Atlanta was one of the sixteen locations chosen for Hugh Hefner's Playboy Club in the 1960s, an extension of the lifestyle brand created by his magazine. The downtown spot was hosted by the Bunnies and welcomed several big names, like Tony Bennett and Dean Martin.

This drink is adapted from one that was on the original menu at the Atlanta club, described as a frothy pink concoction with gin that was served in a stemmed glass with the Playboy Club logo. While we don't know the exact recipe, I imagine it to be similar to a gin-based version of a Cosmopolitan, with the added fizz from egg white. If you're vegan, aquafaba (or the liquid that comes from chickpeas) is a great alternative. I like the gin from Old Fourth Distilling, which lends well to cocktails for its notes of grapefruit and pink peppercorn.

Egg white or aquafaba

2 ounces gin

1 ounce orange liqueur, like
   Cointreau or Grand Marnier

1 ounce lime juice

3 ounces cranberry juice

Simple syrup, for added sweetness
   (optional)

Cherry, for garnish (optional)

Combine the egg white, gin, orange liqueur and juices into a shaker without ice, first doing a dry shake without ice to combine the ingredients. Be careful, as the drink can quickly fizz over. Once the egg white is combined, add ice and give it another shake before straining into a glass. If you like your drinks a little sweeter, add a dash of simple syrup. Garnish as you see fit, but I like a cocktail cherry on a cocktail pick.

Portman Panache

This recipe was created by the Drafting Table at the Hotel Indigo Atlanta and reprinted with permission.

As the "Hotels, Motels and Holiday Inns" section of this book describes, no one had more of an impact on the skyline of downtown Atlanta than architect John Portman. The open atriums and revolving restaurants became some of his signatures. One of the newer additions to the Portman portfolio was the Hotel Indigo downtown, which boasts one of his sculptures. The hotel was opened in 2016 and was one of his final projects before his death in 2017.

His namesake drink at the Drafting Table bar and restaurant, named for where he'd sketch his designs, pays homage to his architectural work in the hotel and around Atlanta. *Panache* is defined as "flamboyant confidence of style or manner," and the way the drink is built, along with its ingredients, speaks to Portman's vision of art and motion.

2 ounces Xicaro Mezcal
½ ounce Grand Marnier
1½ ounces apple cider, ideally from a Georgia company, like Mercier or
   B.J Reece orchards
Dash of cinnamon

Build your drink in a shaker over ice and shake vigorously for a few seconds until it is well blended. Strain into a rocks glass with one large ice cube and garnish with a dash of cinnamon.

S.O.S. Grog

This recipe was created by S.O.S. Tiki Bar and is reprinted with permission.

It's no secret that the early Georgia colonists' favorite drink was rum. It was imported from abroad and loved so much that James Oglethorpe, the colony's founder, and the trustees back in England had to ban it and any other "strong drink" in the first act of alcohol prohibition in America. But despite their best efforts, the colonists' affection for the spirit didn't end there, as it was incorporated into several drinks, like rum punch, toddies and flips, a whole-egg cocktail.[744]

This tropical drink takes its inspiration from the grog that would have been consumed during the colony's early days. This recipe calls for three types of rum, specifically white, aged and overproof, also known as barrel proof, which just means its proof is above 50 percent. S.O.S. Tiki Bar in Decatur rotates its rum selections behind the bar, but Independent Distilling has white and aged rums. I also recommend the top-notch rum from Richland Rum, a South Georgia distillery that has crafted bottles for none other than President Jimmy Carter. The honey syrup is made like normal simple syrup, with one part hot water and one part honey that is mixed until it becomes clear.

¾ ounce white rum
¾ ounce aged rum
¾ ounce overproof rum
¾ ounce honey syrup
¾ ounce grapefruit juice

¾ ounce lime juice
Splash of soda water
Lime, for garnish
Cinnamon, for garnish

Add all ingredients to a shaker with ice and shake well. Strain over four ice cubes and top with a slash of soda water. Garnish with a lime wheel and a charred cinnamon stick.

ACKNOWLEDGEMENTS

This book was written over many a drink—sometimes coffee and, other times, the stronger stuff—and was inspired by several books I read about the significance of bars in places like New York City, San Francisco and New Orleans. The industry celebrates many of these cities as the originators of various cocktails and the home of legendary bars and some of the field's most creative professionals. But I'd never read anything that pays homage to Atlanta's legacy as a party town from its earliest days. So, I decided to write it myself.

It wouldn't have been possible without the generations of Atlantans who partied before I was even a twinkle in the eyes of my teetotaling parents. The archives of the city's newspapers and magazines have been invaluable in my research, especially the work of the *Atlanta Journal-Constitution*, *Atlanta* magazine, Creative Loafing and the *New Georgia Encyclopedia*. In particular, the stories by Charles Bethea, Rebecca Burns, Richard Eldredge, Bo Emerson, Scott Henry, Mike Jordan, Beth McKibben, Chad Radford, Bob Townsend and Yvonne Zussel provided essential information on the city's many watering holes. Franklin Garrett was the ultimate historian on the city's early days, penning the four-volume *Atlanta and Environs*, a lengthy description of Atlanta life that remains unmatched in its attention to detail.

My local library system in Cobb County had invaluable resources, especially at the Switzer branch's Georgia Room and the study rooms where I did my best to pen these pages without distraction. The Atlanta History Center was another crucial asset, which I consider to be the best place to learn about the history of not only Atlanta but the South overall. The Art Farm at Serenbe provided me with a quiet place to finish up this project and test final cocktail recipes.

I appreciate the editors who allowed me to use my stories as part of the research that went into this book, including Chris Walsh, who let me write a deep dive for (the sadly since shuttered) *Fifty Grande* on Underground Atlanta, and Wine Enthusiast, which allowed me to write a story about dollar bills on bar walls inspired by a trip to Elliot Street Pub (also since shuttered). I also wrote a story on the best places to eat and drink at the Atlanta Airport for Thrillist and the histories of Sweet Auburn and the Old Fourth Ward for AFAR and *National Geographic Traveler*, respectively.

My friends in the media offered me support throughout this process and made connections along the way that were helpful—plus, they gave plenty of pep talks when the finish line seemed very far away. My publicist pals and the bartending community have my forever thanks for providing the recipes at the end of this book. My lifelong group of pals assisted in the initial "research" and were present for many of my early Atlanta drinking memories at Manny's, no matter how hazy they may be now.

Of course, I have to thank my family, including my mom, dad, my sibling Rae and my grandparents Sara, Stanley, and Linda. I especially appreciate my sister Sammi, who kept me on schedule and visited many of these bars with me for photographs and taste testing.

Cheers!

NOTES

INTRODUCTION

1. Martin Luther King Jr. National Historic Site, "Ivan Allen."
2. Atlanta Influences Everything, "About."
3. J. Davis, "That Was Then."

TIMELINE OF RELEVANT EVENTS

4. *New Georgia Encyclopedia*, "May in Georgia."
5. Cashin, "Trustee Georgia."
6. Pifer, *Hidden History*, 15–35, 118–29.
7. Coleman, *Colonial Georgia*, 74–88.
8. Cobb and Inscoe, "Georgia History."
9. Ayers/Saint/Gross, "Technical Memorandum."
10. CNN, "UGA Bulldogs."
11. United States Census Bureau, "Georgia 235th Anniversary of Statehood."
12. United States Census Bureau, "Georgia 235th Anniversary of Statehood."
13. Wilson and Ferris, *Encyclopedia of Southern Culture*, 707–8.
14. Ambrose, "Atlanta."
15. McConnell, *Culinary History of Atlanta*, 22–28.
16. Wilson and Ferris, *Encyclopedia of Southern Culture*, 744–45.
17. Buffington and Underwood, *Archival Atlanta*, 30–31.

18. Sismondo, *America Walks into a Bar*, 152–54.

19. Wilson and Ferris, *Encyclopedia of Southern Culture*, 1,452–453.

20. Boyle and Smith, *Atlanta Beer*, 41.

21. Buffington and Underwood, *Archival Atlanta*, 127.

22. Buffington and Underwood, *Archival Atlanta*, 109–10.

23. Washnock, "Prohibition."

24. Boyle and Smith, *Prohibition in Atlanta*, 135–40.

25. Cobb and Inscoe, "Georgia History."

26. Johnston, "Q."

27. Harry, "Jimmy Carter."

28. Boyle and Smith, *Atlanta Beer*, 73–75.

29. Boyle and Smith, *Atlanta Beer*, 74–75.

30. Henry, "Timeline."

31. Uhles, "High-Gravity Beers."

32. Georgia Department of Public Health, "Georgia Smoke Free Air Act."

33. 13th Colony Distilling, "About Us."

34. Butler, "Georgia's Craft Brewers and Customers."

35. McKibben, "Atlantans Say 'Yes.'"

BEFORE GEORGIA AND BEFORE ATLANTA

36. Cashin, "Trustee Georgia."

37. Historical Marker Database, "Horton House."

38. Flatt, "Agriculture."

39. Coleman, *Colonial Georgia*, 74–88.

40. Boyle and Smith, *Prohibition in Atlanta*, 25–27.

41. Cashin, "Revolutionary War."

42. Wilson and Ferris, *Encyclopedia of Southern Culture*, 1,339.

1837–1906

43. Gigantino, "Land Lottery."

44. Boylston, *Atlanta*, 18–20.

45. Russell, *Atlanta 1847–1890*, 24–25.

46. Boyle and Smith, *Atlanta Beer*, 16–17.

47. Boyle and Smith, *Atlanta Beer*, 16–17.

48. McConnell, *Culinary History of Atlanta*, 22–28.

49. Boylston, *Atlanta*, 24; Kurtz, "Whitehall Tavern," 43–47; Boyle and Smith, *Atlanta Beer*, 16–17.

50. Williford, *Peachtree Street*, 10.

51. Cooper, "History of the West End," 72–73.

52. McConnell, *Culinary History of Atlanta*, 22–28.

53. Boyle and Smith, *Atlanta Beer*, 17.

54. Boyle and Smith, *Atlanta Beer*, 17.

55. Boyle and Smith, *Atlanta Beer*, 13–15; Boylston, *Atlanta*, 80; Wilson and Ferris, *Encyclopedia of Southern Culture*, 676–77.

56. Wilson and Ferris, *Encyclopedia of Southern Culture*, 676–77.

57. Boyle and Smith, *Atlanta Beer*, 29–30.

58. Sismondo, *America Walks into a Bar*, 106–9.

59. Boyle and Smith, *Prohibition in Atlanta*, 12.

60. Buffington and Underwood, *Archival Atlanta*, 11.

61. Buffington and Underwood, *Archival Atlanta*, 12.

62. Bauerlein, *Negrophobia*, 45–46.

63. Russell, *Atlanta 1847–1890*, 32–35

64. Pifer, *Hidden History*, 118–29.

65. Buffington and Underwood, *Archival Atlanta*, 13; Mitchell, "Queer Place Names," 26–34.

66. Buffington and Underwood, *Archival Atlanta*, 11.

67. Pifer, *Hidden History*, 118–29.

68. Burns, "Most Lawless Year."

69. Bosworth, "Section of Snake Nation."

70. Russell, *Atlanta 1847–1890*, 73–74; Pifer, *Hidden History*, 126–27.

71. Sumner, "Everybody's Cousin."

72. McConnell, *Culinary History of Atlanta*, 15–19.

73. Bosworth, "Section of Snake Nation"; Boyle and Smith, *Prohibition in Atlanta*, 11–14.

74. Pifer, *Hidden History*, 118–29.

75. Boyle and Smith, *Prohibition in Atlanta*, 11–14; Boyle and Smith, *Atlanta Beer*, 23.

76. Burns, "Most Lawless Year."

77. Boyle and Smith, *Prohibition in Atlanta*, 11–15; Historic Oakland Foundation, "Moses Formwalt"; Kaemmerlen, *Historic Oakland Cemetery*, 24–26; Pifer, *Hidden History*, 135–40.

78. Boylston, *Atlanta*, 43–45.

79. Burns, "Most Lawless Year."

80. Boylston, *Atlanta*, 43–45; Holman, "Castleberry Hill."

81. Boylston, *Atlanta*, 41–48; Atlanta Police Department, "History."

82. Buffington and Underwood, *Archival Atlanta*, 11.

83. *Atlanta Constitution*, "Vigilance Committee."

84. Burns, "Most Lawless Year."

85. Historic Oakland Foundation, "Moses Formwalt."

86. Ward, "Republican Party."

87. Hansberger, "Murrell's Row."

88. W. Range, "Kimball."

89. Buffington and Underwood, *Archival Atlanta*, 43–45.

90. H. Davis, *Grady's New South*, 133–35.

91. W. Range, "Kimball."

92. Russell, *Atlanta 1847–1890*, 138–39; W. Range, "Kimball."

93. Buffington and Underwood, *Archival Atlanta*, 15–16.

94. Kaemmerlen, *Historic Oakland Cemetery*, 44.

95. Russell, *Atlanta 1847–1890*, 234–35; Prince, "Rebel Yell"; W. Range, "Kimball."

96. Prince, "Rebel Yell."

97. W. Range, "Kimball"; H. Davis, *Grady's New South*, 170–71.

98. New York Public Library, "Easter Sunday Dinner"; New York Public Library, "First Annual Banquet"; New York Public Library, "Good Fellowship Dinner."

99. Williford, *Peachtree Street*, 37–38; Prince, "Rebel Yell"; Russell, *Atlanta 1847–1890*, 234–35.

100. Hauk, "Throwback Atlanta."

101. C. Perry, "*Atlanta Journal-Constitution*."

102. Russell, *Atlanta 1847–1890*, 236.

103. Boyle and Smith, *Atlanta Beer*, 37–38.

104. Henry, "Timeline."

105. Plumb, *Unique Eats*, 78.

106. H. Davis, *Grady's New South*, 168.

107. Pendergrast, *For God*, 9–11, 27–28; McConnell, *Culinary History of Atlanta*, 89–90.

108. Giebelhaus, "Coca-Cola."

109. Pendergrast, *For God*, 22.

110. Boylston, *Atlanta*, 161–64.

111. Wilson and Ferris, *Encyclopedia of Southern Culture*, 676–77.

112. Boyle and Smith, *Prohibition in Atlanta*, 51–52; Pendergrast, *For God*, 24–27.

113. Buffington and Underwood, *Archival Atlanta*, 127–30.

114. Pendergrast, *For God*, 25–26; King, "Pemberton."

115. Boyle and Smith, *Prohibition in Atlanta*, 51–52.

116. King, "Pemberton."

117. King, "Pemberton."

118. Boyle and Smith, *Prohibition in Atlanta*, 51–52.

119. Buffington and Underwood, *Archival Atlanta*, 127.

120. Boyle and Smith, *Prohibition in Atlanta*, 51–52; Wilson and Ferris, *Encyclopedia of Southern Culture*, 676–77; Boylston, *Atlanta*, 161–64.

121. McConnell, *Culinary History of Atlanta*, 89–90.

122. J. Levin, *Soda and Fizzy Drinks*, 63–64.

123. Madden, "Long."

124. Kemp, "Candler."

125. King, "Dr. John S. Pemberton."

126. Pendergrast, *For God*, 66–68.

127. Giebelhaus, "Coca-Cola."

128. Coca-Cola Company, "History."

129. Jack Daniel's and Coca-Cola, "The Story"; Tennessee State Museum, "Coca Cola Bottle"; Jack Daniel's, "Our Story."

130. World of Coca-Cola, "Vault."

131. Kuhn and Mixon, "Atlanta Race Massacre."

132. Henderson, "Herndon."

133. Bauerlein, *Negrophobia*, 241.

134. Kuhn and Mixon, "Atlanta Race Massacre."

135. Ambrose, "John Temple Graves"; Summerlin, "*Atlanta Georgian*."

136. Bauerlein, *Negrophobia*, 241.

137. Suggs, "Atlanta Race Riot?"

138. Kuhn and Mixon, "Atlanta Race Massacre."

139. Martinez, *Long Dark Night*, 84.

140. Buffington and Underwood, *Archival Atlanta*, 64–65.

141. Kuhn and Mixon, "Atlanta Race Massacre."

142. Martinez, *Long Dark Night*, 84.

143. Bauerlein, *Negrophobia*, 238–39.

144. Sismondo, *America Walks into a Bar*, 184–89.

145. Bauerlein, *Negrophobia*, 238–39.

146. Maysilles, "Smith."

147. Sismondo, *America Walks into a Bar*, 184–89.

148. Boylston, *Atlanta*, 47.

1907–1920

149. Fahey, "Temperance."

150. Boyle and Smith, *Prohibition in Atlanta*, 60–61.

151. Kuhn, Joye and West, *Living Atlanta*, 172–82.

152. Boyle and Smith, *Prohibition in Atlanta*, 54–60.

153. Moss, *Southern Spirits*, 236.

154. Moss, *Southern Spirits*, 218.

155. Washnock, "Wrestling Temptation."

156. Boyle and Smith, *Prohibition in Atlanta*, 73–76.

157. Boyle and Smith, *Atlanta Beer*, 37–38.

158. Kuhn, Joye and West, *Living Atlanta*, 190.

159. Boyle and Smith, *Prohibition in Atlanta*, 74–80; Kuhn, Joye and West, *Living Atlanta*, 254–55.

160. Boyle and Smith, *Prohibition in Atlanta*, 101–2.

161. Washnock, "Wrestling Temptation."

162. Washnock, "Wrestling Temptation."

163. M. Davis, *Jews and Booze*, 71, 139.

164. Boyle and Smith, *Atlanta Beer*, 46–47.

165. Boyle and Smith, *Atlanta Beer*, 47–48; M. Davis, *Jews and Booze*, 247–49.

166. Boyle and Smith, *Prohibition in Atlanta*, 111–13.

167. Washnock, "Wrestling Temptation."

168. Stewart, "Moonshine."

169. Stewart, "Moonshine."

170. Sismondo, *America Walks into a Bar*, 108–10.

171. Boyle and Smith, *Prohibition in Atlanta*, 121–24.

172. Stewart, "Moonshine."

173. Stewart, "Moonshine."

174. Miller, "The Revenue."

175. Boylston, *Atlanta*, 41–48.

176. Miller, "The Revenue."

177. Buffington and Underwood, *Archival Atlanta*, 125–26.

178. City of Atlanta, "Rose House."

179. Kuhn, Joye and West, *Living Atlanta*, 173–76.

180. Boyle and Smith, *Prohibition in Atlanta*, 126–30.

181. McConnell, *Culinary History of Atlanta*, 92–93.

182. Boyle and Smith, *Prohibition in Atlanta*, 128.

183. Stewart, "Moonshine."

184. Kuhn, Joye and West, *Living Atlanta*, 173–76.

185. Pierce, "NASCAR."

186. Boyle and Smith, *Prohibition in Atlanta*, 130–34.

187. Boyle and Smith, *Prohibition in Atlanta*, 128.

188. Wilson and Ferris, *Encyclopedia of Southern Culture*, 744–45.

189. Boyle and Smith, *Prohibition in Atlanta*, 130–34.

190. Broady, "Photo Vault."

191. Grandaddy Mimm's, "About."

1921–1960

192. Zainaldin, "Great Depression"; Flatt, "Agriculture."

193. *Atlanta Journal-Constitution*, "Customers Line Up."

194. Albright, "Thirsty Fulton Voters."

195. Lemos, *Archive Atlanta*, episode 272, "Cheshire Bridge Road," August 9, 2024.

196. Boyle and Smith, *Atlanta Beer*, 67.

197. Sismondo, *America Walks into a Bar*, 119–30.

198. Boyle and Smith, *Prohibition in Atlanta*, 136–40; Sismondo, *America Walks into a Bar*, 104–5.

199. Boyle and Smith, *Atlanta Beer*, 69–70.

200. WABE, "Cheers!"

201. Atkins Park Restaurant & Bar, "Home."

202. Townsend, "Atlanta Classics: Virginia-Highland Landmark Atkins Park."

203. R. Taylor, "Blue Lantern."

204. R. Taylor, "Blue Lantern."

205. Henry, "Timeline"; Jacobs, "McTell."

206. R. Taylor, "Blue Lantern."

207. White, "Ponce de Leon."

208. R. Taylor, "Blue Lantern"; D'Antonio, "Mildred Lee."

209. D'Antonio, "Mildred Lee."

210. R. Taylor, "Blue Lantern."

211. Boyle and Smith, *Atlanta Beer*, 68.

212. Moe's and Joe's, "About."

213. Moe's and Joe's, "Menu."

214. Townsend, "After 67 Years."

215. Plumb, *Unique Eats*, 56.

216. Burns, "Museum of Manuel's Tavern."

217. Burns, "Museum of Manuel's Tavern."

218. Boyle and Smith, *Atlanta Beer*, 67–68.

219. Burns, "Museum of Manuel's Tavern."

220. Eaton, "Manuel's Tavern."

221. Burns, "Museum of Manuel's Tavern."

222. Monroe, "Maloof"; Blau, "Robert Maloof."

223. Burns, "Museum of Manuel's Tavern."

224. McDonald, *Secret Atlanta*, 24–25.

225. Burns, "Museum of Manuel's Tavern."

226. Burns, "Museum of Manuel's Tavern."

227. Plumb, *Unique Eats*, 56.

228. McDonald, *Secret Atlanta*, 24–25.

229. Atlanta Shakespeare Co., "About ASC."

230. Townsend, "First Look: Is Manuel's Tavern the Same?"

231. *Atlanta Journal-Constitution*, "Manuel's Tavern Added to National Register."

232. Monroe, "Maloof."

1961–1980

233. Mason, *Black Atlanta*, 6–7.

234. Hatfield, "Auburn Avenue."

235. O'Neal, "Great Migration."

236. Kuhn, Joye and West, *Living Atlanta*, 55–56.

237. Mason, *Black Atlanta*, 37.

238. Green, "Gene Kansas."

239. Kuhn, Joye and West, *Living Atlanta*, 55–56.

240. Mason, *Black Atlanta*, 2–7.

241. Dao, "How These Jazz Bars Defined Atlanta."

242. Martin Luther King Jr. National Historic Site, "Sweet Auburn Community."

243. Kuhn, Joye and West, *Living Atlanta*, 293–94; Mason, "Royal Peacock."

244. O'Neill, "Nightclubbing."

245. *Atlanta*, "Little Richard and James Brown"; Mason, "Vanishing Black Atlanta."

246. Dougherty, "Struttin."

247. Mason, "Royal Peacock."

248. Mason, "Vanishing Black Atlanta."

249. O'Neill, "Nightclubbing."

250. Mason, "Vanishing Black Atlanta."

251. Scott, "Group Tries to Revive."

252. Milsap, *Like a Song*, 95–100.

253. Warwick, *My Life*, 25–27.

254. Waterhouse, "Ghosts."

255. Mason, "Royal Peacock."

256. Radford, "Royal Peacock."

257. Goldmon, "Paschal's."
258. Plumb, *Unique Eats*, 6–7.
259. Goldmon, "Paschal's."
260. Paschal's, "Timeline."
261. Plumb, *Unique Eats*, 6–7; Rose, *Lost Atlanta*, 128.
262. Goldmon, "Paschal's."
263. Plumb, *Unique Eats*, 6–7; Opie, *Southern Food*, 99–115.
264. Rozzi, "Riding La Carousel"; Goldmon, "Paschal's."
265. Taylor, *It's a Matter of Pride*.
266. Burns, "Bygone Bars."
267. Plumb, *Unique Eats*, 6–7.
268. Goldmon, "Paschal's"; Rose, *Lost Atlanta*, 128; R. Brown, "Remembering a Soul Food Legend."
269. Goldmon, "Paschal's."
270. Henry, "Timeline"; *Atlanta Journal-Constitution*, "Night Spots."
271. Burns, "Bygone Bars."
272. Zimmerman, *Atlanta in Vintage Postcards*, 68.
273. Henry, "Cover Story: Where'd They Go?"
274. Henry, "Do Not Disturb."
275. Henry, "Cover Story: Where'd They Go?"; New South Associates for Historic Atlanta and the City of Atlanta Office of Design, "Atlanta LGBT+."
276. Burns, "Imperial Hotel."
277. City of Atlanta, "Imperial Hotel."
278. Easton, "Lightning Strike."
279. City of Atlanta, "Georgian Terrace Hotel."
280. Georgian Terrace, "Home."
281. Stafford, "Georgian Terrace."
282. Carter, "Movies Filmed."
283. Georgian Terrace, "Home."
284. Morehouse, "Focus."
285. Kuhn, Joye and West, *Living Atlanta*, 90.
286. New South Associates for Historic Atlanta and the City of Atlanta Office of Design, "Atlanta LGBT+."
287. Albright, "Winecoff Disaster."
288. Emerson, "What Says 'Atlanta'?"; Jillson, "Dinkler Plaza Hotel."
289. Waterhouse, "Ghosts."
290. Lemos, *Archive Atlanta*, episode 273, "Atlanta Playboy Club," August 16, 2024.
291. Swims-Gray, "Playboy Club."
292. *Playboy Club Bunny Manual*, 1–27.

293. ebay, "Playboy Club."

294. Swims-Gray, "Playboy Club."

295. Eldredge, "You Can't Replace This."

296. Georgia State University Library, "Robert Mitchum and Johnny Mercer."

297. ebay, "Playboy Club."

298. Waterhouse, "Ghosts."

299. Lemos, *Archive Atlanta*, "Playboy Club."

300. Bostock, "Polaris?"

301. Rose, *Lost Atlanta*, 139.

302. Bostock, "Polaris?"

303. Wheatley, "After 50 Years"; Craig, "John Portman."

304. F. Allen, *Atlanta Rising*, 152; Eldredge, "Polaris Comes Full Circle."

305. Dazey, "First Look: Polaris."

306. Eldredge, "Polaris Comes Full Circle."

307. Townsend, "Atlanta Classics: Blue-Domed Polaris."

308. Craig, "John Portman."

309. Dazey, "First Look: Polaris."

310. Mah, "Polaris."

311. Wheatley, "After 50 Years."

312. Townsend, "Atlanta Classics: Blue-Domed Polaris."

313. Hansell, "Polynesian Theme Is Newest Twist."

314. McKibben, "Atlanta Boasts One of the Last Trader Vic's."

315. Siegelman, *Trader Vic's Tiki Party*, 79.

316. Hendler, "History of the Hukilau."

317. Daly, "Protecting and Preserving"; Willoughby, "Chattahoochee."

318. Perry, "Ramblin."

319. Willoughby, "Chattahoochee."

320. Heart of Vinings, "Hardy Place."

321. Georgia Rivers Network, "Chattahoochee."

322. Daly, "Protecting and Preserving."

323. Bethea, "Man Who Made Us Float."

324. Rattini, "Big Adventure."

325. Albright, "Chattahoochee Raft Race."

326. Bethea, "Man Who Made Us Float."

327. Rattini, "Big Adventure."

328. Levin, "Mass Mania."

329. Edelstein, "Naked."

330. Edelstein, "Naked."

331. Rattini, "Big Adventure."

332. Bethea, "Woodstock on the Water."
333. Rattini, "Big Adventure."
334. Bethea, "Woodstock on the Water."
335. Bethea, "Woodstock on the Water."
336. Perry, "Ramblin"; "Herbert Graham and Associates," *Billboard*.
337. Chenault, Braukman and Atlanta History Center, *Gay and Lesbian Atlanta*, 82.
338. Surber, "Hotlanta."
339. Cobb, *Georgia Odyssey*, 138–40.
340. Atlanta History Center, "History of Pride Parades."
341. Surber, "Hotlanta."
342. F. Allen, *Atlanta Rising*, 167; P. Range, "Girls."
343. Lasner, "Swingsites."
344. Boone, "That 70's City."
345. Bethea, "Hoochie Koo."
346. P. Range, "Girls."
347. Henry, "30 Years."
348. Bethea, "Woodstock on the Water."
349. Bethea, "Woodstock on the Water."
350. U.S. Department of Housing and Urban Development. "*HUD v. Riverbend.*"
351. Chattahoochee Coffee, "About Us."
352. Buffington and Underwood, *Archival Atlanta*, 11–17.
353. *Atlanta*, "Why Is Underground?"
354. *Atlanta*, "Why Is Underground?"
355. *Atlanta Journal-Constitution*, 81 Theater advertisement; Genius, "Preachin' the Blues."
356. Haley, "Preserving Atlanta History."
357. Bucket Shop Café, "Home."
358. Boyle and Smith, *Prohibition in Atlanta*, 50.
359. Roughton, "Last Act."
360. Emerson, "Nancy Erickson."
361. *Atlanta*, "Why Is Underground?"
362. Henry, "Timeline"; Taylor, "Memories of the Past."
363. Creative Loafing, "Underground Atlanta."
364. Boyle and Smith, *Atlanta Beer*, 28–29.
365. Hayes, "Many of Mayor's Hopes"; Taylor, "Memories of the Past."
366. Henry, "Underground Atlanta."
367. Jones, "Man Pleads Guilty."
368. Creative Loafing, "Underground Atlanta."
369. Badie, "James Philip Ryan."

370. Tony Parenti and His All Stars, *Jazz Goes Underground*; Ruby Reds Band, "Oral History."
371. Hal's The Steakhouse, "Our Story."
372. Boyle and Smith, *Atlanta Beer*, 28–29.
373. *Santa Cruz Sentinel*, "Historic City."
374. *Atlanta Journal-Constitution*, "Tarver Obituary."
375. Scobey, "Armadillo East to Open."
376. Facebook, "Big House Museum"; Jennings, *Ramblin' Man*.
377. Robinson, "Dante's, Other Clubs."
378. McCarty, "Perryman"; Townsend, "Tribute to Piano Red."
379. Roughton, "Last Act."
380. Maddux, "Hammer."
381. Roughton, "Last Act."
382. Roughton, "Last Act."
383. Bulkin, *Frommer's*, 232–33.
384. Rodell, "Dante's."
385. Atlanta History Center, "Down the Hatch Menu."
386. Dante's Down the Hatch, "Home."
387. Eldredge, "You Can't Replace This."
388. Roughton, "Last Act."
389. Latarski, *101 Great Choices*, 232–33; Rodell, "Dante's"; Figueras, "Dante Stephensen."
390. Rodell, "Dante's."
391. Figueras, "Dante Stephensen."
392. Eldredge, "One Last Voyage."
393. Bulkin, *Frommer's*, 158–59.
394. Crenshaw, "Indigo Girls."
395. Horowitz, "Tommy Brown"; Kelly, "Mose Allison."
396. Latarski, *101 Great Choices*, 63.
397. 0405 Photography, "Blind Willie's."
398. J. Davis, "That Was Then."
399. Radford, "R.I.P. Lenny's."
400. McDonald, *Secret Atlanta*, 158.
401. Bulkin, *Frommer's*, 235–36.
402. J. Green, "Little Five Points."
403. Johnson, "Birdsmell, Band of Horses"; Facebook, "The EARL."
404. Radford, "Rest in Peace."
405. Goolrick, "Appreciation: Alex Cooley's Legacy"; Brant, *Join Together*, 106–7.
406. Sprayberry, "International Pop Festivals."

407. Hairston, *Georgian Terrace Hotel*, 41–45.
408. Getty Images, "Kiss Performs"; Goolrick, "Appreciation: Alex Cooley's Legacy."
409. McCoy, "Remembering the Agora Ballroom."
410. Bikoff, "Punk Rocks!"
411. *Atlanta*, "19 Things You Didn't Know."
412. Martin, *Born Standing Up*, 134.
413. J. Davis, "That Was Then."
414. Starrs, "Cooley"; Sams, "Cooley Slates 16 Shows."
415. Goolrick, "Appreciation: Alex Cooley's Legacy."
416. Goolrick, "Appreciation: Alex Cooley's Legacy."
417. Northside Tavern, "History"; Green, "One Night."
418. Emerson, "Northside Tavern"; McKibben, "Heart of Atlanta's Westside."
419. McKibben, "Heart of Atlanta's Westside."
420. Figueras, "What Is the Future?"
421. Green, "One Night."
422. Northside Tavern, "History."
423. Emerson, "Reunion Show."
424. Emerson, "Reunion Show."
425. Cole, *Planet Joe*, 21.
426. Facebook, "688 Club"; Garbus, "Atlanta Queer History Facts."
427. Emerson, "Steve May"; Emerson, "Reunion Show."
428. Emerson, "Steve May."
429. Smith's Olde Bar, "History"; Creative Loafing, "Smith's Olde Bar."
430. Smith's Olde Bar, "History."
431. Moore, "Bowie's Legendary Stop."
432. Smith's Olde Bar, "History."
433. Rose, *Lost Atlanta*, 88–89.
434. Garofalo, "Disco."
435. Latarski, *101 Great Choices*, 29.
436. Padgett, *Night at the Sweet Gum Head*, 300–301; Roughton, "Last Act."
437. Petridis, "Disco Demolition."
438. Backstreet, "Home."
439. Rose, *Lost Atlanta*, 133.
440. Eldredge, "Backstreet."
441. Backstreet, "Home"; Brown, interviewed by Adam Albrite.
442. Eldredge, "Backstreet."
443. Rose, *Lost Atlanta*, 133.
444. Eldredge, "Backstreet."
445. Eldredge, "Backstreet"; Bagby, "Charlie Brown."

446. Eldredge, "Reminisce."

447. Backstreet, "Home."

448. Eldredge, "Backstreet."

449. Rose, *Lost Atlanta*, 133.

450. Henry, "Dead-End?"

451. Henry, "Dead-End?"

452. Saunders, "Backstreet, Jungle Disco Ball."

453. Rose, *Lost Atlanta*, 133.

454. Bethea, "Johnny's Hideaway."

455. Johnny's Hideaway, "About."

456. Bethea, "Johnny's Hideaway."

457. Bulkin, *Frommer's*, 230.

458. Bethea, "Johnny's Hideaway."

459. Green, "Disco Decadence."

460. Green, "Disco Decadence"; Henry, "Timeline"; Owen, *Fabulous Rise and Murderous Fall*, 52–53.

461. Harris, "Having Fun Yet?"

462. Henry, "30 Years."

463. Green, "Disco Decadence."

464. Keenan, "Disco Kroger."

465. Waterhouse, "Ghosts."

466. Owen, *Fabulous Rise and Murderous Fall*, 52–53.

467. Waterhouse, "Ghosts."

468. New South Associates for Historic Atlanta and the City of Atlanta Office of Design, "Atlanta LGBT+"; Padgett, *Night at the Sweet Gum Head*, 230–34.

469. Waterhouse, "Ghosts."

470. Owen, *Fabulous Rise and Murderous Fall*, 56.

471. Henry, "Former Atlanta Club King."

472. Owen, *Fabulous Rise and Murderous Fall*, 16.

473. Henry, "Former Atlanta Club King."

474. Latarski, *101 Great Choices*, 20.

1981–1999

475. Albo, "Gayest Cities in America."

476. Sylvestre, "From Whence We Came."

477. Chenault, Braukman and Atlanta History Center, *Gay and Lesbian Atlanta*, 41.

478. New South Associates for Historic Atlanta and the City of Atlanta Office of Design, "Atlanta LGBT+."

479. M. Brown, "Short Retelling."

480. Rose, *Lost Atlanta*, 133.

481. Glier, "Revamp."

482. Padgett, *Night at the Sweet Gum Head*, 88.

483. Chenault, Braukman and Atlanta History Center, *Gay and Lesbian Atlanta*, 29, 44–49.

484. Sylvestre, "From Whence We Came."

485. Eldredge, "5 of the Most Atlanta Moments."

486. *Georgia Voice*, "'Flash' Back."

487. Malone, "Atlanta Needs Its Gay Bars."

488. New South Associates for Historic Atlanta and the City of Atlanta Office of Design, "Atlanta LGBT+."

489. *Atlanta*, "Queen."

490. *Atlanta*, "Half-Century of LGBTQ+ Milestones."

491. Picard, "This Ain't Texas."

492. Lesbian Bar Project, "About."

493. New South Associates for Historic Atlanta and the City of Atlanta Office of Design, "Atlanta LGBT+."

494. Padgett, *Night at the Sweet Gum Head*, 126–27.

495. Chenault, Braukman and Atlanta History Center, *Gay and Lesbian Atlanta*, 49.

496. New South Associates for Historic Atlanta and the City of Atlanta Office of Design, "Atlanta LGBT+."

497. Padgett, *Night at the Sweet Gum Head*, 277.

498. Padgett, *Night at the Sweet Gum Head*, 277.

499. Burkholder, "Wylie Hotel."

500. Green, "Photos: Inside the Hotel Rebirth."

501. *Atlanta Journal-Constitution*, "Exterior of Mrs. P's."

502. New South Associates for Historic Atlanta and the City of Atlanta Office of Design, "Atlanta LGBT+."

503. Eldredge, "On Ponce de Leon Avenue."

504. Padgett, *Night at the Sweet Gum Head*, 29–30.

505. Padgett, *Night at the Sweet Gum Head*, 30–33.

506. New South Associates for Historic Atlanta and the City of Atlanta Office of Design, "Atlanta LGBT+."

507. Eldredge, "5 of the Most Atlanta Moments."

508. New South Associates for Historic Atlanta and the City of Atlanta Office of Design, "Atlanta LGBT+."

509. Garbus, "Atlanta Queer History Facts."

510. Nodine, *Brick Through the Window*, 307.

511. Historic Atlanta, "Atlanta Eagle."

512. New South Associates for Historic Atlanta and the City of Atlanta Office of Design, "Atlanta LGBT+."

513. Eldredge, "On Ponce de Leon Avenue."

514. Wheatley, "Atlanta Eagle Trial."

515. Hicks, "Red Dog Squad."

516. Wheatley, "Mayor Apologizes."

517. Cheves, "COVID Won't Stop."

518. Garbus, "Atlanta Queer History Facts."

519. Eldredge, "On Ponce de Leon Avenue."

520. New South Associates for Historic Atlanta and the City of Atlanta Office of Design, "Atlanta LGBT+."

521. Silva, Hollis and Abusaid, "No Ill Intent."

522. Locascio, *Flashpoint*, episode 3, "Army of God," August 1, 2024; Armus, "Two Decades Before the Atlanta Spa Shootings."

523. Duncan, "Coming Out on the Other Side."

524. Armus, "Two Decades Before the Atlanta Spa Shootings."

525. Jordan, "Why Atlanta Is the Strip Club Capital."

526. Griffen, "Insider's Look"; Torpy, "Torpy at Large"; The Cheetah, "About."

527. Jordan, "Atlanta's Strip Clubs?"

528. Torpy, "For This Lawyer."

529. Henry, "Do Not Disturb."

530. Henry, "Do Not Disturb."

531. Henry, "Do Not Disturb."

532. Creative Loafing, "Clermont Lounge."

533. Henry, "Do Not Disturb."

534. *Atlanta*, "Blondie Really Publish a Book of Poetry?"

535. Dyer, "Blondie Strange."

536. Dyer, "Blondie Strange."

537. Eldredge, "Mumford, Sons Kicked Out."

538. Rankin, "Magic City Owner Guilty."

539. Jordan, "Oral History of Magic City."

540. Magic City, "FAQs"; Coscarelli, *Rap Capital*, 129–39.

541. Bainbridge, "Atlanta's 'Cult.'"

542. Jordan, "Oral History of Magic City"; Marshall, *Among the Bros*, 125.

543. Jordan, "Oral History of Magic City"; Marshall, *Among the Bros*, 125–26.

544. Colburn, "Drake Had an Armored Truck Deliver $100,000."

545. Friedman, "Make It Reign."

546. Jordan, "Oral History of Magic City."

547. Marshall, *Among the Bros*, 125–28.

548. Lee, *Racket: Inside the Gold Club*, episode 1, "A**hole Naked," August 26, 2020.

549. Jordan, "Oral History of Magic City"; Rankin, "Magic City Owner Guilty."

550. Dator, "Williams' Trip to the Strip Club."

551. Jordan, "Oral History of Magic City."

552. Lee, *Racket*, "A**hole Naked."

553. Lee, *Racket*, "A**hole Naked"; Lee, "VICE TV's 'Sex Before the Internet.'"

554. Lee, *Racket: Inside the Gold Club*, episode 7, "War Trial," October 7, 2020; Henry, "Party."

555. Henry, "Life"; Lee, *Racket*, "A**hole Naked."

556. Henry, "Tao of Steve."

557. Henry, "Life"; Fowler, "Confessions."

558. Raab, "Strip Club Partners."

559. Henry, "Life"; Henry, "Cover Story: The Un-Made Man."

560. Wall, "Bada-Bummer."

561. Bethea, "Stripping for Cash."

562. Henry, "Duh Factor."

563. Henry, "Tao of Steve."

564. Firestone, "National Briefing."

565. Bethea, "Stripping for Cash."

566. Bethea, "Stripping for Cash"; Henry, "Timeline"; Wheatley, "Hobnobbing."

567. Getty Images, "Gold Room."

568. Joyner, "Lawsuit Accuses Atlanta Strip Club."

569. Joyner, "Cheetah."

570. Hansen and Yamanouchi, "Chamblee's Only Strip Club Shuts Down."

571. Capelouto, "Brookhaven."

572. Green, "Construction Activity Spotted."

573. Hansen and Yamanouchi, "Doraville Threatens."

574. Lieberman, "One Last Night."

575. Mason, "1895 Cotton States"; Hatfield, "Segregation."

576. Newman, "Cotton Expositions."

577. Piedmont Park, "History."

578. Hansen and Yamanouchi, "July Fourth, AJC Peachtree Road Race."

579. P.F. Williams, *Freaknik*.

580. Poe, *Skydog*, 119–20.

581. Park Tavern, "About."

582. Boyle and Smith, *Atlanta Beer*, 89.

583. New South Associates for Historic Atlanta and the City of Atlanta Office of Design, "Atlanta LGBT+."

584. Sylvestre, "From Whence We Came."

585. Atlanta History Center, "History of Pride Parades."

586. Sylvestre, "From Whence We Came."

587. Atlanta History Center, "History of Pride Parades."

588. Padgett, *Night at the Sweet Gum Head*, 255.

589. Sylvestre, "From Whence We Came"; Saunders, "Portrait of a Community."

590. Saunders, "Portrait of a Community."

591. Saunders, "Portrait of a Community."

592. *Atlanta*, "Half-Century of LGBTQ+ Milestones."

593. Saunders, "Portrait of a Community."

594. Atlanta Pride, "Home."

595. Coscarelli, *Rap Capital*, 16–27.

596. Burns and Whack, "Freaknik."

597. O'Shea, "From the Archives."

598. Burns and Whack, "Freaknik."

599. Thompson, "Performing Visibility."

600. Suggs, "Atlantans Share Tales."

601. Coscarelli, *Rap Capital*, 42–49.

602. Nickson, *Hey Ya!*, 34–35; P.F. Williams, *Freaknik*; Sarig, *Third Coast*, 128–29.

603. P.F. Williams, *Freaknik*.

604. Hobson, *Legend of the Black Mecca*, 219.

605. "Comparing the Party Habits," 18.

606. Burns and Whack, "Freaknik."

607. Washington, "My People."

608. Thompson, "Performing Visibility."

609. Thompson, "Performing Visibility."

610. Burns and Whack, "Freaknik."

611. P.F. Williams, *Freaknik*.

612. Gomez, "21 Savage Rings in 30th Birthday"; Daniel, "Happening on 4/20"; IMDb, "*Freaknik: The Musical*."

613. Daniel and Van Brimmer, "Orange Crush."

614. Ambus, "Everything You Need to Know."

615. M. Davis, *Jews and Booze*, 34.

616. Boyle and Smith, *Atlanta Beer*, 24–25.

617. Boyle and Smith, *Atlanta Beer*, 24–25.

618. Moss, *Southern Spirits*, 202–6; Boyle and Smith, *Atlanta Beer*, 24–25.

619. Boyle and Smith, *Atlanta Beer*, 87.

620. Nouraee, "There's a Tier."

621. Butler, "Georgia's Craft Brewers and Customers."

622. Nouraee, "There's a Tier."

623. Zickgraf, "FOAM Act Is Dead."

624. Endolyn, "Red Brick Brewing"; Boyle and Smith, *Atlanta Beer*, 78–80.

625. Townsend, "Beer Town."

626. Atlanta Brewing Company/Red Brick Brewing, "Home."

627. Townsend, "Beer Town."

628. McKibben, "One of Northwest Atlanta's Original Breweries Is Closing."

629. Zussel, "Atlanta Brewing Company."

630. Townsend, "Sweetwater Brewing Leads the Way."

631. Georgia, "SweetWater Brewing Crafts Success."

632. Townsend, "SweetWater Brewing Leads the Way."

633. Monday Night Brewing, "Our Story."

634. Wild Heaven Beer, "Our Story."

635. Townsend, "First Look: Hippin Hops Brewery."

636. Esso, "Home."

637. Jones, "OUT THERE: ATLANTA."

638. Barbour, "Club Kaya Reunion"; Wicker, "How Atlanta's Clubs Fueled."

639. Henry, "Party."

640. Eldredge, "Club Rio's 25th."

641. Eldredge, "Club Rio's 25th."

642. Eldredge, "Club Rio's 25th."

643. Eldredge, "Club Rio's 25th."

644. Garbus, "Atlanta Queer History Facts"; Henry, "Timeline."

645. Eldredge, "Back in the Day."

646. Facebook, "I partied (and danced)."

647. Bulkin, *Frommer's*, 231–32; Marshall, *Among the Bros*, 128.

648. Tongue and Groove, "Home"; Shalhoup, "Golden Touch"; Ho, "Recuperated Jamie Foxx."

649. Radford, "Late-Night Magic at MJQ."

650. Henry, "Party."

651. Henry, "Party"; Radford, "Late-Night Magic at MJQ."

652. Dominick, "Genuinely Can't Watch *The Hunger Games*."

653. Radford, "Late-Night Magic at MJQ."

654. Zussel, "Longtime Ponce de Leon Business."

655. Summers, "MJQ Nightclub."

656. Boone, "CDC Study."

657. Henry, "Last Call."

658. Winn, "Bar Review"; Latarski, *101 Great Choices*, 17.

659. Creative Loafing, "CJ's"; CJ's Landing, "Home."

660. Green, "Perspective: 15 Years Ago."

661. Cafe Tu Tu Tango, "Locations"; Steamhouse Lounge, "About."

662. Henry, "Last Call"; Green, "Perspective: 15 Years Ago."

663. Andrews Entertainment District, "Home."

664. Ho, "Atlanta Improv Shutting Down."

665. Spivak, "Buckhead Saloon."

666. Emerson, "Super Bowls."

667. Boone, "CDC Study."

668. Buckhead Village District, "Our Story."

669. Zussel, "Park Bench."

670. Moondogs Bar, "About Us."

2000–2020

671. Coscarelli, *Rap Capital*, 96.

672. Livingston, *The Raven*, episode 1, "Who Is That Dude?," January 12, 2024.

673. Washnock, "Wrestling Temptation."

674. R. Brown, "In Georgia, Some Vote."

675. Holman, "Castleberry Hill."

676. Castleberry Hill Historic Arts District, "History."

677. Ford, "Cover Story: Castleberry."

678. Castleberry Hill Historic Arts District, "History."

679. Zussel, "MAP: Where to Do Karaoke."

680. Figueras, "Take a Food Tour."

681. McKibben, "Elliott Street Pub Is Closing."

682. Boyle and Smith, *Prohibition in Atlanta*, 99–100.

683. Keenan, "Elliott Street Pub Goes Up for Sale."

684. Holman, "Castleberry Hill."

685. Chapman, "Atlanta's Best Bar."

686. Keenan, "Farewell."

687. Figueras, "Take a Food Tour."

688. McKibben, "Elliott Street Pub Is Closing"; Keenan, "Elliott Street Pub Goes Up for Sale"; Keenan, "Farewell."

689. Fuhrmeister, "Details on Cam Newton's Plans."

690. Townsend, "First Look: Dine, Drink and Savor Cigars."

691. Olmsted, "Review: Fellaship."

692. Henry, "Cover Story: Club King."

693. Henry, "Vanquish."

694. Henry, "Cover Story: Club King."

695. Burns, "4 Injured in Shooting."

696. Wheatley, "Vanquish, Reign."

697. Winters, "Brother of Republic Lounge Co-Owner."

698. Miles, "Good Decade."

699. Milk and Honey, "Home."

700. Cooper, "Paper Plane Is Closing."

701. Townsend, "Leon's Full Service."

702. Kessler, "Oral History."

703. Figueras, "Review: Holeman and Finch."

704. Zussel, "Holeman & Finch to Reopen."

705. Watson, "Holeman & Finch Still Shines."

706. Scholz, "Kimball House Partner."

707. Mah, "Review."

708. Chapman, "Tippling Point."

709. W. Williams, "Is This the Best Bar Seat?"

710. Zussel, "Ticonderoga Club Closes."

711. Martin Luther King Jr. National Historic Site, "Sweet Auburn Community."

712. Rose, *Lost Atlanta*, 35.

713. Burns, "Great Fire."

714. Hatfield, "Auburn Avenue."

715. Wheatley, "Atlanta Nightlife."

716. Lauterbach, "Discovery."

717. S. Allen, "Jesus, Karaoke, Bizarre Art, and Queer Family Collide."

718. Stuart, "Sister Louisa's Church."

719. Townsend, "Sister Louisa's 'Church.'"

720. Addison, "Sound Table."

721. McKibben, "Sound Table Closes."

722. McKibben, "Sound Table Closes."

723. The Sound Table, "Home."

724. Figueras, "Atlanta Cocktail Lounge."

725. Figueras, "Wall Collapses."

726. Sedghi, "Why Community Is at the Core."

2020–2024

727. Federal Register, "Establishment of the Dahlonega Plateau."
728. Krewer, "Grapes and Wine"; Nystrom, "Chateau Elan."
729. Townsend, "Take a First Look at Bar Margot."
730. Newmark, "Atlanta's Ranger Station."
731. Townsend, "Leon's Full Service."
732. McDonald, *Secret Atlanta*, 158–59.

WHERE TO NEXT?

733. Wakim, "Music, Cocktails and Food Mix."
734. McKibben, "Chef Brings Decatur Its First Wine and Amaro Bar."
735. Hansen, "Gwinnett Tops 1M People."
736. Allnatt, "4West ATL Planned."

THE DRINKS THAT MADE ATLANTA

737. Boyle and Smith, *Atlanta Beer*, 33.
738. Prism Florida, "Anita Bryant."
739. Padgett, *Night at the Sweet Gum Head*, 255.
740. Levin, *Soda and Fizzy Drinks*, 63–64.
741. Bhabha, "History of the Martini."
742. Fire Island Pines Historical Society, "Origins of Fire Island's Tea Dance."
743. Spataro, "Tea Dance."
744. Wilson and Ferris, *Encyclopedia of Southern Culture*, 676–77.

BIBLIOGRAPHY

BOOKS

Allen, Frederick. *Atlanta Rising*. Taylor Trade Publishing, 1996.

Bauerlein, Mark. *Negrophobia: A Race Riot in Atlanta, 1906*. Encounter Books, 2001.

Boyle, Mary O., and Ron Smith. *Atlanta Beer: A Heady History of Brewing in the Hub of the South*. The History Press, 2013.

———. *Prohibition in Atlanta: Temperance, Tiger Kings & White Lightning*. The History Press, 2015.

Boylston, Elise Reid. *Atlanta: Its Lore, Legends and Laughter*. Foote & Davies, 1968.

Brant, Marley. *Join Together: Forty Years of the Rock Music Festival*. Backbeat, 2008.

Buffington, Perry, and Kim Underwood. *Archival Atlanta*. Peachtree Publishing Company, 1996.

Bulkin, Rena. *Frommer's 1996 Official Guide to Atlanta and the Olympic Summer Games*. Simon & Schuster, 1996.

Chenault, Wesley, Stacy Braukman and Atlanta History Center. *Gay and Lesbian Atlanta*. Images of America. Arcadia Publishing, 2008.

Cobb, James C. *Georgia Odyssey*. University of Georgia Press, 1997.

Cole, Joe. *Planet Joe*. 2.13.61 (publisher), 1992.

Coleman, Kenneth. *Colonial Georgia: A History*. Charles Scribner's Sons, 1978.

Coscarelli, Joe. *Rap Capital: An Atlanta Story*. Simon & Schuster, 2022.

Davis, Harold E. *Henry Grady's New South: Atlanta, a Brave & Beautiful City*. University of Alabama Press, 1990.

Davis, Marni. *Jews and Booze: Becoming American in the Age of Prohibition*. New York University Press, 2012.

Hairston, Julie. *Georgian Terrace Hotel: A Centennial Salute to Atlanta's Modern Classic.* Butler Books, 2011.

Hobson, Maurice J. *The Legend of the Black Mecca: Politics and Class in the Making of Modern Atlanta.* University of North Carolina Press, 2017.

Kaemmerlen, Cathy J. *The Historic Oakland Cemetery of Atlanta: Speaking Stones.* Arcadia Publishing, 2007.

Kuhn, Clifford, Harlon E. Joye and Bernard E. West. *Living Atlanta: An Oral History of the City, 1914–1948.* Atlanta Historical Society and University of Georgia Press, 1990.

Latarski, Ric. *101 Great Choices: Atlanta.* Passport Press, 1996.

Levin, Judith. *Soda and Fizzy Drinks: A Global History.* Reaktion Books, 2021.

Marshall, Max. *Among the Bros: A Fraternity Crime Story.* HarperCollins, 2023.

Martin, Steve. *Born Standing Up: A Comic's Life.* Charnwood Books, 2008.

Martinez, J. Michael. *A Long Dark Night: Race in America from Jim Crow to World War II.* Rowman & Littlefield, 2016.

Mason, Herman "Skip," Jr. *Black Atlanta.* Arcadia Publishing, 1997.

McConnell, Akila Sankar. *A Culinary History of Atlanta.* Arcadia Publishing, 2019.

McDonald, Jonah. *Secret Atlanta.* Reedy Press, 2020.

Milsap, Ronnie. *Almost Like a Song.* McGraw Hill, 1990.

Moss, Robert F. *Southern Spirits: Four Hundred Years of Drinking in the American South, with Recipes.* Ten Speed, 2016.

Nickson, Chris. *Hey Ya! The Unauthorized Biography of Outkast.* St. Martin's Press, 2004.

Nodine, Steven, et al. *Brick Through the Window: An Oral History of Punk Rock, New Wave and Noise in Milwaukee, 1964–1984.* Splunge Communications, 2017.

Opie, Frederick Douglass. *Southern Food and Civil Rights: Feeding the Revolution.* Arcadia Publishing, 2017.

Owen, Frank. *Clubland: The Fabulous Rise and Murderous Fall of Club Culture.* St. Martin's Press, 2003.

Padgett, Martin. *A Night at the Sweet Gum Head: Drag, Drugs, Disco, and Atlanta's Gay Revolution.* W.W. Norton & Company, 2021.

Pendergrast, Mark. *For God, Country, and Coca-Cola.* Charles Scribner's Sons, 1993.

Pifer, Mark. *Hidden History of Old Atlanta.* The History Press, 2021.

Plumb, Amanda. *Unique Eats and Eateries of Atlanta.* Reedy Press, 2021.

Poe, Randy. *Skydog: the Duane Allman Story.* Backbeat Books, 2016.

Rose, Michael. *Lost Atlanta.* Pavilion Books, 2015.

Russell, James Michael. *Atlanta 1847–1890: City Building in the Old South and the New.* Louisiana State University Press, 1988.

Sarig, Roni. *Third Coast: Outkast, Timbaland, and How Hip-Hop Became a Southern Thing.* Hachette Books, 2007.

Siegelman, Stephen. *Trader Vic's Tiki Party: Cocktails and Food to Share with Friends*. Ten Speed, 2005.

Sismondo, Christine. *America Walks into a Bar: A Spirited History of Taverns and Saloons, Speakeasies and Grog Shops*. Oxford University Press, 2011.

Warwick, Dionne. *My Life as I See It: An Autobiography*. Atria Books, 2010.

Williford, William Bailey. *Peachtree Street, Atlanta*. University of Georgia Press, 1962.

Wilson, Charles Reagan, and William Ferris. *Encyclopedia of Southern Culture*. University of North Carolina Press, 1989.

Zimmerman, Elena Irish. *Atlanta in Vintage Postcards*. Arcadia Publishing, 1994.

NEW GEORGIA ENCYCLOPEDIA

Ambrose, Andy. "Atlanta." Last modified June 8, 2022. *New Georgia Encyclopedia*. https://www.georgiaencyclopedia.org/articles/counties-cities-neighborhoods/atlanta/.

Cashin, Edward. "Revolutionary War in Georgia." Last modified September 30, 2020. *New Georgia Encyclopedia*. https://www.georgiaencyclopedia.org/articles/history-archaeology/revolutionary-war-in-georgia/.

———. "Trustee Georgia, 1732–1752." Last modified December 10, 2019. *New Georgia Encyclopedia*. https://www.georgiaencyclopedia.org/articles/history-archaeology/trustee-georgia-1732-1752/.

Cobb, James, and John Inscoe. "Georgia History." Last modified September 30, 2020. *New Georgia Encyclopedia*. https://www.georgiaencyclopedia.org/articles/history-archaeology/georgia-history-overview/.

Craig, Robert. "John Portman." Last modified November 3, 2020. *New Georgia Encyclopedia*. https://www.georgiaencyclopedia.org/articles/arts-culture/john-portman-1924-2017/.

Crenshaw, Holly. "Indigo Girls." Last modified June 6, 2024. *New Georgia Encyclopedia*. https://www.georgiaencyclopedia.org/articles/arts-culture/indigo-girls/.

Fahey, David. "Temperance Movement." Last modified August 26, 2020. *New Georgia Encyclopedia*. https://www.georgiaencyclopedia.org/articles/history-archaeology/temperance-movement/.

Flatt, William. "Agriculture in Georgia." Last modified February 25, 2022. *New Georgia Encyclopedia*. https://www.georgiaencyclopedia.org/articles/business-economy/agriculture-in-georgia-overview.

Giebelhaus, August. "Coca-Cola Company." Last modified June 6, 2017. *New Georgia Encyclopedia*. https://www.georgiaencyclopedia.org/articles/business-economy/coca-cola-company/.

Gigantino, Jim. "Land Lottery System." Last modified September 28, 2020. *New Georgia Encyclopedia.* https://www.georgiaencyclopedia.org/articles/history-archaeology/land-lottery-system/.

Goldmon, Camille. "Paschal's Restaurant." January 7, 2021. *New Georgia Encyclopedia.* https://www.georgiaencyclopedia.org/articles/arts-culture/paschals-restaurant/.

Grem, Darren. "Henry W. Grady." January 20, 2004. *New Georgia Encyclopedia.* https://www.georgiaencyclopedia.org/articles/arts-culture/henry-w-grady-1850-1889/.

Hatfield, Edward. "Auburn Avenue." Last modified September 24, 2020. *New Georgia Encyclopedia.* https://www.georgiaencyclopedia.org/articles/counties-cities-neighborhoods/auburn-avenue-sweet-auburn/.

———. "Segregation." Last modified July 20, 2020. *New Georgia Encyclopedia.* https://www.georgiaencyclopedia.org/articles/history-archaeology/segregation/.

Henderson, Alexa. "Alonzo Herndon." September 20, 2004. *New Georgia Encyclopedia.* https://www.georgiaencyclopedia.org/articles/business-economy/alonzo-herndon-1858-1927/.

Jacobs, Hal. "'Blind Willie' McTell." Last modified June 1, 2020. *New Georgia Encyclopedia.* https://www.georgiaencyclopedia.org/articles/arts-culture/blind-willie-mctell-1898-1959/.

Kemp, Kathryn. "Asa Candler." September 3, 2002. *New Georgia Encyclopedia.* https://www.georgiaencyclopedia.org/articles/history-archaeology/asa-candler-1851-1929/.

King, Monroe. "John Stith Pemberton." Last modified June 1, 2020. *New Georgia Encyclopedia.* https://www.georgiaencyclopedia.org/articles/business-economy/john-stith-pemberton-1831-1888/.

Krewer, Gerard. "Grapes and Wine." Last modified April 3, 2015. *New Georgia Encyclopedia.* https://www.georgiaencyclopedia.org/articles/business-economy/grapes-and-wine/.

Kuhn, Clifford, and Gregory Mixon. "Atlanta Race Massacre of 1906." September 23, 2005. *New Georgia Encyclopedia.* https://www.georgiaencyclopedia.org/articles/history-archaeology/atlanta-race-massacre-of-1906/.

Madden, M. "Crawford Long." May 14, 2004. *New Georgia Encyclopedia.* https://www.georgiaencyclopedia.org/articles/science-medicine/crawford-long-1815-1878/.

Maysilles, Duncan. "Hoke Smith." Last modified November 10, 2021. *New Georgia Encyclopedia.* https://www.georgiaencyclopedia.org/articles/government-politics/hoke-smith-1855-1931/.

McCarty, Laura. "Willie Lee Perryman." Last modified August 24, 2020. *New Georgia Encyclopedia*. https://www.georgiaencyclopedia.org/articles/arts-culture/willie-lee-perryman-1911-1985/.

New Georgia Encyclopedia. "May in Georgia History." Last modified May 4, 2021. https://www.georgiaencyclopedia.org/articles/history-archaeology/may-in-georgia-history/.

Newman, Harvey. "Cotton Expositions in Atlanta." Last modified July 25, 2023. *New Georgia Encyclopedia*. https://www.georgiaencyclopedia.org/articles/history-archaeology/cotton-expositions-in-atlanta/.

Nystrom, Elsa. "Chateau Elan." Last modified March 11, 2020. *New Georgia Encyclopedia*. https://www.georgiaencyclopedia.org/articles/business-economy/chateau-elan/.

O'Neal, Matthew. "Great Migration." Last modified January 16, 2024. *New Georgia Encyclopedia*. https://www.georgiaencyclopedia.org/articles/history-archaeology/great-migration/.

Perry, Chuck. "*Atlanta Journal-Constitution*." Last modified September 11, 2019. *New Georgia Encyclopedia*. https://www.georgiaencyclopedia.org/articles/arts-culture/atlanta-journal-constitution/.

Pierce, Dan. "NASCAR." Last modified May 6, 2017. *New Georgia Encyclopedia*. https://www.georgiaencyclopedia.org/articles/sports-outdoor-recreation/nascar/.

Schmidt, Jim. "Archibald Bulloch." Last modified January 23, 2019. *New Georgia Encyclopedia*. https://www.georgiaencyclopedia.org/articles/government-politics/archibald-bulloch-1730-1777/.

Sprayberry, Gary. "Atlanta International Pop Festivals." February 3, 2022. *New Georgia Encyclopedia*. https://www.georgiaencyclopedia.org/articles/arts-culture/atlanta-international-pop-festivals/.

Starrs, Chris. "Alex Cooley." February 17, 2006. *New Georgia Encyclopedia*. https://www.georgiaencyclopedia.org/articles/arts-culture/alex-cooley-1939-2015/.

Stewart, Bruce. "Moonshine." April 6, 2005. *New Georgia Encyclopedia*. https://www.georgiaencyclopedia.org/articles/arts-culture/moonshine/.

Summerlin, Donnie. "*Atlanta Georgian*." Last modified April 1, 2024. *New Georgia Encyclopedia*. https://www.georgiaencyclopedia.org/articles/arts-culture/atlanta-georgian/.

Washnock, Kaylynn. "Prohibition in Georgia." March 9, 2020. *New Georgia Encyclopedia*. https://www.georgiaencyclopedia.org/articles/history-archaeology/prohibition-in-georgia/.

———. "Wrestling Temptation: The Quest to Control Alcohol in Georgia." December 7, 2021. *New Georgia Encyclopedia*. https://www.georgiaencyclopedia.org/exhibition/wrestling-temptation-the-quest-to-control-alcohol-in-georgia/.

Willoughby, Lynn. "Chattahoochee River." Last modified January 2, 2020. *New Georgia Encyclopedia*. https://www.georgiaencyclopedia.org/articles/geography-environment/chattahoochee-river/.

Zainaldin, Jamil. "Great Depression." Last modified September 29, 2020. *New Georgia Encyclopedia*. https://www.georgiaencyclopedia.org/articles/history-archaeology/great-depression/.

ATLANTA

Addison, Bill. "The Sound Table." *Atlanta*, October 1, 2010. https://www.atlantamagazine.com/reviews/the-sound-table1/.

Atlanta. "Did Clermont Lounge's Blondie Really Publish a Book of Poetry?" November 2019. https://www.atlantamagazine.com/list/you-asked-we-answered-34-things-you-probably-dont-know-about-atlanta/did-clermont-lounges-blondie-really-publish-a-book-of-poetry/.

———. "A Half-Century of LGBTQ+ Milestones in Atlanta." October 9, 2020. https://www.atlantamagazine.com/news-culture-articles/pride-a-half-century-of-lgbtq-milestones-in-atlanta/.

———. "Little Richard and James Brown Cut Their Teeth at the Royal Peacock." November 2019. https://www.atlantamagazine.com/list/things-didnt-know-atlantas-past/little-richard-james-brown-cut-teeth-royal-peacock/.

———. "19 Things You Didn't Know About Atlanta's Past." February 13, 2017. https://www.atlantamagazine.com/list/things-didnt-know-atlantas-past/.

———. "Queen of the Night." September 2019. https://www.atlantamagazine.com/queen-of-the-night/.

———. "Why Is Underground Atlanta Underground?" November 2019. https://www.atlantamagazine.com/list/you-asked-we-answered-34-things-you-probably-dont-know-about-atlanta/why-is-underground-atlanta-underground/.

Bainbridge, Julia. "Atlanta's 'Cult of Lemon Pepper.'" *Atlanta*, July 12, 2017. https://www.atlantamagazine.com/dining-news/atlantas-cult-lemon-pepper/.

Bethea, Charles. "Hoochie Koo." *Atlanta*, November 2009 (archived). https://web.archive.org/web/20110711173250/http://www.atlantamagazine.com/november2009/riverbend.aspx.

———. "Johnny's Hideaway." *Atlanta*, July 1, 2011. https://www.atlantamagazine.com/culture/johnnys-hideaway1/.

———. "The Man Who Made Us Float: A Tribute to Larry Patrick." *Atlanta*, October 27, 2015. https://www.atlantamagazine.com/news-culture-articles/the-man-who-made-us-float-a-tribute-to-larry-patrick/.

————. "Stripping for Cash, Praising the Lord, and Cursing Our Traffic Lights." *Atlanta*, July 1, 2009. https://www.atlantamagazine.com/culture/stripping-for-cash-praising-the-lord-and-curs1/.

————. "Woodstock on the Water: An Oral History of the Ramblin' Raft Race." *Atlanta*, June 15, 2015. https://www.atlantamagazine.com/great-reads/woodstock-on-the-water-an-oral-history-of-the-ramblin-raft-race/.

Bikoff, Mary Logan. "Punk Rocks!" *Atlanta*, August 30, 2014. https://www.atlantamagazine.com/great-reads/punk-fashion-feature/.

Burns, Rebecca. "Bygone Bars." *Atlanta*, June 1, 2012. https://www.atlantamagazine.com/travel-other/bygone-bars/.

————. "The Great Fire of 1917." *Atlanta*, May 21, 2012. https://www.atlantamagazine.com/history/this-week-in-atlanta-history-the-great-fire-o/.

————. "The Imperial Hotel." *Atlanta*, September 1, 2015. https://www.atlantamagazine.com/groundbreakers-2015/the-imperial-hotel/.

————. "The Most Lawless Year in Atlanta's History." *Atlanta*, May 15, 2014. https://www.atlantamagazine.com/crime-city/the-most-lawless-year-in-atlantas-history/.

————. "The Museum of Manuel's Tavern." *Atlanta*, August 5, 2014. https://www.atlantamagazine.com/50bestbars/the-museum-of-manuels/.

Burns, Rebecca, and Errin Haines Whack. "Freaknik: The Rise and Fall of Atlanta's Most Infamous Street Party." *Atlanta*, March 18, 2015. https://www.atlantamagazine.com/90s/freaknik-the-rise-and-fall-of-atlantas-most-infamous-street-party/.

Chapman, Gray. "The Tippling Point: How Craft Cocktails Made Their Way onto Every Menu in Atlanta." *Atlanta*, September 10, 2018. https://www.atlantamagazine.com/drinks/the-tippling-point-how-craft-cocktails-made-their-way-onto-every-menu-in-atlanta/.

Cooper, Carly, "Paper Plane Is Closing, Possible Tropical Theme on the Way." *Atlanta*, August 10, 2015. https://www.atlantamagazine.com/drinks/paper-plane-is-closing-possible-tropical-theme-on-the-way/.

Dyer, Candice. "Blondie Strange." *Atlanta*, May 1, 2011. https://www.atlantamagazine.com/great-reads/blondie-2011/.

Eldredge, Richard L. "Back in the Day: Michael Krohngold." *Atlanta*, March 18, 2015. https://www.atlantamagazine.com/90s/back-in-the-day-michael-krohngold/.

————. "Backstreet: An Oral History of Atlanta's Most Fabled 24-Hour Nightclub." *Atlanta*, October 9, 2020. https://www.atlantamagazine.com/great-reads/pride-backstreet-an-oral-history-of-atlantas-most-fabled-24-hour-nightclub/.

———. "Club Rio's 25th Lures City's Reformed Punks, Yuppies." *Atlanta*, August 23, 2013. https://www.atlantamagazine.com/article/club-rios-25th-lures-citys-reformed-punks-yuppies/.

———. "5 of the Most Atlanta Moments in RuPaul's New Memoir." *Atlanta*, March 8, 2024. https://www.atlantamagazine.com/news-culture-articles/5-of-the-most-atlanta-moments-in-rupauls-new-memoir/.

———. "Mumford, Sons Kicked Out of Clermont Lounge." *Atlanta*, September 12, 2013. https://www.atlantamagazine.com/news-culture-articles/mumford-sons-kicked-out-of-clermont-lounge/.

———. "One Last Voyage for Dante's Down the Hatch?" *Atlanta*, August 9, 2013. https://www.atlantamagazine.com/dining-news/one-last-voyage-for-dantes-down-the-hatch/.

———. "On Ponce de Leon Avenue, 2 Atlanta LGBTQ+ Landmarks Are Being Preserved." *Atlanta*, August 23, 2021. https://www.atlantamagazine.com/news-culture-articles/on-ponce-de-leon-avenue-2-atlanta-lgbtq-landmarks-are-being-preserved/.

———. "The Polaris Comes Full Circle." *Atlanta*, May 1, 2014. https://www.atlantamagazine.com/great-reads/the-polaris-comes-full-circle/.

———. "Reminisce Your Days Partying at Backstreet with This Ultimate Playlist." *Atlanta*, October 19, 2020. https://www.atlantamagazine.com/news-culture-articles/reminisce-your-days-partying-at-backstreet-with-this-ultimate-playlist/.

———. "You Can't Replace This: The Musical Legacy of Dante's Down the Hatch." *Atlanta*, August 19, 2013. https://www.atlantamagazine.com/news-culture-articles/you-cant-replace-this-the-musical-legacy-of-dantes-down-the-hatch/.

Endolyn, Osayi. "Red Brick Brewing Company." *Atlanta*, December 1, 2015. https://www.atlantamagazine.com/drinks/red-brick-brewing-company/.

Garbus, Rachel. "6 Atlanta Queer History Facts You Might Not Know." *Atlanta*, June 23, 2022. https://www.atlantamagazine.com/news-culture-articles/6-atlanta-queer-history-facts-that-prove-this-city-is-gay-af/.

Green, Josh. "Gene Kansas." *Atlanta*, November 1, 2017. https://www.atlantamagazine.com/groundbreakers-finalists-2017/gene-kansas/.

———. "One Night at Northside Tavern." *Atlanta*, September 14, 2022. https://www.atlantamagazine.com/news-culture-articles/one-night-at-northside-tavern/.

Harris, Melissa. "Are We Having Fun Yet? A Chronicle of One Long, Twisted Buckhead Night." *Atlanta*, October 1, 1990. https://www.atlantamagazine.com/great-reads/are-we-having-fun-yet-a-chronicle-of-one-long-twisted-buckhead-night/.

Henry, Scott. "Party Like It's 1996: 7 Iconic Atlanta Nightlife Spots of the Era." *Atlanta*, March 18, 2015. https://www.atlantamagazine.com/90s/party-like-its-1996-7-iconic-atlanta-nightlife-spots/.

————. "Timeline: The Long, Risque History of Atlanta's Nightlife." *Atlanta*, September 19, 2019. https://www.atlantamagazine.com/news-culture-articles/timeline-the-long-risque-history-of-atlantas-nightlife/.

Jordan, Mike. "An Oral History of Magic City." *Atlanta*, September 2019. https://www.atlantamagazine.com/oral-history-magic-city/.

Keenan, Sean. "As the Elliott Street Pub Goes Up for Sale, Its Owners Reflect On Their Long, Strange Trip." *Atlanta*, June 17, 2019. https://www.atlantamagazine.com/dining-news/as-the-elliott-street-pub-goes-up-for-sale-its-owners-reflect-on-their-long-strange-trip/.

————. "Farewell to Atlanta's Elliott Street Pub." *Atlanta*, October 25, 2022. https://www.atlantamagazine.com/dining-news/farewell-to-atlantas-elliott-street-pub/.

————. "Though the Physical Store Nears Its Demise, 'Disco Kroger' Will Never Truly Die." *Atlanta*, July 19, 2021. https://www.atlantamagazine.com/news-culture-articles/though-the-physical-store-nears-its-demise-disco-kroger-will-never-truly-die/.

Lauterbach, Christiane. "Discovery: Sister Louisa's Church." *Atlanta*, April 1, 2011. https://www.atlantamagazine.com/article/discovery-sister-louisas-church1/.

Lieberman, Hallie. "One Last Night at Swinging Richards." *Atlanta*, March 10, 2022. https://www.atlantamagazine.com/news-culture-articles/one-last-night-at-swinging-richards/.

Mah, Evan. "Polaris." *Atlanta*, October 1, 2014. https://www.atlantamagazine.com/reviews/polaris/.

————. "Review: Come for the Drinks, Stay for the Food at Ticonderoga Club." *Atlanta*, April 8, 2016. https://www.atlantamagazine.com/reviews/review-ticonderoga-club/.

Malone, Tess. "Atlanta Needs Its Gay Bars Now More Than Ever." *Atlanta*, October 9, 2020. https://www.atlantamagazine.com/dining-news/atlanta-needs-its-gay-bars-now-more-than-ever/.

McKibben, Beth. "Why Atlanta Boasts One of the Last Trader Vic's Tiki Bars in the U.S." *Atlanta*, August 30, 2019. https://www.atlantamagazine.com/dining-news/why-atlanta-boasts-one-of-the-last-trader-vics-tiki-bars-in-the-u-s/.

Monroe, Doug. "Manuel Maloof." *Atlanta*, May 1, 2011. https://www.atlantamagazine.com/great-reads/manuel-maloof/.

Picard, Lia. "This Ain't Texas, It's Thursday Night at the Heretic." *Atlanta*, June 21, 2024. https://www.atlantamagazine.com/news-culture-articles/this-aint-texas-its-thursday-night-at-the-heretic/.

Wheatley, Thomas. "After 50 Years, Hyatt Regency Atlanta Is Still a Downtown Icon." *Atlanta*, July 10, 2017. https://www.atlantamagazine.com/news-culture-articles/after-50-years-hyatt-regency-atlanta-is-still-a-visual-spectacle/.

ATLANTA JOURNAL, ATLANTA CONSTITUTION AND ATLANTA JOURNAL-CONSTITUTION

Albright, Mandi. "Deja News: Atlanta's Chattahoochee Raft Race Was a Victim of Its Own Popularity." *Atlanta Journal-Constitution*, May 24, 2024. https://www.ajc.com/news/atlanta-news/deja-news-atlantas-chattahoochee-raft-race-trashed-to-death-by-1980/Y7AP3ZKSW5EHJOCN2NXWB6AKHA/.

———. "Deja News: Atlanta Winecoff Disaster Still Nation's Deadliest Hotel Fire (1946)." *Atlanta Journal-Constitution*, December 7, 2023. https://www.ajc.com/news/local/ajc-deja-news-winecoff-disaster-still-nation-deadliest-hotel-fire-1946/SEYhTcBgnuEKzm2QPAz9HI/.

———. "Deja News: Thirsty Fulton Voters OK Alcohol Sales (1935)." *Atlanta Journal-Constitution*, May 15, 2019. https://www.ajc.com/news/local/ajc-deja-news-thirsty-fulton-voters-alcohol-sales-1935/O3Xf5WwUyQ9yPn5pliX5YO/.

Atlanta Constitution. "How a Vigilance Committee Made Attack on Snake Nation." March 18, 1917.

Atlanta Journal-Constitution. "Jackson Tarver Obituary." September 1, 2015. https://www.legacy.com/us/obituaries/atlanta/name/jackson-tarver-obituary?id=23111343.

———. "Manuel's Tavern Added to National Register of Historic Places." June 3, 2020. https://www.ajc.com/news/local/manuel-tavern-added-national-register-historic-places/jRo4CUjz0LjRiMxKOJRlxI/.

———. "Night Spots." February 21, 1949. https://archive.org/details/per_atlanta-constitution_1949-02-21_81_251/page/n11/mode/2up?q=Jennings+Rose+Room&view=theater.

Badie, Rick. "James Philip Ryan, 75, Ruby Red's Warehouse Co-Owner." *Atlanta Journal-Constitution*, June 26, 2011. https://www.ajc.com/news/local/james-philip-ryan-ruby-red-warehouse-owner/zO0poNPfqr8ip5KSCu6poJ/.

Boone, Christian. "CDC Study: Demise of Buckhead Village Led to Major Reduction in Crime." *Atlanta Journal-Constitution*, May 31, 2015. https://www.ajc.com/news/crime--law/cdc-study-demise-buckhead-village-led-major-reduction-crime/tchuDXG54v7281LHsbQaYJ/.

———. "That 70's City." *Atlanta Journal-Constitution*, January 5, 2009 (archived). https://web.archive.org/web/20110604064207/http://www.ajc.com/services/content/printedition/2009/01/05/ev70sriverbend.html.

Bosworth, J.M. "A Section of Snake Nation." *Atlanta Journal*, August 8, 1894.

Broady, Arlinda Smith. "Photo Vault: Tainted Moonshine Killed Dozens 64 Years Ago." *Atlanta Journal-Constitution*, October 21, 2015. https://www.ajc.com/news/local/photo-vault-tainted-moonshine-killed-dozens-years-ago/ar82zln5WxyxQ06p6QxkjJ/.

Burns, Asia Simone. "4 Injured in Shooting Near NW Atlanta Nightclub; Gunman Sought." *Atlanta Journal-Constitution*, January 5, 2020. https://www.ajc.com/news/breaking-news/injured-shooting-near-atlanta-nightclub-gunman-sought/YHRsccNcUJgohfQkxk8D2N/.

Capelouto, J.D. "Brookhaven: Pink Pony Strip Club, Other Businesses Owe Liquor Taxes." *Atlanta Journal-Constitution*, March 5, 2019. https://www.ajc.com/news/brookhaven-pink-pony-strip-club-other-businesses-owe-liquor-taxes/P9alWjtnTQnFjpsAmJToWL/.

Daniel, Christopher A. "Happening on 4/20, Freaknik Reunion 2024 Aims to Be a Community-Centered Event." *Atlanta Journal Constitution*, April 19, 2024. https://www.ajc.com/black-atlanta-culture/happening-on-420-freaknik-reunion-2024-aims-to-be-a-community-centered-event/TJD5MJ637NE7BN4AIPK723G4MM/.

Daniel, Christopher A., and Adam Van Brimmer. "Orange Crush: 'Orderly' HBCU Beach Party Comes to Georgia Coast." *Atlanta Journal-Constitution*, April 20, 2024. https://www.ajc.com/politics/the-new-freaknik-orange-crush-beach-party-starts-quietly/JCG6BH7DGNFLPIJU3EJ3QUOZJA/.

D'Antonio, Maria N. "Mildred Lee, Bar Owner Who Was Tough, Kind." *Atlanta Constitution*, February 10, 1996.

Dougherty, Steve. "Struttin at the Peacock." *Atlanta Constitution*, May 10, 1981.

Emerson, Bo. "Nancy Erickson, 90: First Lady of Atlanta Cabaret Comedy." *Atlanta Journal-Constitution*, December 19, 2012. https://www.ajc.com/news/nancy-erickson-first-lady-atlanta-cabaret-comedy/b5n8wZx1LObkbXMT0VEIIN/.

———. "Northside Tavern, Atlanta's 'Exquisite Dive Bar,' Celebrates 50 Years." *Atlanta Journal-Constitution*, December 6, 2022. https://www.ajc.com/things-to-do/atlantas-northside-tavern-celebrate-50-years/2NKVFOHA6VC27N5PWKOXN3HMVQ/.

———. "Reunion Show Memorializes Atlanta's Punk Scene." *Atlanta Journal-Constitution*, June 15, 2009. https://www.ajc.com/entertainment/music/reunion-show-memorializes-atlanta-punk-scene/SJYSBo1LJgPpZrurnWqLiN/.

———. "Steve May, 688 Club Legend, Avoids Homelessness with Help from Friends." *Atlanta Journal-Constitution*, January 15, 2016. https://www.ajc.com/news/steve-may-688-club-legend-avoids-homelessness-with-help-from-friends/t96ncXXyresh7OaYAFhctM/.

————. "Super Bowls Bookend the Fall and Rise of Buckhead." *Atlanta Journal-Constitution*, January 28, 2019. https://www.ajc.com/lifestyles/super-bowls-bookend-the-fall-and-rise-buckhead/LR6DUGPQfJatehC2z27wWN/.

————. "What Says 'Atlanta'? History Center Wants Your Opinion." *Atlanta Journal-Constitution*, January 9, 2015. https://www.ajc.com/lifestyles/what-says-atlanta-history-center-wants-your-opinion/gSYiUsnNKU8I1Lwzwzp6DO/.

Figueras, Ligaya. "Atlanta Cocktail Lounge the Sound Table to Become Edgewood Dynasty." *Atlanta Journal-Constitution*, October 13, 2020. https://www.ajc.com/things-to-do/atlanta-restaurant-blog/atlanta-cocktail-lounge-the-sound-table-to-become-edgewood-dynasty/7LWU5DX5LNEJJPXRD25HGDEHIA/.

————. "Dante Stephensen, Founder of Iconic Atlanta Nightspot Dante's Down the Hatch, Dies." *Atlanta Journal-Constitution*, July 27, 2020. https://www.ajc.com/things-to-do/atlanta-restaurant-blog/dante-stephensen-founder-of-iconic-atlanta-nightspot-dantes-down-the-hatch-dies/JZKXVFHQ6VAPPIQV4AZJ3RXUVU/.

————. "Review: Holeman and Finch Brings Familiar Menu to Fresh Digs." *Atlanta Journal-Constitution*, May 11, 2023. https://www.ajc.com/things-to-do/atlanta-restaurant-blog/atlanta-restaurant-reviews-holeman-finch/JZPLJLHW7REK3O65RQPGZQ6LT4/.

————. "Take a Food Tour of Castleberry Hill." *Atlanta Journal-Constitution*, February 13, 2020. https://www.ajc.com/entertainment/dining/food-tour-castleberry-hill/NfFuVFsMe5bOTdxQG3ATDM/.

————. "Wall Collapses at Old Fourth Ward Restaurant Slated to Debut This Week." *Atlanta Journal-Constitution*, December 2, 2020. https://www.ajc.com/things-to-do/food-and-recipes/update-wall-collapses-at-old-fourth-ward-restaurant-slated-to-debut-this-week/UK5XTB3L3ZFCTCSWLKFSBQHZCM/.

————. "What Is the Future of Northside Tavern?" *Atlanta Journal-Constitution*, May 15, 2017. https://www.ajc.com/blog/atlanta-restaurants/what-the-future-northside-tavern/8WLrl7Zpo5TMKKUTo2k6NL/.

Glier, Ray, "Revamp of Atlanta's First Integrated Hotel Pays Homage to Its History." *Atlanta Journal-Constitution*, December 2, 2017. https://www.ajc.com/travel/revamp-atlanta-first-integrated-hotel-pays-homage-its-history/3wr2ccJv03Lkdc70ZzgAcP/.

Green, Michelle. "Disco Decadence." *Atlanta Journal-Constitution*, February 1, 1980.

Hansberger, Angela. "Murrell's Row Makes a Gin for People Who Think They Don't Like Gin." *Atlanta Journal-Constitution*, April 13, 2023. https://www.ajc.com/things-to-do/food-and-recipes/a-look-at-murrells-row-sprits-in-atlanta/YIG5FXFM4BCA7F2OYZMYWNR67M/.

Hansell, Sally. "Polynesian Theme Is Newest Twist for Longtime Atlanta Restaurateur," *Atlanta Constitution*, August 15, 1985, https://www.newspapers.com/article/the-atlanta-constitution-george-eng-open/32234529/.

Hansen, Zachary and Kelly Yamanouchi. "Chamblee's Only Strip Club Shuts Down After String of Legal Losses." *Atlanta Journal-Constitution*, September 22, 2020. https://www.ajc.com/news/chamblees-only-strip-club-shuts-down-after-string-of-legal-losses/AM46JBIR4RBVRLYKUD7X5TVUJ4/.

———. "Doraville Threatens to Fine Troubled Strip Club's Alcohol Suppliers." *Atlanta Journal-Constitution*, March 14, 2022. https://www.ajc.com/neighborhoods/dekalb/doraville-threatens-to-fine-troubled-strip-clubs-alcohol-suppliers/KZKJJZG66ZE5LOH56ADDZ6SPTI/.

———. "Gwinnett Tops 1M People, Metro Atlanta Population Booms, New Study Says." *Atlanta Journal-Constitution*, July 10, 2024. https://www.ajc.com/news/business/gwinnett-tops-1m-people-metro-atlanta-booms-new-study-says/SR2WV4YLCZGG5BQ6JYVGPKL2HQ/?utm_source=Iterable&utm_medium=email&utm_campaign=AMATL&utm_content=10426675.

———. "How July Fourth, AJC Peachtree Road Race Give Atlanta an Economic Boost." *Atlanta Journal-Constitution*, July 1, 2024. https://www.ajc.com/news/atlanta-news/how-july-fourth-ajc-peachtree-road-race-give-atlanta-an-economic-boost/XJYSN7H4AJAWHPOETGVCW5MBXU/.

Hauk, Alexis. "Throwback Atlanta: 3 Iconic Places to Dine and Dance." *Atlanta Journal-Constitution*, April 23, 2024. https://www.ajc.com/things-to-do/throwback-atlanta-3-iconic-places-to-dine-and-dance/ESUHEUHB6BCTRMLA2QJ5RDMCOE/.

Hayes, Kathryn. "Many of Mayor's Hopes for City Ride on Underground's Future." *Atlanta Constitution*, December 29, 1985.

Hicks, Victoria Loe. "Red Dog Squad Was a Product of a Very Different Era." *Atlanta Journal-Constitution*, February 7, 2011. https://www.ajc.com/news/local/red-dog-squad-was-product-very-different-era/ssxb0cabvyuylNQZBCuVbN/.

Ho, Rodney. "Atlanta Improv Shutting Down December 31 with Rest of Andrews Entertainment District." *Atlanta Journal-Constitution*, November 30, 2015. https://www.ajc.com/blog/radiotvtalk/atlanta-improv-shutting-down-december-with-rest-andrews-entertainment-district/vDKYBAGnuqWcj490s7aHXP/.

———. "Recuperated Jamie Foxx Is in Atlanta to Finish Netflix Film 'Back in Action.'" *Atlanta Journal-Constitution*, January 24, 2024. https://www.ajc.com/things-to-do/georgia-entertainment-scene/recuperated-jamie-foxx-is-in-atlanta-to-finish-netflix-film-back-in-action/SOWHBL3JO5E25KENM7YCDML3YI/.

Holman, Curt. "Castleberry Hill: Explore the Neighborhood of the New Mercedes-Benz Stadium." *Atlanta Journal-Constitution*, January 15, 2019. https://www.ajc.com/castleberry-hill-sees-creative-renaissance/sdaKNxMshusTTfmaabRaHM/.

Johnston, Lori. "Q: Back in the Early '70s the Drinking Age Had Dropped To 18. When Did That Happen and How Long Did It Stay 18 Until It Went Back up to Age 21?—Johnny Flowers, Lilburn." *Atlanta Journal-Constitution*, December 29, 2009. https://www.ajc.com/news/local/back-the-early-70s-the-drinking-age-had-dropped-when-did-that-happen-and-how-long-did-stay-until-went-back-age-johnny-flowers-lilburn.

Jordan, Mike. "Are Atlanta's Strip Clubs Still Shaping the City's Hip-Hop Scene?" *Atlanta Journal-Constitution*, October 27, 2023. https://www.ajc.com/life/arts-culture/hip-hop-50/are-atlantas-strip-clubs-still-shaping-the-citys-hip-hop-scene/DZM5WLHYVJAUBHEYBEMRU6IQAI/.

Joyner, Chris. "Cheetah, Dancers Settle Lengthy Wage Dispute; Club Alters VIP Rooms." *Atlanta Journal-Constitution*, July 2, 2019. https://www.ajc.com/news/local/cheetah-dancers-settle-lengthy-wage-dispute-club-alters-vip-rooms/JoLaBe8aC5BuBExQfQZz8J/.

———. "Lawsuit Accuses Atlanta Strip Club of Prostitution, Racketeering." *Atlanta Journal-Constitution*, March 3, 2017. https://www.ajc.com/news/local/lawsuit-accuses-atlanta-strip-club-prostitution-racketeering/XhNl5KUqoNbElOb934qeSJ/.

Lee, Christina. "VICE TV's 'Sex Before the Internet' Dives into Atlanta's infamous Gold Club." *Atlanta Journal-Constitution*, January 23, 2024. https://www.ajc.com/things-to-do/georgia-entertainment-scene/vice-tvs-sex-before-the-internet-dives-into-atlantas-infamous-gold-club/OWWSU57QPRGH7GS2GCEXSMGBPU/.

McCoy, Kelly. "Remembering the Agora Ballroom Where Devo and Prince Rocked." *Atlanta Journal-Constitution*, January 27, 2022. https://www.ajc.com/life/remembering-the-agora-ballroom-where-devo-and-prince-rocked/VRXHK5NHCJGAHLBPQ5VD4EJFDQ/.

McKibben, Beth. "Heart of Atlanta's Westside: Northside Tavern." *Atlanta Journal-Constitution*, August 5, 2016. https://www.ajc.com/entertainment/dining/heart-atlanta-westside-northside-tavern/UqT50lBEmoxXsfv3TCCbcO/.

Morehouse, Macon. "Focus on the Winecoff Fire." *Atlanta Constitution*, December 6, 1996. https://www.ajc.com/lifestyles/focus-the-winecoff-fire/UfxBYPGN6dY13NMdjgTOKM/.

Newmark, Avery. "Atlanta's Ranger Station Makes *Esquire*'s 'Best Bars in America' List." *Atlanta Journal-Constitution*, March 30, 2024. https://www.ajc.com/

food-and-dining/atlanta-restaurants/atlanta-bar-named-one-of-best-bars-in-america-for-2024/WUCJDP444FDMNOZDAPAC26XEUQ/.

O'Shea, Brian. "From the Archives: The First Freaknik Was a Picnic, with Music." *Atlanta Journal-Constitution*, March 20, 2024. https://www.ajc.com/news/atlanta-news/from-the-archives-the-first-freaknik-was-a-picnic-with-music/X2OSDCM2ERHBTKIP4VZ4NUPFHI/.

Rankin, Bill. "Magic City Owner Guilty of Federal Cocaine Charges." *Atlanta Constitution*, January 19, 1994.

Robinson, Will. "Dante's, Other Clubs Part of Underground Atlanta's Heydays." *Atlanta Journal-Constitution*, May 1, 2017. https://www.ajc.com/news/dante-other-clubs-part-underground-atlanta-heydays/339LY447pGg1sWzs3dLGCO/.

Roughton, Bert, Jr. "The Last Act." *Atlanta Constitution*, April 21, 2013.

Scott, Pete. "Group Tries to Revive Once-Popular Royal Peacock Club." *Atlanta Constitution*, February 7, 1985.

Silva, Caroline, Henri Hollis and Shaddi Abusaid. "No Ill Intent Behind Fire That Damaged Historic Midtown Gay Bar, Mayor Says." *Atlanta Journal-Constitution*, June 7, 2024. https://www.ajc.com/news/crime/historic-buildings-in-midtown-atlanta-damaged-by-blaze/Z5GB2AC3CRDUXJE5PVTCD7LMO4/.

Stafford, Leon. "Georgian Terrace Has Played Host to Statesmen and Stars." *Atlanta Journal-Constitution*, April 1, 2014. https://www.ajc.com/business/georgian-terrace-has-played-host-statesmen-and-stars/P8Iiie9GXDJxxop1S4yfnL/.

Suggs, Ernie. "Atlantans Share Tales from Attending Freaknik." *Atlanta Journal-Constitution*, March 21, 2024. https://www.ajc.com/black-atlanta-culture/atlantans-share-tales-from-attending-freaknik/ML62E43DMJA6XOZ5F4AU5UU47I/.

———. "Atlanta Race Riot? Or Massacre?" *Atlanta Journal-Constitution*, September 21, 2022. https://www.ajc.com/news/atlanta-news/atlanta-race-riot-or-massacre/XG753DVG6ZAZZGUMX2HXGVDY5U/.

Taylor, Ron. "Blue Lantern to Shine No More." *Atlanta Journal*, January 3, 1986.

———. "Memories of the Past, Hopes for Future." *Atlanta Journal-Constitution*, December 29, 1985.

Torpy, Bill. "For This Lawyer, Naughty Is Nice." *Atlanta Journal-Constitution*, July 6, 2013. https://www.ajc.com/news/crime--law/for-this-lawyer-naughty-nice/dRI5ejnIZCBaZEM14IsUJJ/.

———. "Torpy at Large: A New Kind of Lust at The Cheetah: It's a Hot Property." *Atlanta Journal-Constitution*, July 26, 2017. https://www.ajc.com/news/local/torpy-large-owner-the-cheetah-won-change-his-spots/RFJT5VzPgQrKN2ghvSZ8SP/.

Townsend, Bob. "After 67 Years, Moe's and Joe's Changes Things Up." *Atlanta Journal-Constitution*. March 25, 2014. https://www.ajc.com/entertainment/after-years-moe-and-joe-changes-things/IQIiEjEgaRcwFfcfAaNFlL/.

———. "Atlanta Classics: Blue-Domed Polaris Continues Spinning Atop 'Hotel of Hope.'" *Atlanta Journal-Constitution*, January 24, 2023. https://www.ajc.com/things-to-do/atlanta-restaurant-blog/longtime-atlanta-restaurants-polaris/P3HYLGKXYJEZ7K4EP7ENMOITGU/.

———. "Atlanta Classics: Virginia-Highland Landmark Atkins Park Has Stood the Test of Time." *Atlanta Journal-Constitution*, June 21, 2022. https://www.ajc.com/things-to-do/atlanta-restaurant-blog/atlanta-classics-virginia-highland-landmark-atkins-park-has-stood-the-test-of-time/7KFB2WOXKRBTTGJM7IC535DMJM/.

———. "Atlanta's SweetWater Brewing Leads the Way for Parent Company Tilray Brands." *Atlanta Journal-Constitution*, May 8, 2024. https://www.ajc.com/food-and-dining/atlantas-sweetwater-brewing-leads-the-way-for-parent-company-tilray-brands/HHXWOMAASJA2BFIOB4PEPQLPUA/.

———. "Beer Town: Meet Atlanta Brewing's New President and General Manager." *Atlanta Journal-Constitution*, June 21, 2021. https://www.ajc.com/things-to-do/food-and-recipes/beer-town-meet-atlanta-brewings-new-president-and-general-manager/OFWTMAWUO5HYNPWBF3P35ZXR2A/.

———. "First Look: Dine, Drink and Savor Cigars at Cam Newton's Fellaship in Castleberry Hill." *Atlanta Journal-Constitution*, July 8, 2019. https://www.ajc.com/blog/atlanta-restaurants/first-look-dine-drink-and-savor-cigars-cam-newton-fellaship-castleberry-hill/X1V0ZXYxrErMiapiqj8WRN/.

———. "First Look: Hippin Hops Brewery in East Atlanta Pairs Beer, Seafood." *Atlanta Journal-Constitution*, May 3, 2021. https://www.ajc.com/things-to-do/atlanta-restaurant-blog/first-look-hippin-hops-brewery-in-east-atlanta-pairs-beer-seafood/VXIOXQGNRRBKPD6GRBUF7HMPNQ/.

———. "First Look: Is Manuel's Tavern the Same as It Ever Was?" *Atlanta Journal-Constitution*. August 29, 2016. https://www.ajc.com/blog/atlanta-restaurants/first-look-manuel-tavern-the-same-ever-was/wsR7dwAUCqBFa99QZQz1mK/.

———. "Leon's Full Service Is a Place to Fill 'Er Up." *Atlanta Journal-Constitution*, June 15, 2009. https://www.ajc.com/entertainment/dining/leon-full-service-place-fill/YYy7ZyGSTKpocNTSdlXVKN/.

———. "Sister Louisa's 'Church' Closed by Fire." *Atlanta Journal-Constitution*, September 17, 2015. https://www.ajc.com/blog/atlanta-restaurants/sister-louisa-church-closed-fire/m506cHZ6UkxumJf9FZo0YP/.

———. "Take a First Look at Bar Margot at the Four Seasons." *Atlanta Journal-Constitution*, October 28, 2015. https://www.ajc.com/blog/atlanta-restaurants/take-first-look-bar-margot-the-four-seasons/8scWjKEPKWxCjG3uS0x5jJ/.

———. "A Tribute to Piano Red aka Dr. Feelgood." *Atlanta Journal-Constitution*, August 2, 2010. https://www.ajc.com/entertainment/music/tribute-piano-red-aka-feelgood/oBOHb4wbEnsnpOtpSXqZFN/.

Wakim, Olivia. "Music, Cocktails and Food Mix in These Metro Atlanta Listening Rooms." *Atlanta Journal-Constitution*, July 5, 2024. https://www.ajc.com/food-and-dining/metro-atlanta-listening-rooms-to-try/EPC4ESWKU5CUVL5KK2Q7S7FBQA/.

Watson, Jon. "Holeman & Finch Still Shines After 6 Years." *Atlanta Journal-Constitution*, July 10, 2014. https://www.ajc.com/entertainment/dining/holeman-finch-still-shines-after-years/Mmecor3zW70zynfrYLJtQI/.

White, Gayle. "Ponce de Leon." *Atlanta Constitution*, August 3, 1971.

Williams, Wyatt. "Is This the Best Bar Seat in Atlanta?" *Atlanta Journal-Constitution*, October 13, 2016. https://www.ajc.com/entertainment/dining/this-the-best-bar-seat-atlanta/0DEuSZCI88YcdY65PsZZTO/.

Zussel, Yvonne. "Atlanta Brewing Company Will No Longer Open at Underground Atlanta." *Atlanta Journal-Constitution*, July 13, 2023. https://www.ajc.com/things-to-do/atlanta-restaurant-blog/atlanta-brewing-company-will-no-longer-open-at-underground-atlanta/266GD4MI5FHCHFBT35EVLWBJT4/.

———. "Holeman & Finch to Reopen Next Week in Colony Square." *Atlanta Journal-Constitution*, February 2, 2023. https://www.ajc.com/things-to-do/atlanta-restaurant-blog/holeman-finch-to-reopen-next-week-in-colony-square/VDEAAKKKABGZZHJWPO5FWU6BRI/.

———. "Longtime Ponce de Leon Business MJQ Concourse to Relocate." *Atlanta Journal-Constitution*, December 2, 2022. https://www.ajc.com/things-to-do/atlanta-restaurant-blog/mjq-concourse-closing-on-ponce-in-atlanta/OKG6F647XFAHTPEMBUTMYB3OFI/.

———. "MAP: Where to Do Karaoke Around Metro Atlanta." *Atlanta Journal-Constitution*, July 21, 2022. https://www.ajc.com/things-to-do/map-where-to-do-karaoke-around-metro-atlanta/S3EZW2BGSFEZJEXJH7BG3EE47I/.

———. "Park Bench to Bring Dueling Pianos, Live Music to The Battery Next Year." *Atlanta Journal-Constitution*, October 15, 2019. https://www.ajc.com/blog/atlanta-restaurants/park-bench-bring-dueling-pianos-live-music-the-battery-next-year/rym320BeKRO1v1IPmoHxwJ/.

———. "Ticonderoga Club Closes Temporarily at Krog Street Market After Burst Pipe." *Atlanta Journal-Constitution*, December 19, 2022. https://www.ajc.com/things-to-do/atlanta-restaurant-blog/ticonderoga-club-closed-temporarily-after-burst-pipe/XXZWNQ23FRBEDOVXP45O7VLC2E/.

ATLANTA VOICE AND GEORGIA VOICE

Bagby, Dyana. "Charlie Brown, Former Owner Reminisce on Backstreet's Wild Atlanta Ride." *Georgia Voice*, October 13, 2016. https://web.archive.org/web/20240410233152/https://thegavoice.com/culture/charlie-brown-former-owner-look-back-backstreets-wild-atlanta-ride/.

Burkholder, Katie. "Wylie Hotel Honors Mrs. P's History with Tea Dances All Summer." *Georgia Voice*, June 16, 2022. https://web.archive.org/web/20241204123909/https://thegavoice.com/community/wylie-hotel-honors-mrs-ps-history-with-tea-dances-all-summer/.

Duncan, Dallas. "Coming Out on the Other Side: 20 Years After Atlanta LGBT Bar Bombing, Otherside Lounge Owners, Patrons Revisit Dark Day." *Georgia Voice*, February 16, 2017. https://web.archive.org/web/20240625141516/https://thegavoice.com/news/coming-side-20-years-atlanta-lgbt-bar-bombing-otherside-lounge-owners-patrons-revisit-dark-day/.

Eaton, Maynard. "Manuel's Tavern, a Politician Institution Turns 50." *Atlanta Voice*, August 10, 2006.

Georgia Voice. "'Flash' Back to Gay Past." March 18, 2010. https://web.archive.org/web/20240916193207/https://thegavoice.com/culture/film/flash-back-to-gay-past/.

Saunders, Patrick. "Backstreet, Jungle Disco Ball Donated to Atlanta History Center." *Georgia Voice*, November 17, 2017. https://web.archive.org/web/20240228001534/https://thegavoice.com/community/backstreet-jungle-disco-ball-donated-atlanta-history-center/.

———. "Portrait of a Community: An LGBT Atlanta Timeline." *Georgia Voice*, October 18, 2016. https://web.archive.org/web/20240713101519/https://thegavoice.com/news/georgia/portrait-community-lgbt-atlanta-timelien/.

Sylvestre, Berlin. "From Whence We Came: Our LGBTQ ATL History." *Georgia Voice*, August 2, 2018. https://web.archive.org/web/20240818144035/https://thegavoice.com/community/features/from-whence-we-came-our-lgbtq-atl-history/.

Washington, Stan. "Historic Royal Peacock Reopens on Auburn Avenue." *Atlanta Voice*, October 10, 2010.

———. "My People, My People." *Atlanta Voice*, April 29, 1995.

CREATIVE LOAFING ARCHIVES

Barbour, Shannon. "Club Kaya Reunion a Throwback to Atlanta's Golden Era." January 21, 2011. Creative Loafing. https://creativeloafing.com/content-155445-club-kaya-reunion-a-throwback-to-atlanta-s-golden.

Blau, Max. "Robert Maloof, Manuel's Tavern Partner, Passes Away." July 19, 2013. Creative Loafing. https://creativeloafing.com/content-217229-robert-maloof-manuel-s-tavern-partner-passes.

Bostock, Cliff. "Polaris to Reopen?" January 13, 2009. Creative Loafing. https://creativeloafing.com/content-223691-omnivore---polaris-to-reopen.

Creative Loafing. "CJ's Landing." https://creativeloafing.com/business-7530-cj-s-landing.

———. "Clermont Lounge." https://creativeloafing.com/clermont-lounge.

———. "Smith's Olde Bar." https://creativeloafing.com/business-2423-smith-s-olde-bar.

———. "Underground Atlanta." https://creativeloafing.com/business-5011-underground-atlanta.

Davis, Joeff, "That Was Then, This Is Now." June 18, 2015. Creative Loafing. https://creativeloafing.com/content-168411-that-was-then-this-is-now.

Dazey, Stephanie. "First Look: Polaris." August 14, 2014. Creative Loafing. https://creativeloafing.com/content-198583-food---first-look-polaris.

Edelstein, Ken. "Naked on the Chattahoochee." May 17, 2006. Creative Loafing. https://creativeloafing.com/content-185145-cover-story-naked-on-the-chattahoochee.

Ford, Rebecca. "Cover Story: Castleberry Hill." March 16, 2005. Creative Loafing. https://creativeloafing.com/content-184997-cover-story-castleberry-hill.

Henry, Scott. "Cover Story: Club King." September 7, 2009. Creative Loafing. https://creativeloafing.com/content-185550-cover-story-club-king.

———. "Cover Story: The Un-Made Man." August 8, 2001. Creative Loafing. https://creativeloafing.com/content-184461-cover-story-the-un-made-man.

———. "Cover Story: Where'd They Go?" April 24, 2002. Creative Loafing. https://creativeloafing.com/content-184524-cover-story-where-d-they-go.

———. "Dead-End for Backstreet?" July 29, 2004. Creative Loafing. https://creativeloafing.com/content-170297-dead-end-for-backstreet.

———. "Do Not Disturb…Please!" April 24, 2002. Creative Loafing. https://creativeloafing.com/content-184523-do-not-disturb-please.

———. "The Duh Factor." August 1, 2001. Creative Loafing. https://creativeloafing.com/content-169968-gold-club-trial-the-duh-factor.

———. "Former Atlanta Club King Deported." August 28, 2003. Creative Loafing. https://creativeloafing.com/content-171261-former-atlanta-club-king-deported.

———. "Last Call for Nightlife in Buckhead Village." June 13, 2007. Creative Loafing. https://creativeloafing.com/content-170436-last-call-for-nightlife-in-buckhead.

———. "Life in the Money Pit." June 27, 2001. Creative Loafing. https://creativeloafing.com/content-169953-life-in-the-money-pit.

———. "The Tao of Steve." July 11, 2001. Creative Loafing. https://creativeloafing.com/content-169960-the-tao-of-steve.

———. "30 Years of the Good, the Bad and the Weird-as-Hell." June 5, 2022. Creative Loafing. https://creativeloafing.com/content-184564-cover-story-30-years-of-the-good-the-bad-and-the.

———. "Underground Atlanta Sees Semi-Revival." May 4, 2005. Creative Loafing. https://creativeloafing.com/content-185032-cover-story-underground-atlanta-sees.

———. "Vanquish, Other Half of Dreaded Gidewon Club, Opened on Saturday." August 26, 2011. Creative Loafing. https://creativeloafing.com/content-214464-vanquish-other-half-of-dreaded-gidewon-club-opened-on.

Horowitz, Hal. "Tommy Brown RIP." March 14, 2016. Creative Loafing. https://creativeloafing.com/content-149529-tommy-brown-r-i-p-1931-2016.

Kelly, James. "Mose Allison Plays Blind Willie's Tonight." March 5, 2009. Creative Loafing. https://creativeloafing.com/content-156610-mose-allison-plays-blind-willie-s.

Moore, Bobby. "David Bowie's Legendary Stop at Smith's Olde Bar." January 12, 2016. Creative Loafing. https://creativeloafing.com/content-148722-david-bowie-s-legendary-stop-at-smith-s-olde.

Nouraee, Andisheh. "There's a Tier in My Beer." June 11, 2008. Creative Loafing. https://creativeloafing.com/content-194443-beer-issue---there-s-a-tier-in-my.

Radford, Chad. "Late-Night Magic at MJQ: An Oral History, Part I and II." June 16, 2011. Creative Loafing. https://creativeloafing.com/content-168333-late-night-magic-at-mjq-an-oral-history-part.

———. "Rest in Peace, Alex Cooley." December 1, 2015. Creative Loafing. https://creativeloafing.com/content-149347-rest-in-peace-alex-cooley.

———. "R.I.P. Lenny's." December 23, 2010. Creative Loafing. https://creativeloafing.com/content-165792-r-i-p-lenny-s.

———. "Royal Peacock Reopens." August 5, 2010. Creative Loafing. https://creativeloafing.com/content-154777-royal-peacock-reopens.

Rodell, Besha. "Dante's Down the Hatch." April 5, 2011. Creative Loafing. https://creativeloafing.com/content-186375-review-dante-s-down-the-hatch.

Rozzi, James. "Riding La Carousel to the Black Arts Fest." July 29, 2000. Creative Loafing. https://creativeloafing.com/content-164160-riding-la-carousel-to-the-black-arts.

Shalhoup, Mara. "Golden Touch." July 12, 2006. Creative Loafing. https://creativeloafing.com/content-185219-cover-story-golden-touch.

Stuart, Gwynedd. "Sister Louisa's Church Keeps Getting Famouser and Famouser." December 7, 2011. Creative Loafing. https://creativeloafing.com/content-215002-sister-louisa-s-church-keeps-getting-famouser-and.

Wall, Michael. "Bada-Bummer." April 25, 2001. Creative Loafing. https://creativeloafing.com/content-169921-bada-bummer.

Waterhouse, Jon, "Ghosts of Hotspots Past." April 23, 2003. Creative Loafing. https://creativeloafing.com/content-165126-ghosts-of-hotspots-past.

Wheatley, Thomas. "Atlanta Eagle Trial: Charges Dismissed, Defendants Not Guilty." March 12, 2010. Creative Loafing. https://creativeloafing.com/content-210486-atlanta-eagle-trial-charges-dismissed-defendants-not.

———. "Atlanta Nightlife Gold." March 8, 2010. Creative Loafing. https://creativeloafing.com/content-170573-atlanta-nightlife-gold.

———. "Hobnobbing at the Gold Room." March 10, 2010. Creative Loafing. https://creativeloafing.com/content-230295-hobnobbing-at-the-gold-room.

———. "Mayor Apologizes to Plaintiffs in Atlanta Eagle Raid Case." December 8, 2010. Creative Loafing. https://creativeloafing.com/content-213101-mayor-apologizes-to-plaintiffs-in-atlanta-eagle-raid.

———. "Vanquish, Reign, Midtown Nightclub Hot Spots Close." January 28, 2015. Creative Loafing. https://creativeloafing.com/content-170764-vanquish-reign-midtown-nightclub-hot-spots.

Winn, Amy. "Bar Review—Mike 'n Angelo's: Not Your Typical Buckhead." October 30, 2003. Creative Loafing. https://creativeloafing.com/content-179298-bar-review---mike-n-angelo-s-not-your-typical.

EATER ATLANTA

McKibben, Beth. "Atlantans Say 'Yes' to Sunday Morning Mimosas and Bloody Marys." November 7, 2018. Eater Atlanta. https://atlanta.eater.com/2018/11/7/18071564/sunday-brunch-bill-passes-atlanta.

———. "A James Beard Award–Winning Chef Brings Decatur Its First Wine and Amaro Bar Next Spring." October 6, 2023. Eater Atlanta. https://atlanta.eater.com/2023/10/6/23906186/fawn-wine-amaro-bar-james-beard-chef-terry-koval-opening-decatur-georgia.

———. "One of Atlanta's Original Cocktail Lounges the Sound Table Closes on Edgewood Avenue," October 13, 2020. Eater Atlanta. https://atlanta.eater.com/2020/10/13/21509865/the-sound-table-bar-nightclub-closes-edgewood-avenue-atlanta.

———. "One of Northwest Atlanta's Original Breweries Is Closing in Underwood Hills and Relocating," June 8, 2022. Eater Atlanta. https://atlanta.eater.com/2022/6/8/23158581/atlanta-brewing-company-closing-defoor-hills-road-relocating-new-location.

———. "Yes, Longtime Castleberry Hill Bar Elliott Street Pub Is Closing," October 21, 2022. Eater Atlanta. https://atlanta.eater.com/2022/10/21/23415209/elliott-street-pub-closes-castleberry-hill-atlanta.

Scholz, Laura. "Kimball House Partner Miles Macquarrie Helps Launch a Line of Canned Cocktails." October 7, 2019. Eater Atlanta. https://atlanta.eater.com/2019/10/7/20903060/kimball-house-miles-macquarrie-tip-top-proper-canned-cocktails.

Sedghi, Sarrah. "Why Community Is at the Core of This Edgewood Avenue Bar." September 20, 2022. Eater Atlanta. https://atlanta.eater.com/2022/9/20/23361517/our-bar-atl-sarah-oak-kim-edgewood-avenue-atlanta.

ADDITIONAL ARTICLES

Albo, Mike. "Gayest Cities in America, 2010." *Advocate*, January 13, 2010. https://www.advocate.com/travel/2010/01/13/gayest-cities-america.

Allen, Samantha. "At This Atlanta Bar, Jesus, Karaoke, Bizarre Art, and Queer Family Collide." *Them*, September 11, 2019. https://www.them.us/story/good-wierd-queer-bar-sister-louisas-church-living-room.

Allnatt, Libby. "4West ATL Planned for Moreland Avenue." September 26, 2023. WhatNow Atlanta. https://whatnowatlanta.com/4west-atl-planned-for-moreland-avenue/.

Ambus, Destini. "Everything You Need to Know About Orange Crush Weekend 2024." *Savannah Morning News*, April 4, 2024. https://www.savannahnow.com/story/news/local/2024/04/04/everything-you-need-to-know-about-orange-crush-weekend-2024/73134218007/.

Armus, Teo. "Two Decades Before the Atlanta Spa Shootings, an LGBT Bar Next Door Was Blown Up by a Serial Bomber." *Washington Post*, March 22, 2021. https://www.washingtonpost.com/nation/2021/03/22/bar-bombing-atlanta-spa-shooting/.

Ayers/Saint/Gross. "Technical Memorandum: The History of the University of Georgia." University of Georgia Physical Master Plan. March 11, 1998. https://www.architects.uga.edu/sites/default/files/documents/master-plan-info/sections/i_history_of_the_university_of_georgia.pdf.

Bhabha, Leah. "The History of the Martini." May 16, 2014. *Food52*. https://food52.com/blog/10396-the-history-of-the-martini.

Billboard. "Herbert Graham and Associates, Inc. Entertainment Complexes." July 17, 1982. https://archive.org/details/bub_gb_kCQEAAAAMBAJ/page/n39/mode/2up?q=Ramblin'+Raft+Race.

Brown, Malik. "A Short Retelling of Atlanta's Long—But Radical—Queer History." *Out*, May 12, 2021. https://www.out.com/print/2021/5/12/short-retelling-atlantas-long-radical-queer-history.

Brown, Robbie. "In Georgia, Some Vote to Stay Dry on Sundays." *New York Times*, November 11, 2011. https://www.nytimes.com/2011/11/12/us/georgia-or-most-of-it-ends-sunday-ban-on-alcohol-sales.html.

———. "Remembering a Soul Food Legend Who Nurtured Civil Rights Leaders." *New York Times*, December 5, 2008. https://www.nytimes.com/2008/12/06/us/06paschal.html.

Butler, Chris. "Georgia's Craft Brewers and Customers Thirst for Less Restrictive Laws." April 11, 2024. Georgia Public Policy Foundation. https://www.georgiapolicy.org/news/georgias-craft-brewers-and-customers-thirst-for-less-restrictive-laws/#:~:text=In%202017%2C%20state%20legislators%20passed,state%27s%20craft%20breweries%20stay%20afloat.

Carter, Carol. "Movies Filmed at Hotels in Atlanta," May 30, 2024. Atlanta Convention and Visitors Bureau. https://discoveratlanta.com/stories/things-to-do/the-movies-at-hotels-in-atlanta/.

Chapman, Gray. "Atlanta's Best Bar Started as an Accident." November 28, 2018. Vice. https://www.vice.com/en/article/atlantas-best-bar-started-as-an-accident/.

Cheves, Alexander. "COVID Won't Stop Atlanta's Most Iconic Leather Bar from Queering the South." *Them*, December 21, 2020. https://www.them.us/story/eagle-atlanta-historic-preservation-queer-spaces-covid-19.

CNN. "UGA Bulldogs Its Way to Top of Party Schools List." August 2010. https://web.archive.org/web/20190223145701/https://www.cnn.com/2010/LIVING/08/02/uga.top.party.school/index.html.

Colburn, Randall. "Drake Had an Armored Truck Deliver $100,000 in Cash to Atlanta Strip Club." *Consequence*, November 20, 2018. https://consequence.net/2018/11/drake-future-armored-truck-strip-club-cash/.

"Comparing the Party Habits of Black and White College Students on Spring Break." *Journal of Blacks in Higher Education*, no. 28 (summer 2000): 18. JSTOR. http://www.jstor.org/stable/2678666.

Dao, Dan Q. "How These Jazz Bars Defined Atlanta in the 1960s." March 13, 2020. Vice. https://www.vice.com/en/article/how-these-jazz-bars-defined-atlanta-in-the-1960s/.

Dator, James. "Lou Williams' Trip to the Strip Club During a Pandemic Actually Makes Sense." August 5, 2020. SBNation. https://www.sbnation.com/nba/2020/8/5/21355463/lou-williams-magic-city-wings-nba-bubble.

Dominick, Nora. "I Genuinely Can't Watch *The Hunger Games: Catching Fire* the Same Way Again After Reading These Facts." November 15, 2023. BuzzFeed. https://www.buzzfeed.com/noradominick/hunger-games-catching-fire-behind-the-scenes-facts.

Easton, Terry. "A 'Lightning Strike' in the History of Atlanta's Affordable Housing Development: Revisiting the 1990 Imperial Hotel Occupation." April 6, 2017. Atlanta Studies. https://atlantastudies.org/2017/04/06/a-lightning-strike-in-the-history-of-atlantas-affordable-housing-development-revisiting-the-1990-imperial-hotel-occupation/.

Firestone, David. "National Briefing | South: Georgia: Prison Term for Racketeering." *New York Times*, January 9, 2002. https://www.nytimes.com/2002/01/09/us/national-briefing-south-georgia-prison-term-for-racketeering.html.

Fowler, Ruth. "Confessions of an Ex Scores Stripper." *New York Post*, July 6, 2008. https://nypost.com/2008/07/06/confessions-of-an-ex-scores-stripper/.

Friedman, Devin. "Make It Reign: How an Atlanta Strip Club Runs the Music Industry." *GQ*, July 8, 2015. https://www.gq.com/story/atlanta-strip-club-magic-city.

Fuhrmeister, Chris. "Details on Cam Newton's Plans for Restaurant in Castleberry Hill." *Atlanta Business Chronicle*, September 19, 2023. https://www.bizjournals.com/atlanta/news/2023/09/19/cam-newton-restaurant-n-zone-castleberry-hill.html.

Garofalo, Reebee. "Disco." March 9, 2024. *Encyclopaedia Britannica*. https://www.britannica.com/art/disco.

Gomez, Jade. "21 Savage Rings in 30th Birthday with Second Annual Freaknik." *Paper*, October 24, 2022. https://www.papermag.com/21-savage-freaknik.

Goolrick, Allie. "Appreciation: Alex Cooley's Legacy Looms Large Over Atlanta's Place as a Major Musical Mecca." *ArtsATL*, December 4, 2015. https://www.artsatl.org/obituary-alex-cooleys-legacy-looms-large-atlantas-place-major-musical-mecca/.

Green, Josh. "Construction Activity Spotted at Forcibly Closed Former Strip Clubs." July 28, 2022. Urbanize Atlanta. https://atlanta.urbanize.city/post/sandy-springs-construction-activity-spotted-former-strip-clubs.

———. "Little Five Points Development Canceled, Sparing Landmark Star Bar." December 5, 2022. Urbanize Atlanta. https://atlanta.urbanize.city/post/star-bar-development-little-five-points-canceled.

————. "Perspective: 15 Years Ago, Buckhead Village's Wild Days Died." November 10, 2022. Urbanize Atlanta. https://atlanta.urbanize.city/post/buckhead-village-bar-district-died-15-years-ago-memories.

————. "Photos: Inside the Hotel Rebirth of a Ponce de Leon Avenue Landmark." March 5, 2021. Urbanize Atlanta. https://atlanta.urbanize.city/post/photos-inside-hotel-rebirth-ponce-de-leon-avenue-landmark.

Griffen, Cora. "An Insider's Look at Atlanta's Most-Renowned Gentlemen's Club, The Cheetah." *Jezebel*, August 1, 2022. https://jezebelmagazine.com/insiders-look-at-atlantas-most-renowned-gentlemens-club.

Harry, John. "Jimmy Carter: American Homebrew Hero?" September 30, 2019. Smithsonian. https://americanhistory.si.edu/explore/stories/jimmy-carter-american-homebrew-hero.

Hendler, Kari. "The History of the Hukilau." *Tiki*, January 1, 2007. https://archive.org/details/tiki-mag-2010-6-1/Tiki%20Mag%202009%205-1/page/n29/mode/2up?q=trader+vics+atlanta.

Jones, Anderson. "OUT THERE: ATLANTA; Nightclub Olympiad Takes Shape." *New York Times*, July 14, 1996. https://www.nytimes.com/1996/07/14/archives/out-there-atlantanightclub-olympiad-takes-shape.html.

Jones, Tom. "Man Pleads Guilty to Deadly Shooting at Underground Atlanta." February 24, 2015. WSBTV. https://www.wsbtv.com/news/local/man-pleads-guilty-deadly-shooting-underground-atla/53826766/.

Jordan, Mike. "Why Atlanta Is the Strip Club Capital of America." November 9, 2015. Thrillist. https://www.thrillist.com/sex-dating/atlanta/why-atlanta-is-the-strip-club-capital-of-america.

Kessler, John. "An Oral History of One Flew South." *Garden & Gun*, December 2019. https://gardenandgun.com/articles/an-oral-history-of-one-flew-south/.

King, Monroe Martin. "Dr. John S. Pemberton: Originator of Coca-Cola." *Pharmacy in History* 29, no. 2 (1987): 85–89. JSTOR. http://www.jstor.org/stable/41109874.

Lasner, Matthew. "Swingsites for Singles." October 2014. Places. https://placesjournal.org/article/swingsites-for-singles/.

Levin, Dan. "Mass Mania to Push Ahead." *Sports Illustrated*, May 29, 1972. https://archive.org/details/Sports-Illustrated-1972-05-29/page/n37/mode/2up?q=raft&view=theater.

Maddux, Rachael. "Hammer in Her Hand." *Oxford American*, February 9, 2016. https://oxfordamerican.org/magazine/issue-91-winter-2015/hammer-in-her-hand.

McKibben, Beth. "Atlanta DJ Ree de la Vega Opening Music-Driven Restaurant Pisces in the Sound Table Space This Summer." April 24, 2024. Rough Draft

Atlanta. https://roughdraftatlanta.com/2024/04/24/dj-ree-de-la-vega-opening-pisces-restaurant-music-dance-sound-table-edgewood-avenue/.

Miles, Jonathan. "A Good Decade to Have a Drink." *New York Times,* January 15, 2010. https://www.nytimes.com/2010/01/17/fashion/17shake.html.

Miller, Wilbur R. "The Revenue: Federal Law Enforcement in the Mountain South, 1870–1900." *Journal of Southern History* 55, no. 2 (1989): 195–216. JSTOR. https://doi.org/10.2307/2208902.

New South Associates for Historic Atlanta and the City of Atlanta Office of Design. "The Atlanta LGBT+ Historic Context Statement." April 2023. https://drive.google.com/file/d/1eSF99tEegwzaaZ0CBXhWnYXW2FeX9hxn/view.

Olmsted, Larry. "Review: Fellaship, Atlanta." July 2, 2019. Cigar Aficionado. https://www.cigaraficionado.com/article/review-fellaship-atlanta.

O'Neill, Connor Towne. "Nightclubbing: Royal Peacock." August 18, 2016. Red Bull. https://daily.redbullmusicacademy.com/2016/08/royal-peacock-nightclubbing-feature.

Perry, Whit. "Ramblin on the Chattahoochee." *Tubing,* 1977. https://archive.org/details/tubing0000perr/page/38/mode/2up?q=ramblin.

Petridis, Alexis. "Disco Demolition: The Night They Tried to Crush Black Music." *Guardian,* July 19, 2019. https://www.theguardian.com/music/2019/jul/19/disco-demolition-the-night-they-tried-to-crush-black-music.

Prince, K. Stephen. "A Rebel Yell for Yankee Doodle: Selling the New South at the 1881 Atlanta International Cotton Exposition." *Georgia Historical Quarterly* 92, no. 3 (2008): 340–71. JSTOR. http://www.jstor.org/stable/40585070.

Raab, Selwyn. "Strip Club Partners, Now Ruined, Blame Greed and the Mob." *New York Times,* August 30, 1998. https://www.nytimes.com/1998/08/30/nyregion/strip-club-partners-now-ruined-blame-greed-and-the-mob.html.

Range, Peter Ross. "Girls of the New South." *Playboy,* April 1977. https://archive.org/details/pb-04-77/mode/2up?q=ramblin+raft+race&view=theater.

Range, Willard. "Hannibal I. Kimball." *Georgia Historical Quarterly* 29, no. 2 (1945): 47–70. JSTOR. http://www.jstor.org/stable/40576972.

Rattini, Kristin Baird. "Big Adventure: Remembering the Ramblin' Raft Race." *Georgia Tech Alumni Magazine.* https://www.gtalumni.org/s/1481/alumni/17/magazine-pages.aspx?sid=1481&gid=21&pgid=24690.

Sams, Marilyn. "Cooley Slates 16 Shows for Rest of Year." *Amusement Business* 93, no. 42 (October 1981): 12. https://archive.org/details/sim_amusement-business_1981-10-17_93_42/page/4/mode/2up?q=Alex+cooley.

Santa Cruz Sentinel. "Historic City Beneath the Streets." October 19, 1969. https://cdnc.ucr.edu/?a=d&d=SCS19691019.1.28&e=-------en--20--1--txt-txIN--------.

Scobey, Lola. "Armadillo East to Open in Nashville." *Cash Box*, February 26, 1977. https://archive.org/details/cashbox38unse_39/page/42/mode/2up?q=Muhlenbrink's+Saloon.

Spataro, Joanne. "The Tea Dance Is Part of NYC's LGBTQ Living History." April 23, 2018. Vice. https://www.vice.com/en/article/nyc-tea-dances/.

Spivak, Caleb. "Buckhead Saloon Outdraws for Rio Grande Space." May 10, 2010. What Now Atlanta. https://whatnowatlanta.com/buckhead-saloon-outdraws-for-rio-grande-space/.

Summers, Zac. "MJQ Nightclub to Move into Iconic 'Down the Hatch' at Underground Atlanta." March 3, 2023. Atlanta News First. https://www.atlantanewsfirst.com/2023/03/03/mjq-nightclub-move-into-iconic-down-hatch-underground-atlanta/.

Sumner, David E. "Everybody's Cousin: John J. Thrasher Was One of Atlanta's Founders and Most Colorful Figures." *Georgia Historical Quarterly* 84, no. 2 (2000): 295–307. JSTOR. http://www.jstor.org/stable/40584275.

Thompson, Krista A. "Performing Visibility: Freaknic and the Spatial Politics of Sexuality, Race, and Class in Atlanta." *TDR* 51, no. 4 (2007): 24–46. http://www.jstor.org/stable/25145466.

Uhles, Steven. "High-Gravity Beers Find a Niche Among the Mainstream Brews." Augusta Chronicle, February 23, 2006. https://www.augustachronicle.com/story/entertainment/events/2006/02/23/ent-58910-shtml/14775216007/.

WABE. "'Cheers!' A Toast to Atlanta's Oldest Watering Holes: Atkins Park." September 20, 2022. https://www.wabe.org/cheers-a-toast-to-atlantas-oldest-watering-holes-atkins-park/.

Ward, Judson C. "The Republican Party in Bourbon Georgia, 1872–1890." *Journal of Southern History* 9, no. 2 (1943): 196–209. JSTOR. https://doi.org/10.2307/2191798.

Wicker, Jewel. "How Atlanta's Clubs Fueled the City's Budding Hip-Hop Scene in the '90s." March 11, 2019. Vice. https://www.vice.com/en/article/deep-dive-atlanta-hip-hop/.

Winters, Akilah. "Brother of Republic Lounge Co-Owner Who Was Fatally Shot Increases Reward to Find Killer to $250,000." March 14, 2023. 11Alive News. https://www.11alive.com/article/news/local/reward-increase-republic-lounge-shooting-michael-gidewon/85-53b2c276-2d6c-45ac-9cf7-9659973b04df.

Zickgraf, Ryan. "The FOAM Act Is Dead, But the Glass Is Half Full for Politically Engaged Craft Brewers." February 29, 2024. Atlanta Civic Circle. https://atlantaciviccircle.org/2024/02/29/the-foam-act-is-dead-but-the-glass-is-half-full-for-politically-engaged-craft-brewers/.

ATLANTA HISTORY CENTER

Ambrose, Andy. "John Temple Graves and the Southern Race Problem." July 12, 2023. Atlanta History Center. https://www.atlantahistorycenter.com/blog/john-temple-graves-and-the-southern-race-problem/.

Atlanta History Center. "Dante's Down the Hatch Menu." https://ahc.galileo.usg.edu/repositories/2/resources/224.

———. "A History of Pride Parades in Atlanta." September 30, 2019. https://www.atlantahistorycenter.com/blog/a-history-of-pride-parades-in-atlanta/.

Daly, Kate. "Protecting and Preserving: The Chattahoochee River." November 12, 2021. Atlanta History Center. https://www.atlantahistorycenter.com/blog/protecting-and-the-chattahoochee-river/.

Haley, Claire. "Preserving Atlanta History: The Zero Milepost." December 4, 2020. Atlanta History Center. https://www.atlantahistorycenter.com/blog/preserving-atlanta-history-the-zero-milepost/.

Mason, Herman "Skip" Jr. "1895 Cotton States." Atlanta History Center. https://www.atlantahistorycenter.com/exhibitions/atlanta-in-50-objects/the-1895-cotton-states-and-international-exposition.

———. "Royal Peacock." Atlanta History Center. https://www.atlantahistorycenter.com/programs-events/public-programs/juneteenth/royal-peacock/.

———. "Vanishing Black Atlanta: Atlanta's 'Club Beautiful,' the Royal Peacock." July 7, 2022. Atlanta History Center. https://www.atlantahistorycenter.com/blog/vanishing-black-atlanta-atlantas-club-beautiful-the-royal-peacock/.

ATLANTA HISTORICAL BULLETIN

Cooper, Cornelia E. "History of the West End, 1830–1910." *Atlanta Historical Bulletin* 8, no. 31 (January 1947): 72–73. https://album.atlantahistorycenter.com/digital/collection/AHBull/id/10819.

Kurtz, Wilbur G. "Whitehall Tavern." *Atlanta Historical Bulletin* 1, no. 5 (April 1931): 43–47. https://album.atlantahistorycenter.com/digital/collection/AHBull/id/8866.

Mitchell, Eugene M. "Queer Place Names in Old Atlanta." *Atlanta Historical Bulletin* 1, no. 5 (April 1931): 26–34. https://album.atlantahistorycenter.com/digital/collection/AHBull/id/8866.

BIBLIOGRAPHY

PODCASTS

Lee, Christina (host). *Racket: Inside the Gold Club*. Season 1. 2020.

Lemos, Victoria (host). *Archive Atlanta*. All seasons. 2018–24.

Livingston, Tim (host). *The Raven*. Season 1. 2024.

Locascio, Cole (host). *Flashpoint*. Season 1. 2024.

AUDIO AND VISUAL MATERIALS

Atlanta Journal-Constitution. "Customers Line Up at the Newly Opened Liquor Store After the End of Prohibition." April 22, 1938. Atlanta Journal-Constitution Photographic Archives, AJCP553-124b. Georgia State University Library, Special Collections and Archives. https://digitalcollections.library.gsu.edu/digital/collection/ajc/id/11598/.

———. 81 Theater advertisement. November 26, 1926. https://archive.org/details/per_atlanta-constitution_1926-11-26_59_165/page/n7/mode/2up?q=Bessie&view=theater.

———. "Exterior of Mrs. P's, a Gay Bar in a Hotel on Ponce De Leon Avenue, the Day After It Was Raided by Atlanta Police, Atlanta, Georgia, September 25, 1980." September 25, 1980. Georgia State University, Special Collections. http://digitalcollections.library.gsu.edu/cdm/ref/collection/ajc/id/2767.

Brown, Charlie. Interviewed by Adam Albrite. March 26, 2019. Gender and Sexuality Oral History Project, Archives for Gender and Sexuality. Georgia State University, Special Collections and Archives. https://digitalcollections.library.gsu.edu/digital/collection/lgbtq/id/4770/.

Buckhead Village District. "Our Story." https://www.buckheadvillagedistrict.com/about-buckhead-village.

ebay. "Playboy Club—Atlanta, GA. 1960's Vintage Menu." https://www.ebay.com/itm/155075168813.

Georgia. "SweetWater Brewing Crafts Success in Georgia." https://georgia.org/competitive-advantages/casestudies/sweetwater-brewing-crafts-success-georgia.

Georgia State University Library. "Out in the Archives: Gender and Sexuality Collections at Georgia State University." https://exhibits.library.gsu.edu/out-in-the-archives/.

———. "Robert Mitchum and Johnny Mercer." Special Collections. 1960s. http://digitalcollections.library.gsu.edu/cdm/ref/collection/music/id/196.

Jennings, Waylon. *Waylon the Ramblin' Man*. RCA Victor, 1974. https://archive.org/details/lp_waylon-the-ramblin-man_waylon-jennings/mode/1up?q=Muhlenbrink's+Saloon.

Jillson, Floyd. "Dinkler Plaza Hotel (Atlanta, Ga.)." 1966. Atlanta History Center. https://album.atlantahistorycenter.com/digital/collection/Jilson/id/2548.

Johnson, Dain. "Birdsmell, Band of Horses at The Earl," November 13, 2013. YouTube. https://www.youtube.com/watch?v=awzSbc-ltOQ.

New York Public Library. "Easter Sunday Dinner, Kimball House, 1899." Rare Book Division. https://digitalcollections.nypl.org/items/510d47db-3682-a3d9-e040-e00a18064a99.

———. "First Annual Banquet, Kimball House, 1890." Rare Book Division. https://digitalcollections.nypl.org/items/510d47db-1f33-a3d9-e040-e00a18064a99.

———. "Good Fellowship Dinner, Kimball House, 1901." Rare Book Division. https://digitalcollections.nypl.org/items/510d47db-5cb7-a3d9-e040-e00a18064a99.

The Playboy Club Bunny Manual. Playboy, July 1968. https://archive.org/details/1969-bunnymanual/mode/2up.

Surber, David. *Network Q, Out Across America.* Episode 24, "Hotlanta River Expo." October 1993. https://vimeo.com/87991188.

Swims-Gray, Betty. "Playboy Club Job." June 30, 2015. WABE. https://www.wabe.org/storycorps-atlanta-playboy-club-job-hardest-thing-i-ever-did/.

Taylor, Billy. *It's a Matter of Pride.* Duane Music Inc., 1994. https://archive.org/details/cd_its-a-matter-of-pride_billy-taylor/page/n1/mode/1up?q=la+carousel+atlanta.

Tennessee State Museum. "Coca Cola Bottle." 1911. https://tnmuseum.org/TN225/artifacts/058#:~:text=Chattanooga%20was%20the%20site%20of,expand%20into%20bottling%20the%20beverage.

Tony Parenti and His All Stars. *Jazz Goes Underground: Ruby Red's Warehouse in Underground Atlanta.* Jazzology, 1969.

Williams, P. Frank, dir. *Freaknik: The Wildest Party Never Told.* Swirl Films/Mass Appeal, 2024. Hulu.

0405 Photography. "Blind Willie's Blues Club." December 29, 2022. YouTube. https://www.youtube.com/watch?v=aSPuKPy5OOw.

VARIOUS WEBSITES AND DOCUMENTS

Andrews Entertainment District. "Home." Archived. https://web.archive.org/web/20121002052718/https://andrewsdistrict.com/.

Atkins Park Restaurant & Bar. "Home." https://www.atkinspark.com/.

Atlanta Brewing Company/Red Brick Brewing. "Home." Archived. https://web.archive.org/web/20220816063748/http://atlantabrewing.com/.

Atlanta Influences Everything. "About." https://aie.life/about/.

Atlanta Police Department. "History of the APD." https://www.atlantapd.org/about-apd/apd-history.

Atlanta Pride. "Home." https://atlantapride.org/.

Atlanta Shakespeare Co. "About ASC." https://www.shakespearetavern.com/about/.

Backstreet. "Home." Archived. https://web.archive.org/web/20020602020618/http://www.backstreetatlanta.com/.

The Bucket Shop Café. "Home." https://bucketshopcafe.com/.

Cafe Tu Tu Tango. "Locations." Archived. https://web.archive.org/web/20030218163214/https://cafetututango.com/.

Castleberry Hill Historic Arts District. "History." https://castleberryhill.org/history/.

Chattahoochee Coffee. "About Us." https://chattahoocheecoffee.com/about/us/.

The Cheetah. "About." https://www.thecheetah.com/about/.

City of Atlanta. "The Georgian Terrace Hotel." https://web.archive.org/web/20100528035941/http:/www.atlantaga.gov/government/urbandesign_georgianterr.aspx.

———. "The Imperial Hotel." https://www.atlantaga.gov/government/departments/city-planning/historic-preservation/property-district-information/the-imperial-hotel.

———. "Rufus M. Rose House." https://www.atlantaga.gov/government/departments/city-planning/historic-preservation/property-district-information/rufus-m-rose-house.

CJ's Landing. "Home." Archived. https://web.archive.org/web/20020720111235/http://www.cjslanding.com/.

The Coca-Cola Company. "History." https://www.coca-colacompany.com/about-us/history.

Dante's Down the Hatch. "Home." Archived. https://web.archive.org/web/20010420023343/http://www.dantesdownthehatch.com/docs/opener_noFrames.html.

Esso. "Home." Archived. https://web.archive.org/web/20111001200747/http://essoatl.com/.

Facebook. "Big House Museum." https://www.facebook.com/TheBigHouseMuseum/posts/win-lose-or-draw-poker-game-photo-from-muhlenbrinks-saloon-underground-atlanta-1/10159202203040565/.

———. "The EARL." https://www.facebook.com/EARLav/photos/pb.100067103182713.-2207520000/10157076697361638/?type=3.

———. "I partied (and danced) at Velvet." Post. https://www.facebook.com/phot o/?fbid=84710173037&set=g.39128032910.

———. "688 Club." https://www.facebook.com/photo/?fbid=102276479344865 52&set=g.92683520563

Federal Register. "Establishment of the Dahlonega Plateau Viticultural Area." June 29, 2018. https://www.federalregister.gov/ documents/2018/06/29/2018-14035/establishment-of-the-dahlonega-plateau-viticultural-area.

Fire Island Pines Historical Society. "The Origins of Fire Island's Tea Dance at The Blue Whale." https://www.pineshistory.org/the-archives/the-tea-dance-est-1966.

Genius. "Preachin' the Blues." https://genius.com/Bessie-smith-preachin-the-blues-lyrics.

Georgia Department of Public Health. "Information About the Georgia Smoke Free Air Act of 2005." https://dph.georgia.gov/document/publication/features-georgia-smoke-free-air-act-fact-sheet/download.

The Georgian Terrace. "Home." https://thegeorgianterrace.com/.

Georgia Rivers Network. "Chattahoochee River." https://garivers.org/chattahoochee-river/.

Getty Images. "Gold Room Atlanta." https://www.gettyimages.com/search/2/im age?sort=mostpopular&phrase=gold%20room%20atlanta&license=rf%2Crm.

———. "Kiss Performs at The Electric Ballroom, Atlanta." https://www.gettyimages.com/detail/news-photo/drummer-peter-criss-bassist-gene-simmons-singer-guitarist-news-photo/86547499?adppopup=true.

Grandaddy Mimm's Distilling Co. "About." https://grandaddymimms.com/about-grandaddy-mimms.

Hal's The Steakhouse. "Our Story." https://www.hals.net/ourstory-atlanta.

Heart of Vinings. "Hardy Place." https://vinings.org/vinings-history/hardy-pace/.

Historical Marker Database. "Horton House Historic Site." https://www.hmdb.org/m.asp?m=17445.

Historic Atlanta. "The Atlanta Eagle." https://www.historicatlanta.org/atlanta-eagle/.

Historic Oakland Foundation. "Moses Formwalt: Mayor, Saloon Owner, Atlanta's Rowdiest Citizen." https://oaklandcemetery.com/moses-formwalt/.

IMDb. "*Freaknik: The Musical*." https://www.imdb.com/title/tt1535989/.

Jack Daniel's. "Our Story." https://www.jackdaniels.com/en-us/our-story.

Jack Daniel's and Coca-Cola. "The Story." https://www.jackdanielsandcoca-cola.com/en-us/the-story/.

Johnny's Hideaway. "About." https://johnnyshideaway.com/atlanta-johnny-s-hideaway-about.

Lesbian Bar Project. "About LBP." https://www.lesbianbarproject.com/.

Library of Congress. "World's First Coca-Cola Was Served." https://guides.loc.gov/this-month-in-business-history/may/first-coca-cola-served#:~:text=Back%20on%20May%208%2C%201886,a%20tonic%20for%20common%20ailments.

Magic City. "FAQs." https://www.magiccity.com/faq-2/.

Martin Luther King Jr. National Historic Site. "Ivan Allen." https://www.nps.gov/features/malu/feat0002/wof/ivan_allen.htm.

———. "The Sweet Auburn Community." https://www.nps.gov/malu/the-sweet-auburn-community.htm.

Milk and Honey. "Home." Archived. https://web.archive.org/web/20120425050156/http://www.mlkhny.com/london/.

Moe's and Joe's. "About." https://www.moesandjoesatl.com/about.

———. "Menu." https://www.moesandjoesatl.com/menu.

Monday Night Brewing. "Our Story." https://mondaynightbrewing.com/about/.

Moondogs Bar. "About Us." https://moondogsbar.com/about.

Northside Tavern. "Northside History." http://www.northsidetavern.com/northside-history.html.

Park Tavern. "About." https://www.parktavern.com/about-us/.

Paschal's. "Timeline." https://www.paschalsatlanta.com/timeline.

Piedmont Park. "Park History." https://piedmontpark.org/park-history/.

Prism Florida. "Anita Bryant." June 11, 2024. https://www.prismfl.org/post/anita-bryant.

Ruby Reds Band. "An Oral History of The Ruby Reds Band." https://www.rubyredsband.com/pages/history.html.

Smith's Olde Bar. "History." https://www.sobatl.com/history.

The Sound Table. "Home." Archived. https://web.archive.org/web/20190717121939/http://thesoundtable.com/.

Steamhouse Lounge. "About." Archived. https://web.archive.org/web/20240708024050/http://steamhouselounge.com/about.html.

13th Colony Distilling. "About Us." https://www.13thcolonydistillery.com/who-we-are#AboutUs.

Tongue and Groove. "Home." Archived. https://web.archive.org/web/20090831043352/http://www.tandgonline.com/.

U.S. Census Bureau. "Georgia 235th Anniversary of Statehood (1788): January 2, 2023." https://www.census.gov/newsroom/stories/georgia-admission-anniversary.html#:~:text=The%20area%20of%20Georgia%20was,states%20to%20join%20the%20Union.

U.S. Department of Housing and Urban Development. "*HUD v. Riverbend Club Apartments.*" October 15, 1991. https://www.hud.gov/sites/documents/47_ HUDALJ-04-89-0676-1.PDF.

Wild Heaven Beer. "Our Story." https://wildheavenbeer.com/about-us.

World of Coca-Cola. "Vault of the Secret Formula." https://www.worldofcoca-cola.com/explore-inside/explore-vault-secret-formula.

ABOUT THE AUTHOR

CAROLINE EUBANKS is a writer, author and lifelong Atlantan, not to mention, for a brief window of time, a bartender whose best drink in her repertoire was probably a well-poured pint of Guinness. In her career as a professional writer, she's seen Elvis tribute artists in Mississippi, interviewed a psychic in Florida and attended Cajun Mardi Gras in Louisiana.

Her work on the South and beyond has appeared in *The Washington Post*, *Garden & Gun*, *Chicago Tribune*, *InsideHook*, *Southern Living*, *Atlanta* magazine, *Travel + Leisure* and Wine Enthusiast. Her first book, *This Is My South: The Essential Travel Guide to the Southern States*, won a Lowell Thomas Award for best travel guidebook in 2019. She is a member of the Author's Guild and a board member of the Society of American Travel Writers.

You can follow her work at carolineeubanks.com and on social media at @cairinthecity.

Visit us at
www.historypress.com